I0211709

SPOKE TEN

Publishers:
Kevin Gallagher
Marc Vincenz

Editor in Chief:
Kevin Gallagher

Contributing Editors:
Karina van Berkum
Marc Vincenz

———

spokeboston.com

———

ISBN: 978-1-952335-72-3

Copyright © 2023

———

Cover design by Marc Vincenz
Interior design and layout: MadHat Press

Published in the United States of America

by MadHat Press
PO Box 422
Cheshire, MA 01225

———

madhat-press.com

SPOKE TEN

BOSTON, MASS.

TABLE OF CONTENTS

POETRY

ESSAYS AND REVIEWS

TEN

The mission of *spoKe* is to advance a better vision of the world through poetry and poetics. Founded in response to the Boston Marathon bombing, we are strong to advance:

1. A global poetry that engages with or is from the world's places, cultures and literary traditions: past, present, and visions of futures.
2. American poetry that sees the English language and literary tradition as core but one of many roots and paths for poetry.
3. A poetics that attempts to innovate language, idiom, sensibility, and poetic form while maintaining a public presence.

We publish in the great tradition of Boston-area independents most notably Cid Corman's *Origin* that gave full features of the work of individual poets but also including *Poems for a Dime, SET, Measure, Fire Exit, Exact Change, compost, LIFT, Polis, The Poker, Let the Bucket Down* and many others.

—*Kevin Gallagher and Karina van Berkum*

POETRY

Sabine Huyn, tr. from the French by Charlotte Mandell

Speaking Skin

"We have fragile bodies because they are immensely generous, supported by an immensely generous heart, and that's also what makes us strong, that total gift of us!"

"Nothing, apart from the transformation of the body into language."

"And my body remembers all its wounds, draws up the inventory of all its sufferings, physical and moral, and consigns them to the ocean […] I am healing. I don't know what from. But I am healing. My shadow is clearer. My light too."

—Philippe Rahmy-Wolff

(Physical reunions for H.)

il y a tant à dire si peu de mots
intacts — pliée elle tousse exile
résiste et cale — mal et répare
— bouche insensible — n'arrive
nulle part — langue raidie sur les
cicatrices du palais

débris de mots à son corps dé-
fendant devenus siens — de-
dans elle bute contre les blocs
de silence

tu — manques — de moi

There's so much to say so few words intact—curled she coughs exhales resists and stalls—wrongly then rightly—unfeeling mouth—arrives nowhere—tongue stiff on the scars of the palate

wreckage of words on her reluctant body had become hers—inside she stumbles against blocks of silence

you—are what is missing—from me

tous ces jours figée dans la
bouche la langue rompue
abrite mots mordants guerres
marques de naissance d'os

carcasse grippe hoquète et râle
rampe rampe sur l'asphalte noir
de rues sans issue où l'usure
se confond à celle du corps où
rugit la gravité de collisions
d'astres défunts

le coeur plus — une chambre
d'attrition

all those days frozen in mouth the
broken tongue shelters mordant
warlike words bone birthmarks

carcass seizes up coughs and
rattlescrawls crawls on the black
asphalt of one-way streets where
erosion merges with that of the
body where there roars the gravity
of collisions of dead stars

the heart nothing but— a room of
attrition

nuit — j'ai faim — juste secondes
avant la pluie sur mes
paupières froissées envie de
l'amitié ronde des arabesques
en boule au fond d'un bol de
sabi depuis toujours la faim
tendue vers l'offrande bouche
de sel ouverte

night—I'm hungry—just seconds
before the rain on my creased
eyelids desire for the round
friendship of arabesques curled on
the bottom of a bowl of sabi always
hunger reaching for the offering
open mouth of salt

entre deux murs tombés en gra-
vats au détour d'un regard inat-
tendu quelque chose luit plus
fort qu'une éruption solaire un
sourire en retour doucement se
grave dans les coeurs solitaires
et redresse les corps

né du courage des sculpteurs
l'orage allège l'air

between two walls fallen in rubble
at the intersection of an unexpected
gaze something gleams stronger
than a solar flare a smile in return
gently is engraved in solitary hearts
and rights bodies

born from the courage of sculptors
the storm lightens the air

viens nous connaissons l'eau la
pluie nous attend elle coulera
de nos fronts à nos yeux à nos
lèvres à nos cous pour dispa-
raître là où nos mains iront
chercher le chaud et le brûlant
des corps où nos langues iront
laper la source d'un monde re-
commencé viens c'est fortune
de mer c'est éternel ça vole pa-
pillons partout dessus dessous
dedans ça entre et sort et n'ar-
rive et n'appartient qu'à nous
viens

come we know the water the rain
waits for us it will stream from our
foreheads to our eyes to our lips
to our necks to disappear where
our hands will go to seek the heat
and burning of bodies where our
tongues will go to lap the source of
a world begun again come it's the
perils of the sea it's the eternal it
flies butterflies everywhere above
below inside it comes and goes
and only arrives and belongs to us
come

émue et vent dans le cou la
langue va craintive et fervente
traverse vivement la ville fardée
de poussière foule les pé-
tales maculés sol ou ciel c'est
pareil partout s'étale son visage
cent-cinquante frissons par mi-
nute dans le vertige nouveau
l'unique où se lover

moved and wind in her neck her
tongue goes fearful and fervent
eagerly crosses the city powdered
with dust treads on the spattered
petals earth or sky it's the same
everywhere spreads out her face a
hundred fifty shivers per minute
in the new vertigo the only one in
which to cuddle up

le corps frémit de l'envie de tou-
cher la peau pense aux mains
— vibrer encore et encore par-
ler peau — contre peau écou-
ter peau pencher vers demain
peut-être les caresses com-
posent ce qui ressemble aux
premiers serments

the body trembles with desire to
touch the skin thinks with hands—
vibrating still and still speaking
skin—against skin listen to skin
lean towards tomorrow perhaps
caresses compose what resembles
the first pledges

il y a temps — de peau à mordre
— presque un peu de mots sim-
plement sans dire beaucoup ça
bourdonne   durablement   ça
contient — tout —forcément

there is time—so much skin to
bite—almost a few words simply
without saying much hums for a
long time contains—everything—
necessarily

grand écart par-dessus les
flaques de mémoire la langue
défie le vide se frotte au silence
délie ses doigts dégrafent re-
cueillent et plantent la douceur
— elle avance avec ce trésor son
coeur bat l'indifférence des rues
le désespoir et l'espoir tapis en-
semble sous les marches où
assise elle attendra le regain ses
mains toutes aux ondulations
de sa peau sous les traces indé-
lébiles

big gap above the puddles of
memory the tongue defies the
void rubs against silence unties her
fingers unfasten gather and plant
gentleness—she moves forward
with this treasure her heart beats
the indifference of streets despair
and hope lurking together under
the steps where she sits waiting
for the renewal of her hands all
with undulations of her skin under
indelible traces

elle n'arpente plus elle nage en
écartant — les ronces ses lèvres
— dans la touffeur des coeurs
aphones s'ouvrent des clairières
d'embrasser de répondre oui —
toi — mon ébranlement — ain-
si cette beauté ou ne sera pas

she no longer paces she swims
spreading—the burrs her lips—in
the swelter of voiceless hearts open
clearings to kiss to say yes—you—
my trembling—thus this beauty or
will not be

sur le dos l'appel des paysages
tes mains pulpe et plexus veines
grosses   marginales   vaisseaux
trajets
flexueux   arcades
enroulements   tension
renversements   pression
chaleur doigts confluents ou-
vrant le feuillage lumière lacis
de nous tension du tendre le
monde en toi rassemblé

on the back the call of landscapes
your hands pad and plexus veins
thick peripheral vessels pathways
winding   arcades
whorls   tension
reversals   pressure
heat fingers confluences opening
the greenery light tracery of us
tension of the tender the world in
you gathered

il y a des portes sous
la peau   qu'enfoncent
nos effleurements au mi-
lieu d'illusions urbaines nous
sommes là nous aimant nous
endormant en vie nous dor-
mons à plein corps innocents
comme des enfant

there are doors under the
skin   which
our caresses push in the
middle of urban illusions we
are there loving each other to
putting each other to sleep
in life we give ourselves with
all our bodies innocent as
child

dehors l'horizon les grues
rongent — les corps vulné-
rables exposés derrière les vitres
de tours éphémères dedans
l'amour que nous faisons serine
l'impossible qu'il prenne son
temps nous oublie nous laisse
nous parler ce langage d'amants
tout en mosaïque d'égarements

outside the horizon the cranes
are gnawing—bodies vulnerable
exposed behind the windows of
ephemeral skyscrapers inside
the love we make teaches the
impossible to take its time forget
us let us speak to each other the
language of lovers made all of a
mosaic of derangements

le sommeil une autre plage du
don de soi blottis enlacés douce
lassitude   loin   des   pudeurs
l'abandon met en relief les mots
qui trouvent demeure dans la
chair — ce grand poème

sleep another shore of gift
of self huddled intertwined
sweet weariness far from
shame abandon brings out
words that find a home in
flesh—*that great poem*

Guy Rotella

Epitaph

Rutland bore me.
I hid or lied,
pretended to be bored,
then left
and died.
Home again
my plan
is to lie here
quiet
as long as I can.

Guy Rotella

Sentence

In life as in Italian,
Non ho l'opportunità
di praticare;
and therefore: error—
running on,
endlessly repeating,
always young.

Guy Rotella

One Bad Day Deserves Another

Musky oligarchs.
Rape and murder in Ukraine.
Fouled-up seas;
ratcheted storms.
Osmotic junk of siloed news.
The bears, a plague,
and jestered courts.
You're right. Bad's bad.
But go ahead. Relax.
We'll fix it: make a list, get
all the things a culture needs:
a coroner, a vivisectionist.
Some masks.

May 12, 2022

Foundation Myth

This ground
was a battlefield
in a war of revolution:
attack, retreat, parlay,
make peace.
Then, for two long centuries,
a hayfield
cut by hand, by horses,
by machines.
It's a playfield now.
Two shield-shaped kites
fly placidly above it,
frail as the solid-seeming breeze
that lifts
and drops them.

Toy catalogues
reliable as history
mock
whatever the ideals we wield:
"Fighting kites,"
declare their plaything lists.
Somewhere in the wings
war planes idle
anxiously at airfields.

Beware

when counting praise as tokening survival.
Appraisal's kin's reprisal.

Faith

To the unenticed,
affliction's lack's
affliction: useful, sweet.
They would not change it.

They boast the nest's
an inn, not residence;
the tender tree
no consolation.

Blunt knives, the others say.
Rehearsing stoutly safety's part
they take, for flower,
the bleeding heart.

Gospel

on Dürer's Nativity

Behind the scree of our reflection, faithful in the glass,
subservient and focused on his simple task
a workman transfers water from the courtyard well
into a jug. He's a sign, though of exactly what's unclear.
Indifference, perhaps, miraculous or plain
refreshment, or perhaps our own confused attention
to what's central and what's not. He's turned away,
both from the refugees, accommodated on an open porch,
and from the outcrop, partly ruin, partly hill, that towers
skull-like up behind him. Meanwhile, securely old, Joseph's
praying in the background. A preternaturally alert or startled
cartoon ox is at his shoulder. *Their* eyes dwell on Mary,
not the perfect child Mary gazes on. Astonished, overwhelmed,
adoring, lost, she kneels, sublime beneath the lintel,
her infant boy held up on a table altar-like before her,
she about to change or nurse or bathe him in his earthly aspect.
Her crossed arms cradle emptiness as if to say that he's
already all beyond her, she who's as sure as he of where they're
    bound.
Their future takes us in with its predictable surprise;
one more variation in an ancient repertoire (fistful of nails,
spread-winged finch, bracelet of thorns, swaddling shroud),
it repeats the forecast histories of art all school us to expect,
an architecture we naturally believe and knowingly reject:
on the etched rear wall of a foreign inn
half-timbered crosses rise in certain prospect.

Guy Rotella

At Gallarus

i. m. Seamus Heaney

Good sharp stink of cow and sheep, dewslick grass,
and a gritstone stone tent, wall-roofed, impervious—
give or take—a thousand years to history or weather
(Vikings and Norman raiders sluiced away its makers).
"Like an upturned boat." Just so. Stranded,
but buoyant, a corbelled ark of hand-worked rock
cut and stacked and tipped exact and incremental.
The Gaelic name means church (or home, or shelter)
of the strangers' place. Built for God or man or beast,
for the sheer good of dressing stone, or for the stone itself,
to mark a big man's grave, it posits prayer and permanence.
From the hill behind a hundred year old fuschia hedge from Chile,
a tractor (power take off set to augur holes for posts that might
see out a generation) echoes hard off in- and outside walls
its ominous antique ordinary capable native refutation.

Guy Rotella

At Dickinson's Grave

Bang spice for cakes,
words for weight,
eternity for soundings,
then sight beyond:
off soundings--
there's where
ships
sail safe
(in pews'
lee shore
insistent bromides
wreck and founder;
wreckers haul).

Fly and flounder,
winged and pinioned.
Homework, verse;
comets, puddings:
ratchet, pawl.

Solitary now as never,
intensity,
distinctest noone,
ladders ladders
deep as tall.
Vocation
and the phoebe's call.

The sea,
the land,
however vast:
coffined cupboard,
vaulted halls.

Housed here in boughs,
one
surpassing surplus
compassed
some things
less than
though provoking all.

Poem not nearly enough in the style of Billy Collins, who says that poems will go on being written until everything in the world has been compared to every other thing, and toward that end, some minor contributions

His poems
are taken in
in handfuls,
hands full,
like peanut M&Ms.
Invitingly thin
familiar pretext shells
lead down
through milky detours
to a central nut,
and eaten properly,
like bacon:
tasted, chewed, devoured,
they deliver—
each layer altering
deliciously the others—
more than simple punch line jolts
or sugar-junkie payoffs.

Yes, poems like peanut M&Ms.
And yet
(since by their nature
similes insist
that difference is the complement
of likeness; likeness' condiment),
these affable sweet treats
—they're not available in stores;
in bookstores, yes, if you can find one,

otherwise, on line—
provide sometimes
quite startling exceptions
in the mix:
bittersweet and dark
exotic whiskey flavored truffles,
even now and then the heavenly,
infernal down and dirty,
mouth and tongue and mood
and mind transforming kind
trained pigs in Italy or France
are said to find.

Little Mirror

It's one of those
perfect
days,
storm passed
and sea and sky
all white
on blue on white.
A clean wind scrapes
the harbor,
beach, and air.
The moored boats
skate and waddle,
waddle and skate,
as Schuyler says somewhere.
Dead serious ospreys
squeak like toys.
I'm 69, that
impressionable age,
the world
serene but
joyful
just because
I feel
that way.

Guy Rotella

Aging in Place

Death is closer every day. It always has been,
or so we say, taking up the all-day chores
that once were child's play, laughing at the paucity
of our devices. We let the garden go last year;
maybe the year before. The roto-tiller's rusting in the barn.
These days house room's all the yard we want or need;
it shuts us in. And to be shut-in feels almost right.
Wanting's banked, an old account to draw on, or like a fire
we pretend we'll stir again come morning. Does us good
to think it. Need is something else, but even that's
contained. The kids all live away; they come back when they can,
and do what they can from a distance. When they call
they ask us what we ask ourselves, "Are you OK?"
Most of the time we are. Memories keep us entertained;
some we retrieve, more of them fetch us. There's television,
but it doesn't make much sense: people are wolves or fools;
the wars seem just the same. Meanwhile, we talk and read,
nod off, play music, cobble lunch and dinner. Clean-up's haphazard.
Lost loved ones, places, friends, they're as real as ever: wish you were
     here,
the way the postcards say, and in a way, you are. That's right,
we're fine. The shrubs we planted when we came here crowd the
     house.
Our trees outgrow us; darkness gathers in their crowns.

Ice Dams

We might say to the roof what, headed south,
Frost told his apple trees: keep cold. The house throws off
the excess heat we generate by keeping things inside
just warm enough for going on. And it can leak away
so snow that's gathered at the eaves will melt and freeze,
and melt and freeze again. It's the old, old story:
forcing its way out, ice-blocked unseen familiar water's
turned back in; it runs upslope against its grain, brims
over ice-shield, then seeps between the shingles and the sheathing,
pouring down to sap our walls and windows from above.

We know what's needed well enough: open up
and vent the soffits so the roof's well chilled.
We put it off in fall; it's too late now: a job for spring.
There are roof or snow rakes. We could try those,
but it'd be like trying to shovel leaves and might well
make things worse, since clearing all the way from peak
to eave's beyond our reach. Anyway, it hasn't happened
yet. We know it can. We've read enough that just the thought
awakes us separately from sleep to listen overheated
at the dormer. For now, our hold's still tight; might be,
when one or the other of us leaves the house, we'll look to the
     snowed-in
roof and cast ourselves that pilfered spell: good-by; keep cold.

Guy Rotella

Mesh

for Mark and Mary Anne

Wakened by the flick
of a fleeting, maybe fatal
phrase I hope to catch,
I see the tracery
 where overnight
 an orb weaver has cast its net,
cornering a wedge of deck,
webbing flower pot and railing,
chair, umbrella base, and table leg
in a skein that hints
almost invisibly at its intention.
Only predawn dew
and the spider's thick-set,
centered, curled-asleep
or shamming self
give the shape away.
It's lithe, alert, and lethal,
no more a metaphor
than the careless,
unintended feeder trap
the sleek and subtle
sharpshins strafe.

Tossed

under the deck
for a night
that runs to weeks
the tarp becomes
a habitat,
a staging-ground, a refuge:
termites in the logs laid on
to hold it down,
mosquitoes—wigglers and tumblers
in water-filled folds,
spiders, ants, rolled-up
or scurrying wood lice,
the usual homegrown cast
but featuring a star:
limax maximus,
domestic interloper
in a motley leotard,
the giant great or gray
or leopard slug
famous for the mucus
thread it, partnered,
hangs from
in the intertwining, fainting
pas de deux
a willing audience
lets stand
(too easily
perhaps) for love.

Guy Rotella

On Yellowed Postcards

Being together
we were told
would one day
gather and condense
into togetherness
and stay and stay.
It might be so.
Makes sense.
Although
the famous
other hand
may feel compelled
to write to say,
Together? Well,
adjacent, sure,
but ironbound
like islands
in an empty bay.

Framing Aftermath

Taut consent impelled us, the way an oar's stroke drives
then melts on water put behind. Reason enough
to be abashed if not ashamed. Abject
Francesca wept her fact, a fixed spike,
fletched joy blown back in time of sorrow. Ours
is something else, not that; say, temperament
expressed in an acquired gesture tinged
with sacrament. Perhaps. Whatever it was,
it caught us right up into paradise,
where hearing unspeakable words we thought
for a while we could speak them back.

Well, that's a start, but not quite right, wrong footed,
headed wrong, too serious, inflated, even grim,
consoling, too, derived. The flow was otherwise,
more ordinary, funnier, and sad.
Details, perhaps, since you put faith in them.
Snug in his solitary habitat
the pygmy hippo flinched when mated, matte-
black forest ducks crashed the drowsed contentment
of his pool. A sign explains. It says the hippo's
temperamental, wants to be alone; the wings'
unfolded flash, sky blue, is speculum.
It is the very mirror, shade and texture,
of your writing paper curing in a desk.

An open stretch of shore. A couple stands.
He holds her lightly, like a dancer, from behind,
and leads her through the steps, the fly rod's
forearm flick that sends the line inscribing air
in firm and cursive loops, as if, with hand on hand
and rapt in their bodies' overlap, they thought
by linking stroke on stroke to catch some word

equating craft with, what?, say ethics? Well and good.
Beyond, a single swan fills out the pretty picture.

Better yet? Perhaps. It does depend
on temperament. Meantime, there's this much certain
to be said: Dante's still right: love pardons
none who's loved from loving; whatever ache
imprints us will outlast the shallow season,
remnant wind, this psalm that holds us up;
and this: while a weave of whimbrels carols lovely
in your lively hair, their whicker's our assent,
unstinting yes to all that's ordinary,
funny, sad: the tapered oar, the water's mark,
and some of what we said and did and meant.

Cynara

That island trip we took,
what were we, 82?
I spent days sunning,
napping with my book,
dreaming now and then
of freestone brooks
I'd fished for years
but then forsook
when slippery rocks
and currents
made my steps uncertain,
even with a wading staff,
that folding shepherd's crook
I thought—with
all the stiff
surefooted arrogance
of long protracted youth—
embarrassing as worms
or spinning gear.
Sorry, dear.
I'm wandering again I know,
and running on.
What I meant to say
was this:
when I awoke
from fitful dozes
in those lovely island nooks,
it wasn't sun-enameled
topless girls in thongs,
but the sidelong look
of your still girlish slouch,
bright eyes,
and proper suit—

the memories
those things shook loose—
that sent old passion
threshing through me
like a leaping rainbow trout
on yet another run,
cold blooded, dancing
hopeful, desperate,
hooked.

Vestige

You suffer,
sheaf of symptoms
not yourself.
I watch
and feel
you're ill so I am
(greed that makes
your illness, even, mine).
I know,
even so,
hope watching's watching over,
trust that underneath
your hollowed voice,
its pleading
"*Please.* Go home,"
that other, hallowed voice
is yet once more, as ever,
making rainment
(okay, raiment, my mistake) of remnant,
remembering that ember isn't ash,
or flesh a fiction of the soul.

Guy Rotella

Stages

for MMD

Beyond the ward, forsythia, perennial
ingénue, perennial veteran, rehearses
one more time the role it's had line-perfect
from the start: brash youth to antique gold
in a brief, repeatable arc: curtain up; curtain down;
encore. Within, flesh frayed, perplexed and proud,
spangled in losses, you shimmer and bow
to improvise a final act, as scene by scene
you've improvised your whole life long
your own and everybody's
singular much precedented part
half cribbed from past performances,
half ad-libbed on the fly. Shimmer and bow.
We listen and watch, audience of understudies
primed for laughter, tears, applause,
our practiced, crossed-up wishes: end and endlessness—
our meager repertoire of exits: Play on; Go now.

For J.B.G., in Irons

A proper little woman.
With unexpected pleasures:
mock lasciviousness,
fire scenes,
vodka, Canadian Mist.
Fond and malicious, your Irish wit
could take the piss,
as when you pegged your pupils
sideshow geeks:
Sam the Fail; The 300-Pound Boy.
You hated sailing. If impressed
you faked the woodwork, brightwork, flaking,
or drank yourself insensible to stay on shore.
Too vehemently instructed once
to keep new seeded lawns
from drying out,
you pulled the hose straight through
the house from back to front.
What was that?
Getting your own back? Protest?
Some ladylike confusion about taps
and spigots? Delight in the absurd.
Now you're absurd yourself. Phase five.
The body's hull's deserted,
conn abandoned,
all your rigging down
with nothing left to do but sink and drown.
Stupefied and stupid, we stand by,
no more to say beyond goodbye
and wordless wishes:
full glasses, soft and soaking rain,
light winds, fair sailing
on the long reach out.

Progress Report

Five stages of grief
the comforters
would exchange for peace:
Denial's first. We still say No.
So that one's right.
Then *Anger.* Much the same:
We're recruited to your rage
all unappeased at 98
for more and yet more light.
Turn the page?
Depression's next.
We're in it, night on night,
a hole too deep for *Bargaining,*
though looking up from here
we see where in the distance
steep *Acceptance* lurks
beside his dismal twin Relief.

Of simplicity

my mother made,
predictably, a virtue,
making of it, too,
an explanation,
a style and deed,
even a barrier with banner
(defensive, yes;
although, cornered,
she could,
as the poet says,
wound
with her shield);
then, near the end,
nothing simple about it,
given plainer,
plainest stuff
to work and wield,
she,
as if hardly trying,
made of it a cloak
to wrap herself
and us
all up in it as well
to ease us into dying.

Epitaph

Much as I wandered here and there,
the bit of me beneath this stony roof,
bound by native earth and native air,
signals loyalty beyond reproof.

The Source of What We Do with Words: An Interview with Maxine Chernoff

Lea Graham

LG: I'd like to start with talking about narrative in these recent poems. I often feel—whether I'm reading your prose poetry or your "skinny poems," as you've called them, that we only get a glimpse of narrative before it turns the corner and disappears. Even early poems like "A Vegetable Emergency" where a head is found sprouting in the garden doesn't fully turn as a story turns. Can you talk about your relationship to narrative generally (because you spent many years writing fiction) and to these newer poems specifically?

MC: I do not like to tell "clear" stories because they are anything but lifelike. Life is filled with complexities and mixed motives. There are more Hamlets than people of action among us. So whose story do we tell and how? Our own personal circumstances do not usually rise to moments of such insight (except to our mothers) that they must be told in poetry or fiction. So what should narration then do? It can serve as a "doorjamb," so that what we glimpse through the half-open door takes on meaning and depth, or we can tell complex, broken, flawed, tangential, partial stories, which feel more like life filtered through the consciousness of the writer. (My MA thesis was about narrative methods in Beckett's *Watt* and Woolf's *To the Lighthouse*—alternate tellings always intrigued me.)

Everything can be a story in that we have witnessed or experienced or imagined something, but there is no master story of our times, which are so perilous and seem more and more out of our control with nascent dictators, global climate crisis, perilous migrations, wealth inequality as was never fathomed, plagues, war, etc. We who work from our intentions as creative artists are writing in the margins of peril, which can be personal but is often universal and increasing in severity. But even "small" topics can stand in for "the whole" as emblems of or entries to larger questions. Think of Emily Dickinson rarely if ever mentioning the Civil War, yet her poems about death are deadly and convincing even when they are playful. That was her way to account for her times. The engagement needn't be direct for it to be credible and often moving. I think that good narrative opens rather than limits possibilities. In that way poems and novels are probably more similar in their possible strategies than short stories. Short stories are often singular views of a circumstance, most often narrated by the main character. Their need is for succinctness whereas poems and novels more favorably work with fragmentation or abundance.

LG: In other interviews, you've talked about the use of "I" by contemporary poets, wondering why it always has "the last word." In *Diary,* your latest work, you rarely use the first person. There seems a kind of resistance to the personal nature that we associate with diaries. Talk about your decisions around speaker(s) and addressees.

MC: Diaries are traditionally personal. But as someone fully aware of Rimbaud's statement, "I is another," I know that poems needn't be the single truth of an individual writer. What happened to me isn't what I try to account for—I am more a witness to my moment in the world and feel powerfully attached both to my own consciousness and the circumstances of the moment that shape my orientation. But anyone's experiences are as interesting as mine. It's something deeper I want in my work, and that is the lyric mode and approach that also shines a light on an object or locale or situation that has gained the writer's attention. The writer is the medium. The poem is the approach—the trail of words, the path, be it a lineated piece or a poem in prose. When I wrote novels from approximately 1985 to 1997 (in addition to poetry), my books were always multi-valent, with at least two and once, five narrators. Every perspective can inform; one that aspires to command the story isn't of great interest to me. The overlapping realities and moments are what interest me in creating any piece of writing, be it a poem, a story, or a novel. In my novel *American Heaven,* a former gangster; his caretaker, a Polish mathematician living in Chicago; a woman who lost her baby and cares for a retired Black jazz musician; and the grandson of the former gangster all get to narrate their stories, which of course enrich each other's and overlap over time.

But back to poetry. So many first-person poems are reportorial, which can be interesting but are stacked in the speaker's favor. I keep wanting to hear "the other side" or alternate versions. I think of Ashbery and Stein, abstraction and indeterminacy figure here—but many approaches spurn the mimetic. Hyperrealism as seen in wonderful painters who can make a dish and glass look more real than an actual dish or glass are also flirting with what constitutes showing—

we come to appreciate the daring of the painter who reproduced "reality" with such confidence and ability, yet we know that the real glass is dust-flecked and maybe slightly cracked near the base. *Diary*, then, is a document whose "main character" is our moment. In writing I am in service to that intention.

LG: When the "I" comes out in *Diary*, they are dealing with actual memories—those of your Bubi and her vigilant eye at the door as you ate, hiding snacks when your friends came over. The effect is like photographs that float to the surface amidst the less specific. How does this diary operate between the abstract, the "you," the "we" and the spare use of "I"?

MC: I am interested in my own consciousness as it is shaped by forces within me that I don't fully understand, but also, my alignment with or misalignment to the world. I am one of nearly eight billion voices on this planet. So what I say as "I" is not all that significant. The use of the "I" in the poems is reserved as you notice for the specific personal memories I include such as childhood experiences, but I am more interested in a collective voice in the poems and the way they can "write" the listener or reader into the work.

Experience is universal, and the hope in the poems is to invoke that by using either "you" or "we." To depersonalize the personal without losing specificity is a goal. If you look at the work of Dickinson, for instance, she doesn't tell about herself—rather, even as an "I," she is impersonal, observing a sunrise or the unwanted thought of a "funeral in [her] brain." "I is another," again! And the reader is made part of the experience by the generosity of the writer who offers it to the reader. I tell my students, "You are not on a witness stand." You can embellish or omit details from the real event if the piece elucidates deeper states of being in the world—writing as an act of attention.

LG: Dreams play a part in this new work as well as your past. Can you talk about your thoughts on bringing dreams into your poems? Some writers keep a notebook by their bed for just this reason; others, denounce dreams in that they are predictable in their strangeness. What do you have to say about them as a focal point?

MC: When I was a younger writer, I sometimes wrote prose poems that feel dream-like in their narrative content: a boy enters a room, turns off a fan, but begins to chant *air air air* in its place. A woman straddles a globe. Fred Astaire, influenced by the movie *Royal Wedding*, holds his daughter upside down, nostalgic for when he danced on the ceiling. Those were simulations of dreams, but like narratives of an episode in life, they are too clear and "manufactured" for my taste. The parts of real dreams we forget nightly are surely as interesting as what we remember. Maybe poems are a way of bringing the forgotten scenes back into view. When I did write down actual dreams, again many decades ago, I never used them in poems. Committed to the page, they seemed complete in themselves, and that was fine with me.

LG: Some of the poems in *Diary* seem like riddles:

> *I know you exist in books I take up just to find you, often just a footnote*
> *or entry in an index* (6).

Talk about your relationship to riddles and how you think they intersect with poems.

MC: Riddles, runes, chants, spells—all are the territory of poetry, which sometimes works as an expanded riddle, almost a prophecy. We see this often in poems with a metaphysical stake in things—Donne, Dickinson, Simic, Popa, Vallejo, countless others, all deal in such scenarios and play constantly with parts standing in for the whole. When the poet May Swenson writes, "Body, my horse, my house, my hound..." she is posing riddles. How is a body like these three other entities? It carries her through life, it encloses her, providing safety, and it accompanies her and searches for objects of meaning in the world. Naming is mysterious and richly satisfying. We like to talk about our possessions, and for writers those possessions are often the abstractions of words translated into the materiality of context and design. If we are good "translators," poems can appeal on various levels and lead to linguistic connections that both satisfy and complicate matters. I appreciate that quality and think that the prose poem with its lack of attention to line raises the image to a higher level of notice. That has been important in my work in the form.

LG: I know that the Vietnam War was a large presence in your teenage life. You've written about your cousin's young husband who was killed there after just three weeks and the effect it had on you and what you wanted to say in poetry. But the War shows up even here in this later work:

> I wanted to be a cowboy and shot my father from behind the couch and between the legs of the Formica table. I had silver guns and a fake-leather holster. On my Schwinn I was Lieutenant Cable, tumbling onto the Ornstein's lawn in a Hammerstein fantasy of young love destroyed. Mostly I was a rabbi, reading the inscriptions on my temple wall to do Justice and love Mercy. When the actual war on Vietnam arrived, I remembered that wall and how we create suffering, even in play (Diary, 6).

Other poets have told me that the War and its time period brought poets together who might not otherwise have been in the same room (e.g., Robert Bly, Robert Creeley, Galway Kinnell, Diane Wakoski, Denise Levertov, etc.). Talk about that period for you and what you saw in terms of its connection to poetry—your own early work and/or other poets' work. But also, what ways do you think about the Vietnam War and its legacy now nearly 50 years later?

MC: The Vietnam War began under the French in 1954; we entered in '64 when I was 12 and it continued until 1975 when I was 23—so many years of my adolescence and young adulthood occurred during that war. Also, and more importantly, people of my generation first came to understand what massive lies our government used to create a continual state of military involvement around the world when Ellsberg (who just died) published the Pentagon Papers, and we discovered how the Gulf of Tonkin incident was a convenient invention of our government for the purpose of entering an undeclared and unwinnable war. What were we doing thousands of miles away conducting an intervention in a civil war? We were acting as the imperialists that we have always been. It was an awakening for people of my age, particularly boys of my era, whose lives were threatened by the draft. If you had a "low number" in the draft lottery, you either served or went to Canada or ended up in prison. Not only my cousin's husband, but a handful of boys from my high school, often Hispanic kids, ended up as cannon fodder. Meanwhile, on "the home front," there was Kent State and a highly emotional debate between people like my father who had served in WWII and were pro-military and anti-communism (which they connected to the Domino Theory of nations in SE Asia falling without our intervention). In my household, my father and I would battle over this. An additional source of anxiety for him as an American

Jew was the Holocaust, whose lesson to him was one of fear: don't let the ruling class know what you think—they may come for you. He actually feared for my safety. Meanwhile, I was provocative to him by not heeding his warnings. I attended the Conspiracy 7 Trial some mornings after college, hung out with the accused, and often went to anti-war demonstrations. Ironically, in my life as a waitress in college, I often served the Conspiracy 7 judge, the now infamous Julius Hoffman, who in his earlier years sided with anti-censorship forces and desegregation forces in key rulings. But the aged jurist had no appetite for the Conspiracy defendants and famously gagged Bobby Seale, the only Black defendant.

One area in which my father was right and my generation mainly wrong was our attitude toward returning soldiers: we scorned them and their service while people like my father supported them. We couldn't get past the bad taste of the war and recognize their sacrifice. I think our actions caused further wounds to lives already made precarious. It was unkind.

Regarding your question about how the war changed the poetry community, I was too young and new to poetry to fully understand that people against the war could also be opposed to each other's poetics. Thank goodness there aren't wars about that, at least in the United States.

LG: You have pieces in this work that deal with the Civil Rights Movement and the history of the Trans-Atlantic Slave Trade. Just as with the Vietnam War, the Civil Rights Movement was an ongoing event in your young life in Chicago. Talk about how you see connections between the history of slavery in this country and the route to the Civil Rights movement and now, the Black Lives Matter movement.

MC: We are a culture tarnished by our slave-holding past—this is clear to me. But having lived more than half my life in Chicago, a city rich in Black culture, it was also clear to me through art, music, writing, dance, community—all of these areas have been enriched through years of struggle over Civil Rights with activism. And it has led to many cultural advances. But as we know, this is never settled in our land with its fearful and often out of touch white ruling class and myths about race which are often highly ignorant and remarkably transparent for their racism: the fear of the 1600 Project, Critical Race Theory, the history of Civil Rights as it's taught in the world come to mind.

I grew up with all of this swirling around me even as a child. I recall watching King's famous speech in 1962 at age 10, reading Malcolm X, protesting the sentence Muhammad Ali (a neighbor at one point) received, being censured with the girls in my eighth grade class in 1965 by our Irish Catholic teachers for playing kissing games at a mixed-race birthday party. But I also recall how my Southeast Side neighborhood was a site of white flight and redlining after the 1968 riots in Chicago which occurred after the murder of MLK. Once again, my father and I were at odds—he wanted change without protest and feared violence more than repression.

But what I most like to recall of Chicago and Civil Rights is how one splendid alderman named Harold Washington became mayor, supplanting years of white mayors pre and post-Daley, and how Barack Obama celebrated his own momentous victory in the same park where anti-war demonstrators had their heads bashed during the Democratic Convention in 1968. Now it was 2008, and it seemed like a new era. The crowd was enormous and ecstatic, and I'll never forget Jesse Jackson's joyous tears as Obama became president, an ascendancy no one had predicted in previous years when Chisholm and Jackson himself had staged a run for the presidency.

So, the Black Lives Matter movement which began before George Floyd grew to new power when the world witnessed his killing, and the police were actually held accountable. Do we need to discuss the backlash with Trump? Let's not. But the recent radical Christian takeover of the state legislatures throughout the country, the insane policy at our border, the new push toward censorship and reproductive interference are all examples of the backlash. One step forward, three back seems the pattern for the fight between justice and White Privilege, which is always secretly or not so secretly veiled racism.

LG: Let's talk about the Ukrainian War. You have pieces in here— maybe the driving pieces of the work that focus on Ukraine. How do you see this war within the scope of other wars in your lifetime? Does it connect with you personally in some way or is it yet another part of the "arrogance of men and their bullets" that you need to write about and against?

> They had always wanted a son, the young couple, so the grandma, the dog, and the small boy cross the border into Poland. She makes use of a stroller abandoned at a train station to push the child, who holds the small dog on his lap.

Rituals like morning tea are memories. Everything she had is lost. An
empty calm fills her, makes her able to press forward, find a tiny room
for the three of them—one mattress, no stove, a bathroom shared by 14.

As they wait in line for supper, her phone rings. It's her daughter, telling
her that the child's father has been killed, her plan to wait behind now
senseless.

They are both widows of different wars. Outside embers stir a bonfire
that lights the spring night with vagrant ghosts. There is no Heaven,
she thinks, only the infinite arrogance of men and their bullets. The dog
snores in the corner, twitches in his sleep.

MC: There are many angles of inflection with Ukraine. First, I am from the Jewish Pale of Settlement in Eastern Europe through my grandparents who came from various parts of Russia or Poland and Ukraine around 1900 to 1910. Part of the family settled in Chicago, the others in Toronto. But more importantly, that Ukraine is in a tug-of-war between dominating forces in Russia and the former US President, who seems to represent Russian interests more than those of our country, hence, the first impeachment. On the other side stands Ukraine and people who believe in a country's sovereignty. But mostly Ukraine entered the work because it began when my *Diary* poems began. It is the backdrop to all the writing in that manuscript. And it is an interruption of what most people want in their lives, a safe place to live and raise their families. If governments can't guarantee this and more powerful countries don't defend those in peril, what are they for? So yes, there it sits right in the middle of my project, which is a diary of our times more than a diary of me.

LG: Your poem about "lies" that begins with: "She lies about her beagle and its pedigree" (9) progresses to the point where what is being lied about threatens the future of humans. How do you understand this period of "alternative facts"? As a poet and fiction writer, your medium is language that, perhaps, "lies in order to reveal the truth." Can you characterize this relationship between truth and lies?

MC: Lies are not good. Imagination is. If one lies in service of the overall good on a personal basis (telling someone their suit is attractive when it's not, for instance), it needs to be harmless or advance a good motive, not hurting the feelings or security of a person you value. To create baseless lies that scare people or embolden insane delusions (e.g., Pizzagate, Q-Anon, Replacement Theory, etc.), is always wrong and confuses many people of questionable moral standing or critical thinking skills. It is altogether dangerous—as is the news media when they report as if there were only two sides and one side is "batshit crazy." How MAGA thinking has shaken our country's solid-seeming base continues to horrify me.

Now to imagination. When one invents in writing without an intent to harm that isn't lying. It's the source of what we do with words, which can speak the truth even if the examples are hypothetical.

LG: You've said that you inverted sonnets in your manuscript *Zonal*, the poems you wrote during the pandemic (and included in the newest book *Light and Clay: Selected and New Poems*, MadHat 2023) since the world seemed to have turned inside out.

> *make morphemes sing and white space*
> *speak: we stay inside, watch news, make*
> *soap, tend windowsill gardens of dill*
> *and anise, hoping the illness will not find us,*
> *hoping we are as tissue, flimsy and invisible.*

Talk about the relationship in these poems between content and form which is something you are so thoughtful about—though, perhaps, most readers know you for your prose poems.

MC: When Covid began and we lived as shut-ins, I found myself wanting to write in a way that somehow mirrored my circumstances. I wanted a project I'd never attempted before because we were living under conditions that were completely new and strange. (A token of the strangeness is the fact that for the first few months I baked (which I never do, and embroidered a cloth square, totally atypical for me). I had maybe written two sonnets in my life—one in high school as an assignment and one while trying out forms now and then over the years. I realized that the poems would be accounts of the moment we were sharing and that because the natural order was overturned, there might be a reason to regroup the lines in a sonnet to reflect that, so I took the 14- line form in the 3 quatrains and a couplet mode and stood it on its head: 4,4,4, 2 became 2,3,4,5 regarding stanzas. The conclusion therefore came first and the examples followed. Somehow this not only seemed emblematic of the moment but also responsive to how the world had changed— even the old form of the sonnet could be imagined differently. I also wanted a form that could include long or shorter lines if I wished, so metrics didn't hold over from the original. I found these broad constraints freeing at the time and useful for the series I wrote, which is filled with heartbreak and news of myself and the world. And it occurs to me now, language in a set form is in a sense "trapped" with a purpose not its own but assigned—so, too, our circumstance as shut-ins during Covid.

LG: Talk about the title "Zonal" as this section seems to reveal some of what you were after:

> And now in surfeit we have loss: planet shifting
>
> on its axis to shoulder all the waste: redundant
> fracking zone/ birdless vector of regret:/ what are you
> in this late day? / What sound issues from the glass
> place you call mirror or self in a world of shattering, /call
> it Zone, or Area N: /how we make songs to suture space.

Where is the connection for you among space, disease, language and the other circumstances that we encountered during the lockdown?

MC: The social fabric quickly frays when the world is a vector of contagion and no place is finally safe. We think of Zones as we imagine how the disease is flaring here or there, but with the fluidity of travel and people's movement there is no safe place. Zone and therefore, "Zonal" has a sense of irony to it. How to continue a meaningful life with the threat of sickness or even death, how to reassure our children, how to keep on with creativity, how to help those less comfortable than ourselves, how to stay close to those we love—all were lock-down issues. Suturing with words is no different from the idea of repairing the broken world offered in Judaism. Our language can bolster notice and perhaps healing—though, in this case the disease was randomly deadly and severe.

LG: Let's just talk generally how these last years since 2020 have been for you. We've had a pandemic and with it, a lockdown of our lives. There's been the Ukrainian-Russia War and with that, a destabilization, I think, of what we thought Europe was. But also, the Trump-inspired assault on the Capitol and, more generally, on information. I keep seeing these ads for news "like Walter Cronkite" and while I'm not sure that's good or more so, even possible now, it seems very inviting to me after these years where "alternative facts" and misinformation are the new normal.

MC: Yes. Total agreement. We have slipped into a zone in which nearly half of all Americans agree with the liar-in-chief and think the liars are telling the truth. How to combat stupidity and intentionally fake news? It's shocking to me that the Supreme Court, generally erudite people from Ivies, are as misguided as meth addicts, aluminum-hat wearers or as evil as Trump. What has gone wrong? I think the little worlds we carry in our hands (phones or tablets) give people access to so much junk they must sort through, and some are not seeking the truth; but, rather methods to oppress, stoke fears, and bully others. Unless there are harsh penalties against government officials beyond Trump, I see no reason why this new orientation will change. If more lawsuits like those against Fox are adjudicated, maybe the climate for truth will change but as long as those in power want to obfuscate and complicate serious issues such as global warming for fear of losing money or control, there is little hope.

Zonal

"What of writing itself as a passion?"
    —*Geoffrey Hartman*

1.
Photo of a hand, shadowed by a hand.
Inside the eye of a fly, worlds and breaches

of security: how we've come to witness
quieter still, slow awakening of spring,
outside of history's grasp or need to show.

What grows and what burns is design.
You will lose your way in liminal drifts:
Amid the signs and warnings,
Indecipherable forms/systems disabled

in the reaching and the grasping.
Have you come to notice fog's
conspiracy? Is there method
in your breathing? Time to grow
wings and set out for the obvious.

2.

It is all introduction now: the notes,
and signs of comprehension.

Take Marx's giant head at Highgate.
Unimpressed, the children were, too tired
from the trek. They focused on the morning

when the carriage horse had taken
the apple, green and welcoming,
from their hands: all circumference there.
In Westminster behind the velvet ropes

I told my son, who wanted explanation,
on our "wasted," sunny day: "You're right.
Lots of dead people." How the press of
dappled leaves and early magnolia shedding
on the Serpentine became the story too:

3.

Roll over, Oscar Wilde. Meet Gertrude Stein
and the Little Sparrow. Meet Jim Morrison and

Chopin too. Deeper and deeper our travels
took us: there was Crete, whose indoor toilets
were the first preserved. The tourists

from the cruise had sea legs, as Knossos listed
right or left. The Mexican economist hated
America's presumptions, he confessed at dinner,
before the ping pong ball disappeared into the Aegean.

I thought *Ship of Fools,* how doomed
our journeys, felt comfort in moss roses curled
around a railing where men worked sums.
The castle from the Crusades, rehabbed by Mussolini:
palimpsest of wrong ideas: and no plot to save us.

4.

When worlds collide choose stillness, choose
green's waning days, or footprints in the mud;

choose a planet such as ours, whose carbon holds
an engine of rebirth. For those awaiting signs, like
the recluse in his hut awaiting God, no more

wrong than the fisherman with his slack,
dark line awaiting silverfish on Oakland's pier.
Under sea's repose, a slowness and a speed.
The bleached-out coral knows a crime. When smallest

mouths are open, it's nativity or war. The skirmish
never ends. Nothing restive but our minds awaiting
legibility. You too will stumble into simplifying by degree,
grow lazy with solutions on a breezy night when truth
gives way to forces of desire. Know this too is measuring.

5.

We choose to live, choose love as beacon,
choose names for fat, slick infants, mucousy

with birth, choose kindness for a few, invisibility
for the many, whom we honor with our obliviousness.
How can you claim to have made a choice when

tendrils reach around your shoulders, and one creature
eats another, beyond sight of our eyes? "I have my preference,"
she told me on the phone, though days outnumber choices
in the end. And in the end you have no say, as breath

comes slow, then fast, then seizes in the bellows of
your lungs. He said he watched his father die at the rural
hospital, where oxygen was running low. In Wuhan
the sun rose and roosters crowed as ever. Strange
to die at daybreak. (He shut his father's eyes.)

6.

Time speeded up is comedy—and time slowed down
its opposite. To know the ending is right is a nod

to convenience. What can sympathy mean when children
die at sea and parents weep and shake a fist?
There is a border crisis, where borders don't exist

any more than perfect love or painless birth.
The harms accumulate, until you gather
a lifetime of torn cloth. On the loom she knew
the truth, as white and black combined their powers.

The death of the artist, the death
of the critic, the death of the language. The last
speakers, two sisters who wouldn't speak to
one another. The tragi-comic gods own all the real
estate and in the end the blackness too.

7.
Born to find yourself surrounded,
a Kurdish girl in March, in winter's

 tent, whose single book reads
Nursing Practice, since you were
living too, among the others, before
the onslaught powdered existence and filled
blank pages with the language habits we
 have come to know as grief. Try a little
 defamiliarization if it feels too close:

 make morphemes sing and white space
 speak: we stay inside, watch news, make
 soap, tend windowsill gardens of dill
and anise, hoping the illness will not find us,
 hoping we are as tissue, flimsy and invisible.

8.

Riding this same subway/ planet Earth/
a young woman/ (dressed only in a Hefty bag)/

had trained her eyes on me/ Now nurses wear the same
to treat the ill, whose last words won't be heard
by loving ears. Cue the narrative, friends:

dystopia now (I watch a documentary about the painter
whose work I'd seen that year: how she had continued/
her disease slower/than our current plague/
her paintings large/ and glistening with life/:

"I can't believe I have to leave this world!")
But must we trade economy for love?
When worlds mourn at a distance, nothing
to hold except our worry beads and lists of needs:
from Lysol to goodbyes / deliver us, we pray/.

9.

Examples thick with meaning of a boy who left sweet
 William at her gate and of a woman with gray braids

who sewed cat masks for her many friends, uninvited lens
descending on our spring, old solstice in a new
 world of refrigerator trucks and spreadsheets tracking

viral load while lotuses bloom and swans make
stillness seek its center. We do not know how we'll
 discourage the jasmine until a proper window – or
Marvin Gaye from playing "Ain't No Mountain"

--on satellites circling over tallies of the dead.
 My friend watches "Pride of the Yankees," Iron
 Horse, taken in the middle of his day, life limping
 toward spectacle, grandiloquent, or stumbling out
 of reach. Be brave for the newsreel. Be grace.

10.

You carry with you like a shell, the heaviness
of words surrounding what we've come to call

"environment." A student years ago had written
of an "ecology walk," his story set in the '50s,
anachronistic term in finite time. I told him

   how we had thrown our bottles in the pond, lit matches
   in dry fields, ignored translucent moths the texture
   of our skin peeling in summer delirium of sun.
   And now in surfeit we have loss: planet shifting

 on its axis to shoulder all the waste: redundant
fracking zone/ birdless vector of regret: / what are you
in this late day? / What sound issues from the glass
 place you call mirror or self in a world of shattering, / call
 it Zone, or Area N: / how we make songs to suture space.

11.

The older woes were beads of plastic ocean cramped with string
and oil tankers circling in the soup. We pastiched our needs:

bought flotsam at the jetsam store to make a proper flag for life
before our current limit: how nothing we predicted came
to be, and everything we'd never guessed has come to pass,

how friends were spared and not, in the ellipsis of a season,
sirens scorching air on radiant April days. On Hart's Island
ghostly work attends the barges of white shrouds,
whose proper lives get captioned by their fates: to look at all

the dying and yet not find the proper words attendant to
the grief. How in the future they will sing the loss,
in ballads to their children, of a world just opened as another
died outside of myth and theory: magnolia blanketed in dew,
moss- thickened gate of a mute and humbled spring.

12.

But who is speaking now, and how to Zoom the edges of the text?
  Can meaning take its storied place on suddenly vacant shores?

The middle goes missing from the plot of how we train our
      minds to follow
 all but tragedy, mortality pressed behind the ropes of well-
      earned fears.
While we try light and bleach and llama's blood to seek a cure,

 history shifts its weight. We pass markers for the losses we endure,
 whole Viet Nams of endings, cities falling ill, as fruit begins to form
in winter's face, and seasons pass in reference to our moons.
 April 15 lilacs bloom, the flower moon is pink and low in what

 we call a firmament of words and signs. We choose to read and
      "voice"
our fears though legibility encounters bewilderment, makes
 sense of time outside of time, experience upended, the week
      coyotes
 take LA, flamingos claim Mumbai, and monkeys loot Nepali
      shrines:
 how the millions missing from the tale agree to disappear.

13.

Or choose to be an orchid, blooming in a loamy patch
of earth, your fate a devolution--Ovid for our times.

Our stealthy state of being (the conditional)—while men with
signs think arrogance can chase away a plague. We are lonely,
 says the chorus of shut-ins in their robes. Posed before our screens,

 we play Saint-Saëns and Otis Redding; we play the Reverend
Gary Davis, gravel-voiced and certain, "Death don't have no
mercy…." And is there actual need for *world* when decades are
    reborn
 before our eyes? We live daily in our youth; we live our dying too.

 While under bushes growing at the verge, a nest is raided by a
    Steller's
jay, who eats the bluish eggs; cypress tree outside my beveled
glass witnesses the advent of new clouds. I take the photo on
    my phone of
 yellowish orchids angling toward the light. I have no name for
    what I feel,
 my dear: despite our life receding, no devolution when it
    comes to love.

14.

On the calendar of missing days, bright May passed
 in a firmament of haze, while our other selves roamed

avenues, remembering how feelings swelled and oceans
too. Subject to memory and its children, we find our best
selves in a mirror of belonging—crowds swarm behind us

in scenes of slow time, absence itself a destination,
as the future goes missing, lost in shrubs or budding groves.
Boats wobble ghost-like in slips and clouds roll overhead,
 unseen by captive multitudes who save their lives

 by simply losing hold. How hands slacken, drinks stay full,
 the castle sleeps—but this is not a tale. While sheep graze as
 ever, the brindle dog wonders where the neighbor's
  gone, the one who tended zinnias and daily asked
his name. Forgetting as an art: silhouettes, ideal forms.

15.

New death enters from a place of utmost hate: how
none are safe but some are even less. Then call it murder, sim-

ply put, a life was taken by a man--while others watched.
 Complicit world, half on fire as "president" spouts
 the nonsense he wants heard / It's nothing new

that leaders lie and hurl their viral loads into the air each time
they speak. / When cameras focus on one deed so ugly it halts all
time, the people pause to take a breath / the breath he needed
while a knee was placed upon his mortal neck. Now stores burn

 and those who want restraint must know how they have waited
centuries and more. / How even in our season
 of disease the world must stop to say his name: George
Floyd / was 46. / He had a life / went to a store / lost all
 chance for justice on a street/ phones recorded/ sisters wept.

16.

While signs proclaim the madness of the king,
 the world spells its name in summary/

summer of woes/ and nature's worldly
 face: how fledglings enter seasons rich
with song, first notes the ear has

never heard or failed to hear: We found you,
 world, when we were new, and you were
snow on roof, black branch of unfilled space,
absence to which we lent a listening ear.

Days painted green within a globe
 that also holds the song. Only amber
 colors world's past display of how we
 lived before the map was red with death:
 eyes peer out from story's unknown end.

Diary

A new day opens with all griefs known, patient eyes resting on the face that you love. Trees touch underground, roots interlocking as tendrils curl over the lip of a jar in the sun. So easy to enumerate our sorrows in the early light of the new year. Still, we hold onto hope as if it were a key and find the missing door. When we step inside, a table is set and candles lit.

Diary

Twig-baby, leaf baby, Ice-baby, who melts in her arms. She must be half-asleep or delusional with cold in the sparsely covered field, which could as well be a narrative regarding dirt. She sits on a discarded chair wrapped in her coat, feet draped with a blanket, thick oven mitts as gloves and creates more children to comfort her: moon-baby, snow baby, whispering baby, who sings her to sleep.

Diary

You were not there when the rift appeared or the sinkhole that held another miniature world. You made nothing new to stand on or peer into. The bottom didn't drop out: you gained new abilities to see beyond the edges, into the narrow heart of things, under the woes to the hearthstones warmed by your looking. Comfort creates heat. Which comes from our deepest pains, our tender notions. You are a stone warmed by the sun, hope resting in the hollow of your shadowed palm.

I awake with the world still upon me, a blanket, a fog, my own mother's slow death.

How can I tell you how I want to take away your pain? How can you appreciate my efforts, given the apex of your misery ("apex" a word conjuring Sir Edmund Hillary, *National Geographic*, 1957?

But wait.

I can offer you the stillness of the moment: let's cover our ears and hear silence swell as in an undersea cave. Or, to say it more simply, let me share the pain that engulfs you. I will be your birch forest dappled by sun and "slow time": rest here until the root of your grief is unearthed by hope.

Diary

In a house I've never seen, I tell my (dead) mother there is a (dead) cat I have mistakenly left behind, which she must feed. From dream to dream, our ghosts follow us, awaiting a call to action. Here is my father in his '60 Chevy Impala, the one with the big wings, telling me the same corny joke he told whenever we were alone: it doesn't bear repeating. And there is my Bubi, always at the stove, always cooking something meaty and bland: the shtetl wasn't a place for subtle cuisine. We sat and ate silently, her watchful eye on the door, worried that someone would arrive to imperil our food. When I invited friends to play, she hid our snacks. Family got fed: her ghosts taught her caution and fear of want. Now I am painting my dream house beige. So far it is empty, maybe invisible, as leaves in winter. But my ghosts will find me to populate it with all the memorized perils.

Diary

You write "Diary" and suddenly the room opens like a hinged shell. In it are the sorrows of the world. What to attend to as one lone voice? There are children to love, imposters to expose, flowers wilting in the sun, too warm for September, and worse, a catalyst for fire. A man has published a photo of a dead Steller's jay among leaves in his yard. Another corrects him on the species of bird. Pedantry has a long history, but birds will outlast us all with their petulant wings and shiny button eyes. Those with talons will fare better still with their unyielding grasp. You are not here to mend the world but to observe the pages as they burn slowly, slowly, as in a lit cathedral.

Diary

You, who fill the space, sliver between the running and the leaning, the lasting and gone star—becoming feldspar, landing near storm. You, who ask nothing of me but my arms, held and holding—but only in theory. You are seaweed and starfish, harp to my hands, ear to my song, blinking lighthouse in the cortex of nebula, billions of years distant but also not far. You are.

Diary

You cling to the objects of your life: that bracelet, that vase, knowing there are no proper amulets for warm no talisman for damage control. Who are you to feel their lives so acutely as they wane on a Friday in March? Here the moist magnolia buds give off their fragrance. The blood tree grows elsewhere. You will need an axe.

Diary

Another possible hole in the story.

Seasons tear the surface with their scratch marks, avalanches, and echoes, but under the ground Earth's core cools faster than imagined: what will become of our ancient planet, shrouded in stillness? No lovers or neighbors to write the history of how we disappeared.

Diary

I wanted to be a cowboy and shot my father from behind the couch and between the legs of the formica table. I had silver guns and a fake-leather holster. On my Schwinn I was Lieutenant Cable, tumbling onto the Ornstein's lawn in a Hammerstein fantasy of young love destroyed. Mostly I was a rabbi, reading the inscriptions on my temple wall to do Justice and love Mercy. When the actual war on Viet Nam arrived, I remembered that wall and how we create suffering, even in play.

Time's sutured notions of release played on yellow-fingered sleep. Under the harp of spider webs' weaving irises turned. Vines grew conspicuous. A small space opened in summer's span. Scarves of no consequence shook the light at noon. A reason stanched the bleeding hour, replaced by glittering eyes and slow speech. Day bleached carapace replete with words.

Diary

You slept on library desks with sun on your back or between the darkness of rows, elbows splayed, then rushed home in the twilit cold. That was your girlhood. Today as the warmth of a March day bleeds into your clothing, you open a book. You feel the length of hours and days.

Years? What are they?

Diary

Ants invaded the peony bulbs while under the vast face of sky, fireflies sent their signals. We lit sparklers and ran in joyous circles. Bedtime came and went. While in the world, napalm ravaged a jungle, and in our own South, dogs and water cannons spread their hate: that too, your childhood. No paradise: only time and its casual indifference through which you see the ravaging ants, their persistence.

Diary

In their dream bed blending boundaries and endearments, the known world is a bridge of rotted planks over murky water, which they are crossing together, the lovers, holding life's promise in their arms, as armaments pummel the air. Love and war, partners in their story of escape: Now they are awake in the windowless basement, hunched between others, no chance to feel the eternal sun warm their cheeks.

Salvos and Salve: Poems of Humor

Danielle Legros Georges

When Kevin Gallagher invited me to curate a special section of this volume of *spoKe,* among the many issues we were facing as poets and self-avowed global citizens were the effects of a world-wide pandemic and its devastating consumption of so many lives; the implications of international supply chain challenges; the rescinding of federal protection of abortion rights in the U.S.; a war against Ukraine; a failed state in Haiti (my native land); deadly conflicts raging around the world accompanied by their creation of large numbers of refugees; and an existential threat to the human species that is the global warming of the planet—among other worries, none less pressing than the other.

How were poets carrying on in the face of such events, and in a world that could be frustrating, crushing, or even inconceivable at times. *How do we manage the weight of such concerns and "do" literature?* This perennial question. What were some of our tools in addition to and beyond witness and documentation? Beyond lament. The use of humor struck me as a powerful response and a vital form of human knowledge, whether employed darkly and magnificently in the most awful situations, in wry analytic ways, or raucously as a celebration of life. I was interested in the opposite of tragedy, in the many forms of jesting, in the way humor can transgress boundaries of decorum and propriety.

To explore this topography, I reached out to a few handfuls of poets I knew (or suspected) would be willing to engage the question of comedic expression in/through poetry. How might incongruity, surprise, and the absurd present themselves? And how might irony, double entendre, parody, and the understated and overstated serve inquiry or revelation? One word I haven't mentioned heretofore is *fun. What might be the value of that?*

I'm grateful to each of the poets whose work appears in this section: Indran Amirthanayagam, Sharon Amaguni, Jennifer Barber, Daniel Bouchard, Linda Carney-Goodrich, Chen Chen, Susan Donnelly, Wendy Drexler, Magdalena Gómez, Holly Guran, Natasha Labaze, Gavin Moses, Melissa Peters, and H. Preston Soss. I'm especially happy to have the work of Anne Riesenberg, whose witty visual juxtapositions serve as section heads for the groupings of poems presented here.

depend   *deep end*

Astonish

There will be a time when you will color your
hair bright orange and act like a fool.
Better to do this now.
You can join the circus,
or at least go to the mid-life women's circus summer camp.
Learn to ride a unicycle on the tightrope.
Have an affair with the lion tamer and the bearded lady.
Go on a retreat and howl at the moon,
while sitting naked with 12 crones at the beach,
call them your disciples. Write your holy book.
Come home with damaged vocal cords,
or not come home at all.
You could learn to hang glide!
Feel what it is to fly while you still can.
Today you are the youngest you will ever be.
You could learn Russian. Backpack Europe.
You know how to survive.
You've proven it!
You can live on air and raindrops.
Skinny dip and hug trees naked.
Why don't you get a tattoo and sleep with strangers?
You could get lice from hostel beds, journal about it,
        and perform it at slams.
Wouldn't you love to join a biker gang and try your first hit of acid?
You are a golden beam of light that has not yet touched land.
Let secret parts of yourself out of the dark.

Inculcate

—to instill by persistent instruction
from Latin calc: heel; calcare: to tread

If a drag queen
can come forward,
in her spangled stilettos,

mid gunshots and screams,
to stomp on the back
of the Club Q killer—

let me come forward,
though suspicious before,
in favor of drag queens

and let those
high heels inculcate
and pound me,

till I'm dragged,
kicking and screaming,
into a new Gospel.

Jennifer Barber

On the Last Day of December

I can't find the gift book
a friend sent me, *Gratitude,*
which I wasn't planning to read

but isn't it true nobody wants
a book called *My Simmering Despair,*

despair in a flask
I set on a Bunsen burner
in the chemistry class I never took

and doesn't joy sometimes rise
like steam from the same flask
when the sidewalk
is clear of ice,

my smoothly wondrous skeleton
moving me down the block

Indran Amirthanayagam

Drunk in Paradise

We are going down to party. On the shore,
by the Caribbean Sea. We have worn

shorts and t-shirts and we are stepping
into the water balancing long tall glasses

on our noses. Goodbye arms merchants.
Goodbye kidnappers. Goodbye white collar—

roll your sleeves, get your Venezuelan cut—
oil for banana commodities exchange.

Goodbye all of you and all of that. We
are on the neighboring island's beach

and we drink and dance here without
fear until the morning Sun wakes

street cleaners, bus conductors
and schoolkids, and nobody will

shoot a stray bullet or direct one
straight between the eyes. We are

sober now and nobody worries.
Even the local priest imbibes

more than is necessary
to turn his wine into blood.

Linda Carney-Goodrich

God Tree

I planted a communion wafer in my front yard.
A grand tree erupted the very next day
with thick and tangled branches.
Tiny gods sprouted in place of leaves.
At first, they were all happy and singing songs.
Some hummed, some sang high, others did a little oompa, oompa.
A few of them bellowed great calls of OOOHHHHMMMMMM!
It was a heavenly choir blended with the special gods of all the world.

Mostly, it was perfect for three days, which seemed
      three hundred years.
Then some of them started screaming and proselyting.
Don't do this, don't do that, they warned passersby.
Cars slowed down. Dogs barked. A priest came to question.
The mail carrier asked, *mind if I pluck one of these?*
On the third night, it was silent 'til around 3 AM when
the gods cried together through my window.
They formed sections, argued about scripture, threatened
to cut each other's branches or to send each other viruses and plagues.

Next morning, they started in about mortal sin,
deadly sins, venial sins, which sins are permanent,
which are sins that will put the committer in old-timey purgatory,
Some insisted sinners could pay to have sin
      removed from their souls,
others said sins weren't sins if the right kind of person
      committed them.
Oh, they grew loud and shook my house to its very foundations.
I went to out to soothe them, *All right, boys*
(did I mention they were all boys?) *where is the love?*
Be silent, woman! they hollered in unison.
And that was it.

I started to give them away like zucchini in fall.
I harvested them and baked them into pies.
What are you doing with us? one asked. *It hurts.*
See how you like it, I said.
I created my *pièce de resistance* in the kitchen.
Of course, I used extra butter and sugar, but I added
secret ingredients from an ancient family recipe,
I did the steps, I cast the incantations at the exact time,
and baked at just the right temperature.
When I say my pie was divine, oh, I mean it.
I sent pies out far and wide. One to the governor
    and another to the pope.
I sent one to the president and all the judges supreme,
Here, I wrote, *have yourself a little sweet nothing.*
And all was good in the world.

 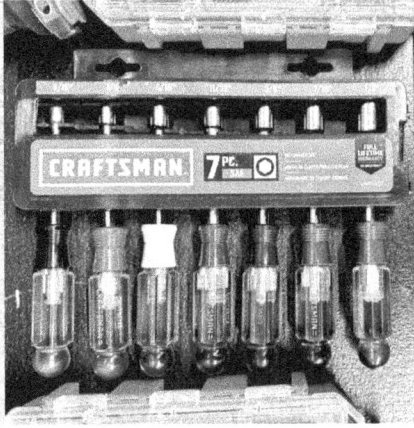

skillet   *skill set*

Apricot Jam from Vanak's

It's way too luscious.
Must be a sin—
to mouth and smack

half-apricots, aswim in jam
dark orange as the smear
of sun on the horizon

before it disappears.
Too sweet, I fear,
this *confiture d'abricot.*

Yet given, not bought—
so for me perhaps
a lesser fault. And humbled,

should it boast, upon
an ordinary piece
of wholegrain toast.

Wendy Drexler

Clover Food Lab

This place is as spotless as a chemistry lab, not one dirty dish in sight,
not one crumb, as the barista pours a scoop of ice into my plastic cup
which rests beneath a silver metal frame that holds a paper-lined gold filter.

He's trickling hot water meticulously over the grounds of my decaf pour-
over iced coffee, four or five passes but it's the slowness I crave, the waiting
for this coffee and I bet the black, grey, and white speckled counter is made

of an environmentally friendly non-toxic composite. I've had a hell of a day,
and while I wait I marvel at the tidy displays, bags of roasted beans,
the El Salvadorian Monte-Carlos, the Costa Rican Tarrazo, each color-coded,

printed label curated like an exhibit at MOMA. It's the order I crave, away
from the books piled so high they sway beside my bed, the stacks of
New York Times, the checkbooks I've hidden from my husband and don't

know how to tell him, the three times today he's asked what day today is,
it's the sinuous shape of the four beakers lined up on the counter I want
with the ripe pulp of pureed juice waiting to be mixed with sparkling water.

Actually, I want everything here, the stainless-steel stove, the covered
cauldrons of chickpea fritters, the unblemished white tile, the minimalist,
blond good looks of the designer chairs, as if we have all day to be

at our best. I want the Pesto Breakfast Bowl with organic longwind farm
(lower case) tomatoes (why clutter up lunch with capital letters?),
a soft-boiled egg and massaged kale, I want a massaged back

and a massaged mind, for dessert I'll want the egg-free, peanut-free,
soy-free, milk-free, wheat-free Pistachio Halva. I'm going to walk out
of here scot-free and easy as a new-born babe who's played all day in Clover.

True Crime

for Rachel

You who took the Hippocratic oath
often have no other self-prescription
for a cold, overwork, or feeling blue
than to loaf with cats upon a couch
and watch a crime. Although true,
the harm all happens on a far-off day
the mystery's solved, despite unanswered
questions. The perpetrator's locked away.
And pharma ads break in occasionally
to chat of drugs with murderous side effects
"ask your doctor if X is right for you."

Tea Break

A pineapple is embossed in stainless steel
at the upper right quadrant of the closed

elevator door. It catches my attention while
I roll my eyes at the hospitality of this

establishment. The pineapple flirts with
thistle and pine cone, breaking the tedium.

Give me my mind back I muse on what to say
to my employer. The elevator doors open,

taking back the proffered bowl of grapes.
Somewhere near the four silver rosettes

on the ceiling, a disembodied voice chirps
Going Down.

Daniel Bouchard

Half Pound

A cadence is catching,
  an eye not. After
evening conversation ends,
  voices carry over to sleep,
half-dream state echoes
  on the count of four
and the glare of a silver rooftop
  glinting and scored like fish skin
sits in the sun, a gunmetal
  layer to cover three floors
of apartments and pizza shop
  at ground level.

No pizza now, not anymore,
  no subs since last year, shut down
for tax evasion. Now a new place
  making souvlaki and gyros,
producing subs and heroes
  under relentless battleship gray.
Strange roof, like a hull hung upside down,
  enormous dormer jutting out like a prow.
Does hero derive of gyro?
Immigrant neighborhoods
  work as language grinders,
grease the gears of idiom
  plink new words out onto the world,
fly like sparks from a welder's torch.
(Hoagies were invented in Chester,
  stromboli too.)

Many folks would trade big slices of western culture
  for a good sandwich.
"The delivery trucks," he sd, sweeping an arm,
pointing in the wrong direction,
  "came from the east, up Menotomy Avenue."
The dumpling place owner tells us
  the pandemic killed off the soup
and fortune cookies, and the distributor
  warehouses are packed
with people unable to fill orders.

Coffee

I love coffee,
I love coffee,
I love coffee—
                    I love juice.
Coffee-Juice.

February. Little girl
with twisted dreads,
Boston's

Red Line train, on her
mother's lap, sings, *I love*
Coffee-Juice.

People sit facing the Charles
like silver Chieftain-heads
on an old Pontiac.

Joy, quicker than a tongue
down a dripping ice-cream
cone, cascades off the child's
words. Her feet kick as if
on a swing.

The people on the bus
go up & down, up &
down, she sings.

She giggles. *The doors on*
the bus go—open & shut—
all through the town.

I love coffee, the girl tells a man
sitting next to her. *But you don't
drink coffee,* her mother says.

I know, says the girl.
But I like it. The whole
train laughs. There's
Truth in it: Some things
we like, are yet to be
known.

*She's going to tell all
your secrets,* says a man
next to her mom. *Uh huh,*
the mother agrees.

The train rumbles out of a
tunnel.

Her mother tickles her.
In her laughter, doors open,
smile after smile people
come out.

American Cauliflower Sonnet

for S

The cauliflower, rather the cauliflower bush, round, thick and deeply
mature seized my mind. Besides salivating and shifting in my seat
I could not resist telling the cook that this is no ordinary vegetable,
that she has found a rare example of how fruits and vegetables once

sprouted on this ancient grained earth—before the combine,
and nitrogen fertilizer. I refer to wild growth, stoked by mysterious
wormy loam, fed in turn by thousands of dinosaur pounds rotted
into rich fertile minerals feeding the mother and father

of cauliflowers, which appear as if by magic and miracle today
on an InstaCart order from the local super, on the island
of Paumanok where American poetry got its start and
flourishes again, with each pulling off the massive bush,

into delicate yet whole flowers, before tossing into the cast
iron pot, olive oil sputtering, eyes and ears and tongue dancing....

Bread

1.
4 a.m., thin cloud, mid-
August, early morning,
Cerulean-Blue sky.
63 degrees. I like it just
the way it is. Crickets
playing their maracas.

Air conditioner hum.
Cars on distant highways
strumming. One outside
the convenience store,
idling.

*Coffee, everything
bagel, French cruller*

Under the florescent *7/11-
Dunkin Donuts* sign, curbside
a man rubs lottery tickets.

Did you win? I ask.

He holds one up, smiling,
Amigo, Look, I won $1,000.

Hallelujah, I say. *Gracias, Dios.*

He's happy. I'm happy.
Our momentary mountain.

2.

I had woken up from a sudden
post-pandemic rent increase.
$50 every month, $50 added
to last month's rent.

Four weeks waiting for
a check the postman never
delivered. Two of them—
ramen & rice.

Most days, I did not want
to go home.

But this morning, the ATM says,
In the bank. Woodsy air,
still clouds. Inhale the pristine air.
Music in me like crickets now
playing—all the unseen stars.

Water

Today I do not take you for granted
although usually I do.

When I was naked and vulnerable
you did not run out.

The shower, generous with its healing,
released my neck, warmed my shoulders.

Between my toes, you licked away the dreck.
I did not need to fear a well running dry

or a drought robbing me
of one single meal in the long day.

I count on you to cover the potatoes
and bubble gaily in the pot, to spray the lettuce,

the tomatoes into a glistening crop,
and when rain releases you,

to run freely down the street
Let me not waste a single drop.

Anne Riesenberg

whole   *hole*   *holey*

A Day in the Life

Oops. I have been destroyed
once more by my own impossibility.
Plus a strong wind
      bearing down on the gleaming idea of a car

      with new safety features.
It may have been a Honda. Beyond that, I haven't the foggiest.
Tax season, it's coming right up. Right after

Pisces season. What's that about?
      Meanwhile, every dude in workshop
keeps dutifully writing autoerotic autofiction. 12% of which is
alright. To my phone's camera I practice saying, Don't

call me. I revise my face to look pissed
      but not pained.
Precision is a type of pleasure. A type

of grief, too. Meanwhile, I am holed up
in the hole of myself. So busy. An art monk, worshipping
at the altar of mischief-
      multiplication. If only I had better

safety features. Newer, at least.
      I can rarely play it cool, but my extremities
always get way too cold. It's weird, how the day can go

from warm to way too cold.
People, too. Every day, people
lose each other
      to each other. It's hard, telling another person

exactly what you need. The exactly
is the hard. Sometimes, it's ketchup. Sometimes,
        slowly repairing a sense of trust

        that may never be fully restored but you both want
to try anyway. Why is life so often
irreparable? Even the best of ketchups cannot reverse
the most ordinary of sads.

        But am I sad because sitcoms,
romcoms, plus my mom have trained me to believe
that people who truly love me should totally be

able to read my mind? Are my neurons sad
because they've tried to say my needs, only for all that trying
to be misinterpreted,
        altogether missed? Are my synapses sad

because they'd rather do art 24–7 but they, too, know
        that to art even a second requires being
a part of life, which means trying to say the simplest things

to the unsimplest others?
Am I sad because of how many times I've said I'm sad
        without I myself et moi knowing my true needs?
Am I sad, desperately, because despite my love

for words, I don't know which
can truest say the love my needy neurons
        want? To this or that person-shaped

        particularity I love? Who in all probability
also has this sneaking
suspicion of a sinking feeling that they will be
asking these questions every single day

for the rest of their mopey but at times totally miraculous
mortal existence? Isn't it time
>for bed?

>It's time for bed.
For my neurons, my synapses, my every
brain fold to talk amongst themselves
at their symposium on the memory of a breathtaking drive

to a distant buffet. For the eerily remixed recollection of sitting
>there. For my actual gluteus, however maximus, to maxiless
a small while—if at all possible.

Jennifer Barber

Propelled by the urge

for air beneath my feet,
I leapt along the walk.
People stared. I didn't care.
There were years of this
restlessness and flight,
hanging for a moment
with gravity at bay.
Later I walked like anyone,
my muscles in check,
invisible, unlaunched.
Now there is no way
to leave the ground
for fear of landing. The air
no longer knows me.
Out my window, in the sun,
three boys flourish their
Star Wars light sabers
between the parked cars,
falling dead, leaping up.

As I Wake

The wind moans openly.
The blue jay who declaims
from the top of the fire escape
flies off into the din.

Alone onstage, the wind
keeps up its soliloquy.

To be or not to be is beside the point
for the lit window
in a dark house.

Wind remembers me
walking down a hallway
in the shadow
of my footfalls.

Indran Amirthanayagam

Desire and Book

I have overcome
desire. I do not
need a hug or kiss.
I am self aware
to the point

of disappearance.
Nobody new,
or returned,
from the old
country

will know
the taste
of my unique
spit, to bond
with passing

mynah,
parrot fish,
or human,
happens
now only

here in this
safe space
bound by
lines hidden
behind stanza

walls, the
naming of
those parts
and the covers
always of

a book. Except
trade editions
have no
dust jacket,
so help us God.

Thank You for Attending This Ongoing Cosmic Error

Aka my life. Aka my perpetual

leaving, peppered with drizzles & amateur
embroidery. Then filled
with downpours & amateur cross-country.
These adidas that need
replacing. Those doc martens that have long
been gobbled by hunky ghosts. Must I fill out
another questionnaire about how amorous
one finds the woods? Hello, scales of 1 to

too much. Plethora of noons,
prolific midnights.   Moons
on button-downs, precum on lips, aka moonlight
on lips. In midsummer. Through midwinter.
While middling
salads. Meddling moi. My question mark

mouth, perpetually turned
on: why is français the standard dialect for moonlit

jobs, both blow & rim? why
not 普通话? in which lunar bright
arrives as 月光 or 月色aka   mooncolor, moonlook,
moonlust. You're welcome, amorous
linguists. My pleasure, amateur
selenologists. Aka poets. Aka how perpetually

pissed off I am
that this dead person   I'm reading
loves me this hard.

129

Daniel Bouchard

Grayscale

A Pharaoh's face, as if dozing
or reading lines from the book
inscribed on his own sarcophagus.

I like the big ears, the columns of script,
vertical and orderly, containing the dust
of the dust that once was blood and nerve.

Suddenly the eyes open, ablaze
with ancient light, illuminating
wraith-like life, reflected
from the adjoining exhibit.

The visage takes in the shocked faces
and the cameras held up like salute.

Now he rises from out of the wall,
history come alive, asks if everyone
would like to be schooled in religion.

But the patrons only scream and run
conditioned by horror movies more
than the horrors of history. He takes
a step forward, cracks the marble floor,
stretches a heavy arm out and sings
"Hello young lovers, whoever you are."

The placards can be pretty loose
with provenance, now they uniformly read
I hope your troubles are few.

Wendy Drexler

I Ask My Husband's Neurologist about Alzheimers and the Uncanny Valley

Q: Sometimes I think I love my husband more when he's clearly lost in the fog of his forest, instead of when he most resembles the person he used to be. Why?

A: *When he is most like his old self, you may feel sad remembering how dust bowl your soil is now, a candle that could blow out with the slightest whiff. When he is fully alpine to himself you become most protective.*

Q: Is this like the uncanny valley, you know, the way people are attracted and responsive to a very human-looking robot until the robot looks too human and then they are repulsed?

A: *If something looks a little like us we trust it. If something looks too much like us we are unsure if it's really a human and think someone is trying to pull a fast one. If he's lost in the fog, that's very human. Fogs, shadows, the valley of the shadow of death. Thou shalt not be replaced, in other words, by any robot.*

Q: Do I have my own uncanny valley?

A: *I would explore the junction where your empathy locks horns with your frustration.*

Q: How far must each of his synapses travel to remember where to find the tea bags in the kitchen?

A: *Each synapse takes I-95 North to Manchester, NH, exits, and heads south on 93 to Route 2, exit 52, formerly exit 29A, through the rotary out Concord Avenue past the high school, turn left at Goden Street and come straight to your front door to the kitchen to the cabinet to the left of the stove, bottom shelf.*

Q: When I ask him how he's slept, why does he say he doesn't know yet?

A: Sleep is an uncanny valley and he has to check his Apnea-Hypopnea index to know how many times he's stopped breathing. He needs to know how many trees fell in the forest to believe he heard any one of them fall.

Q: I first noticed his symptoms years ago, when he asked me what time we were having dinner, what time we were having dinner, what time was dinner. Why is time the first thing to go?

A: Time corrals us like a barbed-wire fence, and the brain begins to snip holes in the wires. That lets the night inside, and the hours fly out like bats at dusk.

Q: Do the hours leave you sooner than the minutes?

A: No, minutes are a triumph of versatility. Seconds are filled with weather on all sides.

Q: Where and how will this all end?

A: The ending can be a thousand versions of itself. Loosestrife, firestorm, lichen, a leg trap, hail, a slow creek, a sigh of light at the edge of a blue heath butterfly's wing.

beyond   *reach*

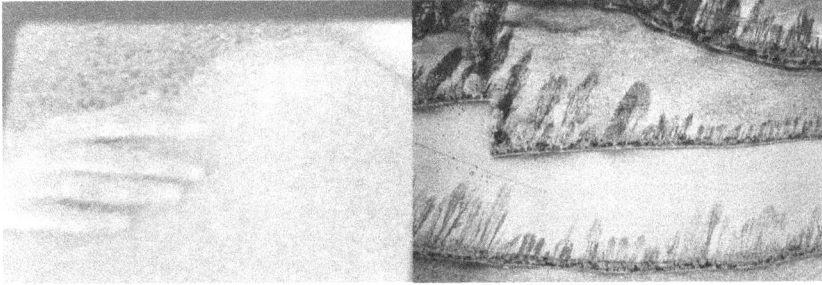

reach   *beyond*

Little Laika, Space Dog

Chagall's cow flying high over a stupefied village
Stood a better chance of surviving than Laika did,
Her liquidly expressive eyes having darkened to singularities.

No Khrushchevite was ever a dog's best friend. Bladder full
And looking for a curb or hydrant, she believed she was being taken
For a walk with her Leninist pup pals, Albina and Mukha.

Nobody asked her if she wanted to roll over and play dead in Soyuz II.
They didn't so much as throw her the bone of a heads-up,
Just strapped her in and off she went, with a one-way ticket to pee the moon.

Did anyone bother to give her a medal,
Order of Lenin, Hero of the Soviet Union? Or stoop to gush
"Good canine cosmonaut!" as might have been expected?

No, not even that. No shoe-thumping speechifying by Nikita
Preceded her entry into Wikipedia, only some fur-loving bureaucrat's wife
Absently petting her in lieu of a more elaborate send-off.

Nor did Laika's handlers, usually affectionate
And good for a belly scratch when she trustingly exposed it to them,
Offer a juicy veal chop or two as a last meal, liquified kibble

Comprising both the before- and in-flight menu, yet still better
Than many dog-eat-dog Soviets had it, babushkas icing over
As they huddled on day-old bread lines in hopes of a crust.

Had she known what a test it would be to void in space,
How difficult it would be to lift up her hind leg in weightlessness
Without fear of floating into her own doggone mess,

She might have slipped her leash like that lucky mutt Bobik did in '51:
A coward, yes, but still alive. As our little Laika in '57 might have been
Had she run for her life, pledging bark and bite to the anti-Soviet resistance.

Sharon Amaguni

Thank God It's

What did you even laugh about
in the TGI Friday's parking lot
Showy as you shuttled a gloss soggy cigarette
between you.

Bellies already swashing
with long island iced-tea.
Nips clinking against the house keys
in the Sears purse you got for Christmas.

Inside your laughs ricochet,
all of you, too drunk for anyone's good.
Not quite whispering about boys you met,
or are meeting, or have always known
in the archives of your baby lives.
Buzzed and giddy
with the adolescence of it all.

Before you learned how to sop up the whir of rum
under the callous lights of a strip mall.
Before you learned that childhood
unfolds like a fitted sheet
always caught in itself,
you learned these simple joys as street remedy
for the house where a pot of tea,
brown as sap, is overboiling.
And your parents are in their bedroom
quarreling about visas, and citizenship.
How the state you lost every baby tooth in
still sees you as a foreign mass.

Tonight you are grateful for the secrets
of girlhood, bad jokes, the scent of nicotine.

You're thankful to sneak into your house
without waking any worn sleepers.
Lightly stumble down the stairs
clipping the tail of a woozy laugh.

The room dark and day softened,
You, momentarily as American teen as you can be.

"This is for Ayiti: Don't Touch"

—a bop

We can't invite our Park Avenue friends
to our apartment, our home. Even though for my mother,
Home is Haiti. Any new silverware or
Precious thing is instructed to be put
Aside pou Ayiti … for Ayiti … not for here …
Our home with the triple locks in Queens, New York.

This is for Ayiti: Don't touch.

She never throws away the bulky phone books.
Name the year … We have it. Open the front closet,
The one meant to greet guests with empty hangers
And there they are: a contorted pile of yellow and white pages.
Summers bereft of paper-coned roasted peanuts sprinkled with
sea dust
Away from the shady solace of our almond tree's broad leaves.
I whine, my mother repeats, "You are bored. Clean the closet."
No Great Adventure: "We do not pay to be terrorized. We fled
danger."

This is for Ayiti: Don't touch.

We come home one day to find a gargantuan machine
In the middle of our kitchen. We have to squeeze around it
To get to the stove, the sink, or the fridge. "This machine
Can save lives," my mother, the nurse anesthesiologist, beams.
"The hospital said as long as I can get it to Ayiti, it is mine."
So for weeks, we squeeze around the life-saving machine.

This is for Ayiti: Don't touch.

Apnea

I tell you I would rather tape my mouth shut than have a Velcro kind of strap around my head or one of those horseshoe things that keeps off the wind tunnel effect that my daughter told me the sound was like so the only alternative is to go with a mask but everybody I know who's tried them doesn't like them besides I sleep on my side and when I'm still awake you know before I finally go off I experiment but no I just don't want anything over my chin somebody tells me this guy on the internet knows about the airway pressure kind and can tell you how to read the graph that lets you see just how you're breathing like if the pressure goes up or goes down and why but I don't want some guy on the Internet telling me what's going on or what I'm feeling so it's hard because another friend who uses it says she gets up every morning and goes "I feel great!" And who needs a friend like that?

H. Preston Soss

Secret Life of Sidekicks

Ventriloquists had best beware their dummies.
Headliners, their chums lurking in the subscript.
Just when you think they're satisfied with second place,
With daffodils instead of roses after a Kentucky Derby race,
That they have no expectations above their pay grade,
Boom, they burst into your room, guns blazing with live ammo.
Then it's, "Oh, Cisco!" "Et tu, Pancho?"

On posters it seems sidekicks are always the other guys,
The also withs.
As in, Also with Jay Silverheels, as Tonto;
Also with Leo Carrillo, as Poncho.
Burt Ward as Dick Grayson (Robin).
There's not a mother's son among them
Who doesn't want to be a Batman, a Number One.

They want to be seen as their mothers see them,
GYNs having assured Mrs. Silverheels, Mrs.Carillo,
That they had birthed A-listers not B
After hard pushing that outrivaled the exertions
Of any marquee-worthy mom. And, as regards Mrs. Grayson,
A son more deserving than the Caped Crusader
Of a hero's welcome at Comic-Con.

Second bananas, generally viewed by us as fungible,
Dream of fanzines dedicated to their every move, whether on-screen
Or in the bathroom. With a need to be listed, and paid, as protagonists
Building in them like water pressure in an overheated junker.
What Numero Unos who want to keep top billing should know
Is that one of these days it's going to blow, the next Lou Costello
Already planning to nip the next Bud Abbott in the bud.

Executive Options

I hear he's an avid hunter. He trades
lives like he trades stock, with swagger.

He's equally at ease looking through you
as he is looking through a riflescope.

He's climbed high enough up the ladder
his way of life is in danger. You avoid him

in the hallway. He's planning his next safari.
He plans to be on safari until he retires

every last lion & tiger into extinction.
He invests in private equity and dabbles

in crypto coin and black markets.
Living wages are obsolete. He intends

to hunt the offspring of big cats until
their eyes flicker on & off, bloodless

and robotic. If he plans to pull the trigger—
or face what we all face, our ability

to be heartless—he'll need to lift a finger.

Melissa Peters

The Horse Casts a Vote

I was talking to the horse across the street.
We have a long history. We like to commiserate

about the way he's been cemented into his post
guarding a rich man's property. That, and the way

he & his kind can only survive by being in our
good graces. Imagine, after roaming free for

three million years. Call me crazy. I call me
born with my feet on the ground and my head

in the stars, if that's an acceptable way to say
you don't own me. Your friend owns a gun

& your employer wields a hammer that pounds
repeatedly on your head. There are 3 companies

that stand to benefit while on their way to causing
the end of life as we know it. Corporations being

people, that means three people (or whatever fraction
of humanity) who stand to benefit—and be damned

the horse and his planet. I'm making numbers up,
but maybe it's closer to reality than anyone cares

to calculate or contemplate. The horse believes
in survival, even if it's against all odds.

Maybe it's more than 3 companies, maybe it's 20
if you analyze the statistics. There are lonely souls

who compile data and analyze statistics, who speak
truth to power, if you think I'm only on the side

of poets. When the stress gets too much, it is good
for employee morale to buy a lottery ticket.

If you travel outside your own circles, you might
be surprised by how far up the free-market food chain

you will need to be, how rarified the air you breathe,
to be exempt from the anxiety you & yours can survive.

There's an old curse from way out West, from way
back in history, I think it goes something like,

fuck you and the horse you rode in on. Bad news!
Every *great* leader knows how to mount a horse.

Chen Chen

Asian American Weather Forecast

It will snow.
In a cozy corner of a college library, somebody will hold
somebody else close while saying, I love
your culture.

It will stop snowing.
Somebody will walk all around campus, up the big hill,
then down,
before returning to their dorm's common area
to say, Hey. Cantonese? It's not Mandarin.

It will be hot out.
Somebody will shout in Mandarin to somebody on a bicycle
going to lunch, You're hot.
Somebody will try again in Korean with a big smile.

The heat will break.
Somebody will realize at the gym, in the dining hall, by the pond,
how their body is

not a body but a shiny
forever mirage to some whose bodies
get to say, Oh wow your hair, can I touch it
while touching it.

Being fetishized is being told can I touch it. Being told but I just like
your features so much, what's wrong

with that. Being fetishized is to be
that. Studied at length, in detail, by somebody who can't stop smiling.
To be liked
so much, not loved.

It will rain.
But it will be the right temperature
for me. I will be
my body, in a raincoat I got myself.
I will have thrown out the raincoat
he got me in college. I will have stopped thinking of that raincoat
every time it rains. I will stop
by a pond to listen to the rain greet its cousin.

The Theme, I Was Told, Is Humor

Or humer?
Or humerus?
Or was it hubris?
Humid?
Tumor/Rumor/Goomer?

Anything but humor.
Few things make me laugh in times of war.
Life's jokes.
Paying for the massage
that damaged my neck.
Apologizing to the therapist
for making her feel insecure.
She winced with pity
as I sat unmoving in my car.
      Are you okay? Are you okay? Are you okay?

She cashed the check.

      George Carlin, is dead.
      Now what?
                Remember.

Dare to play the violin at Auschwitz.
Dare to rosin the cello bow in Sarajevo.

Drones set by sociopaths
     just following orders
kill bakers, mothers, doctors, teachers.
Infants deboned like baby lambs for veal
vaporize truckloads of tomorrows.

The most gruesome thoughts
are buried in vegan jokes —
The LOL's of white supremacist yoga;
            eat a steak, buy a gun, grow a pair.

Coney Island.
Skeeball Lanes.
Wooden balls.
The real thing. Nostalgic lust.
A solo hotdog
rolling on a '50s grill
Its Miami wrinkles
reminiscent of my aunt
who died of melanoma
tanning to darken
while passing for Greek.

I didn't like her.
Laughter arrived hard.
It dripped a little.

Grief isn't for everyone.

Daniel Bouchard

Lines of Type

This is an appliance   shall I continue
  to park it here for occasional use
or free up two square feet by its absence?
Writing is an appliance
I need a physical book now to finish
  the line of Bernadette's stuck in my head
"Writing poems is really dumb but fuck it"
dragging thought, crashing sound down
  up or over   I cannot pick lines up
and wing them into cloud
I cannot actually do anything with this writing
  before digitizing the text

The *Correcting Selectric* hums
  with a heavy patience that vibrates the desk
I salute the impetus of switching it on
Arrogant laptop nearly slips into my coat now
  like an envelope
Many machines got tossed into
  Marx's dumpster of history
a bin that holds mountains of art as well

This keyboard pressing is an ode to value
This hulking ribbon winder is a toss back
  to the notion that one cannot toggle
to headlines or shopping or
  obliterate the 'y' I keep making
when 't' is meant

I need music now to overpower
  the hammer strikes and relentless noise
that reminds me of the electric current
  necessary to work

I tap into the digital ether
where the bass nudges a melody
and reanimates a voice in my ears
finished long ago

The Phoenix

I have heard it is far   away from here
in the eastern reaches   of the noblest realms
well-known to many.   Across Middle-earth
part of the region   is past the reach
of the lords of lands,   but walled off as well
from sinning people   by sacred power.
The plain is beautiful,   blessed with bliss,
with the finest fragrances   found on Earth.
That island is unique;   the noble Creator
who molded its dirt   is mighty yet measured.   (10)
Happy harmonies   are there for the holy
at the always-open   gate of Heaven,
a pleasant place,   a grove of green
beneath spacious sky.   No rain or snow
no breath of frost   no fiery blast
no harm from hail   no hoary gale
no fevered sun   no frigid run
no humid weather   nor wintry shower
is doing damage,   and grasslands stretch on,
blessed and unscathed.   This regal realm   (20)
is blooming with blossoms.   No barrow or peak
is standing steeply,   no craggy cliff
is hanging overhead   as they do with us here,
no ravines or valleys   no cave in the clouds
no rise or ridge there   is looming large,
no rough terrain,   just a fine field
burgeoning below clouds   bursting with joys.
In the clear-eyed counsel   of serious scholars,
as told in their works,   this is a lustrous land
twelve fathoms taller   than the highest height   (30)
of hills shimmering   here with us
looming aloft   below high heavens.
The plain is peaceful,   the grove is gleaming,

and the woods are wondrous.   The fruit does not fall,
the blossoms are bright,   and trees are bound
to remain green   as God commanded.
In woods in winter,   and the same in summer,
fruit is hanging;   below the heavens
no leaf will rot,   no flame will ravage them
before a change   forever and always   (40)
enters the world,   as when waves of old,
a flood of water,   overwhelmed the world,
the orb of earth.   This stately stretch,
wholly unharmed   by the surge of sea,
remained safe   from the manic surf,
blessed and unblemished   through the grace of God,
so it abides while blossoming   for the blaze to come
when God so judges,   when in burial grounds
grim graves   of the good are unlidded.
That land is lacking   in unfriendly foes: (50)
no weeping or suffering   nor signs of worry
no aging or agony   nor drear of death
no loss of life   nor demons nearing
no sin or strife   nor sorrowful life
no laboring with want   nor lack of wealth
no stress or sleep   nor sickness in bed
no winter storm   nor struggle with weather
no havoc from the heavens   nor heavy blizzard
cudgeling anyone   with a cold icicle.
No hail or ice there   falls on the Earth,   (60)
no drifting cloud   nor dripping water
driven by the wind,   but a strangely stunning
river running there   comes gushing
from dazzling springs.   It drenches dirt
with wondrous water   from within the woods,
which bursts sea-cold   from sandy soil,
then every month   sweetly seeps
throughout the grove;   the will of God

151

is this gorgeous river   must run gloriously
twelve times each year   through this lovely land.   (70)
Flower blossoms   dangle in the forest;
the finest of fruit   never fades there,
since yields of this grove   under Heaven are holy
and don't fall to the ground   as flowers grow
on brilliant branches,   but in beautiful ways
the limbs on those trees   stay laden
with refreshing fruit.   All throughout the hours
it is always green   on this grassy plain,
the most glittering glade   bedecked in gladness
by The Holy One.   The woodland holds   (80)
its colors constant;   there a sacred scent
throughout the joyous land   will be left lingering
for ever and ever   until the toppling
of the hallowed handiwork   that He began.
Those woods are watched   by a wondrous, delightful,
strong-winged fowl   called a "phoenix."
It lives in that place   alone in a lair
in steadfast style.   Death will not harm it
on that pleasant plain   while the Earth endures.
There it must scan   the cycle of the sun   (90)
and keep on coming   toward God's candle,
that joyous gem,   to observe zealously—
until the rise   of the most regal star
above the brilliant   eastern sea-waves—
our Father's legacy   gleaming gorgeously
as God's bright sign.   The star is hidden,
lurking below   the waves in the west.
It stays through sunrise,   and the black night
glides into gloom,   then the stately bird,
strong of wing,   searches below the sky   (100)
and over the ocean   for mountain streams
until the heavens' rays   arise from the east
gliding over   the open ocean.

With changeless beauty   this charming bird
dwells near waters   that well from the spring
where the blesséd one   bathes in a brook
twelve times until   the coming of the sign
of heaven's candle,   and always as often
at every soaking   sips from the sumptuous
sea-cold water   of the surging wellspring.   (110)
After water-play   the prideful one
then heads up high   into a towering tree,
where it can behold   the huge sweep
of surf to the east   as the torch of the sky,
a beam of brilliance,   glows brightly
over churning chop.   The dirt is gilded,
the globe more begraced,   once the sublime star,
a glory of a jewel,   lights up the land
of Middle-earth   as it arcs over ocean.
As soon as the sun   is soaring above   (120)
the salty streams,   the darkly drab
bird takes off   from a branch in the trees.
Fleet in flight,   it flashes through air,
sings harmonies   and hymns heavenward,
then the very beautiful   voice of the bird
with inspired spirit,   exultant in ecstasy,
warbles wondrously   in a well-crafted way,
a more amazing melody   than a child of man
has heard under Heaven   since the highest King,
The Worker of Wonder,   founded the world   (130)
of Heaven and Earth.   That hymn's harmony
will be finer and sweeter   than any song-craft,
with lyrics lovelier   than any other,
yet nothing we hear   from trumpets and horns,
no hush of the harp,   no human voice
of anyone on Earth,   no organ strains
with sweet refrains,   no feathers of a swan;
no melody can match   that which God makes
for mankind's joy   in this mournful world.
Thus, blessed with bliss,   it warbles and trills   (140)

until the time the sun   starts to sink
in the southern sky,   then it falls still
and takes to listening,   lifts its head
with prudent purpose,   and fluffs its flight-ready
feathers three times;   the fowl hushes.
It notes the hour,   day and night,
always twelve times;   as ordained, this dweller
in the woods will exploit   the pleasures there
of the grassy plain,   savor the plenty
and bounty of the land,   and life's delights,   (150)
until this guardian   of the woodland grove
has endured in this world   a thousand winters.
Feathers faded,   wizened but wise,
burdened by years,   the most glorious of birds
then leaves the lushness   of the blossoming land,
and starts to search   for a solitary stretch
of Middle-earth   unoccupied by men
for its home and homeland.   With a potent presence there
it serves as sovereign   for all breeds of birds;
it thrives in this throng   and ensures their safety   (160)
for a while in the wasteland.   Set on wandering,
weighed down by winters,   it heads to the west
as its feathers beat.   Birds are flocking
near their noble one;   they each want to be named
a liege and servant   of their illustrious lord
before it leaves to seek   the land of Syria
with the biggest of flocks.   The innocent bird
abruptly hastens there   to hide in a shelter
in a lonely spot   in a leafy grove,
sealed off and hidden   from the mass of men.   (170)
There in wilds of these woods   beneath Heaven's vault,
in a towering tree   fixed by its roots,
it perches and settles;   people call
it the "phoenix tree"   from the name of this fowl.
Glorious God,   Maker of Mankind,
has granted this tree   uniqueness in number
is what I am told.   Of all the timber

that rises high   by roads of the world,
it blooms the brightest.   Nothing bitter
can harm it with evil,   but forever shielded   (180)
it lives undamaged   as the world endures.
When the wind fades,   the weather is fair,
Heaven's bright gem   gleams with holiness,
clouds are cleared,   the raging rapids
are standing still,   every storm
is soothed below the sky,   the weather-wick
blazes from the south,   and people are beaming.
It then prepares to make   a nesting place
built on a branch.   Since old age
is coming closer,   it is strongly set   (190)
on transforming its fate   through a surge of spirit.
To revive its body   it then gathers and gleans
from far and near   the sweetest fruit
from the woods and spice   filled with flavor
for its roosting place,   overjoyed by every
fragrant succulent   which the Father of all,
the King of glory,   created on Earth
to bring His blessing,   honeyed from Heaven,
to the masses of men.   Alone there, it loads
glimmering treasures   inside the tree,   (200)
where that untamed bird   builds a lair
in the barren wasteland   atop that tree,
beautifully and blissfully,   and settles itself there
in the sun-drenched space   and surrounds itself,
body and feathers,   in that forest bower
on every side   with sacred incense
and the finest flowers   of all the earth.
It is roosting restlessly   while Heaven's jewel,
the sweltering sun   at the peak of summer,
shines on the shelter   and fulfills its fate.   (210)
The world watches,   then the bird's house
becomes combustible   in blistering sun.
Twigs are warming;   the refuge reeks
of a sweet scent   as heat scorches it.

The nest ablaze,   the bird is burning.
The pyre is kindled,   then fire enfolds
the dreary dwelling   and races through it.
Orange fire overwhelms   and at long last burns
the ancient phoenix,   then flame digests
its languishing frame;   the fleeting life   (220)
of its soul-hoard is doomed.   The pyre then swallows
bone and flesh,   but following a break
it returns again,   soul regained
after the blazing assault.   As soon as the ash
begins once more   to bind into a mass,
dwindling to a ball,   the noblest nest,
the hero's home,   is wholly ravaged
by fierce flame.   Body broken,
the corpse is cold   as the blaze ebbs,
then in the pyre's ash   something like an apple   (230)
is often found   in the fire's aftermath,
from which a larva grows,   a lovely wonder,
as if it had been hatched   out of an egg.
Bright in the shell,   it then grows in shadows
so it seems at first   a splendid fledgling,
like an eagle's chick,   then even more greatly
it flourishes in happiness   since it has the form
of an aging eagle,   and then even later,
adorned with feathers,   it clearly flourishes
as it was at first.   Fully reformed,
its body becomes   born again,   (240)
sundered from sin,   somewhat akin
to men at a harvest   bringing home
fruit of the soil   for needed nourishment,
flavorful food   at reaping season
before winter arrives   so no rainfall ruins
it beneath the clouds.   There they know comfort,
like the joy of food   when frost and snow
with fearsome force   garb the ground
in winter-wear.   From those crops the wealth   (250)
of mankind shall grow   once more in line

with the grain's nature,   so as soon as the seed
is sown it is cleansed,   the sun gleams
in the season of spring,   a sign of life
that wakes the world-wealth,   which is the yield
of fruit from the ground.   Farmed again,
it keeps burgeoning,   just as the bird,
old in years,   restores its youth
recloaked in flesh.   It eats no food,
no meat on Earth,   just a tiny taste   (260)
of sugary dew   that sometimes drips
in the dead of night,   thus the noble one
sustains its life   until it seeks again
its ancestral home   in its own homeland.
Proud of its plumage   amid the plants,
the bird flourishes;   its flesh will be fresh
with youthful grace.   From the dirt of its grave,
it then collects bits   of its lithe body
that the mayhem of fire   had formerly demolished.
It carefully gathers   the crumbled bone,   (270)
and afterwards brings   bone and ash,
the seared scraps,   together again
to cover the beautifully   embellished corpse
with ceremonial spice.   It then becomes eager
to seek again   its native soil,
and its claws clench   the scorched scraps
its talons grab,   and again it searches
for its happy homeland,   a sun-drenched homestead,
and its closest kin.   Its soul and plumage
are wholly restored   to what they were   (280)
when triumphant God   began to settle it
on that proud plain.   It brings its own bones there,
as well as its ashes,   to the place where earlier
the surge of fire   upon the pyre
was overwhelming,   then it bravely buries
bone and ash,   all of it combined,
right on that island.   It is resurrected there
by the sign of the sun,   the most sparkling gem,

a stellar delight,   as light from the sky
shimmers from the east   up over the ocean.   (290)
In the front the bird   is beautiful in appearance,
arrayed with colors   all around its breast.
Behind the head   there is a green
that varies beautifully   with blended violet,
then there is that splendid   split-in-half tail
artfully speckled   with resplendent spots,
some brown, some red.   The wings are white
toward the tips   and the neck emerald
above and below,   and the beak glows
like glass or a jewel   with jaws gleaming   (300)
inside and out.   The essence of its eye
is stark in look   and stony in color,
a joyous gem   like one encased
in a gilded setting   with a goldsmith's skill.
A brilliant ruff   burnished with feathers
surrounds its neck   like the sun's ring.
Below its gorgeous gullet   it is strangely stunning,
luminous and lovely.   The crest is covered
with adornments all down   the back of this bird.
Both of its thighs   are obscured by scales;   (310)
its feet are flaxen.   This fowl is utterly
peerless in appearance;   joyfully raised,
it passes for a peacock,   as told in the texts.
It is not sluggish   nor is it slothful,
neither leaden nor languid   like birds of some breeds
that slog with their wings   slowly through sky,
but strong and swift   and awesomely agile,
winsome and winning,   special in splendor.
The Lord is everlasting   who bestows such delight!
It then takes flight   from this foreign turf   (320)
to find the plains   of its former home.
As the fowl is flying   it is seen by the people,
the masses of mankind   throughout Middle-earth,
then it gathers together   from east and west,
north and south,   an assembled flock.

From far and near   they travel in force
to gaze upon God's   astonishing gifts
to that fine fowl,   since triumph's true king
created from the start   this exotic species
with more beautiful features   than all breeds of bird,   (330)
thus men from all   the Earth marvel
at its brightness and body,   and tell in texts,
inscribed with their script   in marble stone,
the day and time   that the fleet-flyer's features
were shown to the throng;   birds of all breeds
then crowd into flocks   on every flank.
They dive from a distance   and praise it in song,
exalting the beast   with robust voices
as they all encircle   the saintly one
while aloft in flight.   The phoenix is among them,   (340)
mobbed by a crowd.   Many watch,
marveling in amazement,   as a joyous group,
one flock after the other,   honors the loner
and carefully declares   their beloved leader
the best of kings.   Blissfully they bring
their hero home   until that fleet-feathered
loner has left,   which thwarts revelers
from following their lord,   then the flocks' delight
seeks a homeland   away from this world.
With the death-hour gone   the begraced one   (350)
heads out again   to its former home,
that rapturous region.   As it goes back,
birds abandon   their brave warrior,
soul-sorrowed,   then their fledgling sovereign
makes it home.   Only almighty God
the King comprehends   what gender it is,
male or female,   so among mankind
no one knows at all,   only the Creator.
How marvelously wondrous   matters were
with that ancient explanation   of the bird's gender!   (360)
There the happy creature   can savor its haven
beside swelling waters   in the woodland grove

and thrive on the plain   until a thousand winters
have run their routes,   and the end of life
comes to pass.   The pyre engulfs it
with kindled fire,   but weirdly awakening
it revives once more   with no fretting or moping
in wondrous ways,   and does not dread death
and its raw rattle;   it always understands
that after flame's fury   a sudden flash   (370)
refashions the flesh   for life after death
in a hatchling's image;   it is restored
again from the ash,   goes on refreshed
under Heaven's cover.   It is his own
dear father and son   and also always
forever the heir   to its mortal remains.
The mighty Maker of   mankind allowed
him to stunningly   remake itself
back to the way   it had been before,
arrayed in feathers   but surrounded by fire.   (380)
So too each of the blessed   decides to pursue
everlasting life   after the terrible torture
of dismal death,   so each might enjoy
after days and years   the grace of God
in unending ecstasy   and then ever after
dwell in glory   as their works' reward.
The bird's manner   bears a remarkable
likeness to how Christ's   elect believers
have held their hold   on glorious gladness
on Earth under Heaven   through the Father's help   (390)
in these treacherous times,   and gained for themselves
the greatest glory   in their heavenly home.
All of us have fathomed   that The Almighty fashioned
men and women   through His wondrous means
and then He settled   them in the best spot
of all of the Earth,   which their heirs called
"The Paradise-plain,"   where none were deprived
of any blessing   while The Everlasting Word,
His Holy Commandment,   was upheld by them

with renewed happiness.   Envy harmed them there   (400)
through spite of a foe   who offered them food—
fruit from the tree—   as they partook foolishly
of the apple's evil   against God's grace
to taste the forbidden.   It was bitter there
after gluttonous sin,   and the same for their offspring,
a doleful feast   for their sons and daughters;
their grinding teeth   were grievously tortured
as post-judgment punishment;   they felt God's rage
as savage sorrow.   Since that time their offspring
have paid in grief   for that gift eaten   (410)
against God's word,   thus, sick in spirit,
they were forced to flee   their happy homes
due to the serpent's evil   when he craftily conned
our earliest elders   in olden times
with his deceitful spirit,   so that far from there
they sought a settlement   in the Valley of Death,
a harrowing home.   A happier life
was shrouded in shadow   and the holy plain
was firmly sealed off   through the foe's deceit
for many years   until the joy of mankind,   (420)
consoler of the haggard   and their single hope,
the King of Glory,   by coming forth
opened it up   again for the saints.
As teachers tell us   and explain in texts,
for us this is   closely akin
to this insightful fowl   with its journeys forsaking
its home and homeland   as it grows old.
Weighed down by years,   it flees weary-hearted
to the shelter it finds   high in the forest.
In that place it builds   with branches and plants   (430)
a new, most noble   dwelling place,
a nest in the woods.   Its intense wish
is that its ageless body   be allowed to embrace
life reborn   through blasts of fire,
in a blazing bath   after one has died,
then pursue a search   for a sun-drenched home,

its former dwelling.   So after our forefathers,
our elders of old,   had left behind
the pleasant plain   and the seat of splendor
that lost its loveliness,   they undertook a trek   (440)
into hellish hands.   In that place old foes,
evil wretches,   often inflicted injuries,
yet there were many   who strictly served
The Maker under the heavens   with many good works
and holy rites,   so Heaven's high King,
was well-disposed   toward them in spirit.
That is the tall tree   where true believers
now make their home,   where no ancient enemy
can harm them at all   with a poisonous potion,
a sign of sinfulness,   in this terrible time.   (450)
Against every evil   The Lord's soldier
makes his nest there   with commendable deeds
when he doles out alms   to the down and out—
those mobs without money—   calls to Our Lord
the Father for help,   hurries on from there,
blots out the faults   of this fleeting life
and his dismal deeds,   upholds stoutheartedly
the law of The Lord,   strives through prayer
in righteous reverie,   and bends its knee
to the ground with grace.   He flees evil,   (460)
all the grim guiltiness,   for fear of God.
Glad-heartedly he yearns   to do deeds
for the greatest good.   The shield of God,
vicar of victory,   joy-giver to people,
is always for his kind.   These are the herbs,
the products of plants,   which the untamed bird
harvests under the heavens   far and wide
and takes to its bailiwick,   where it builds a nest
wondrously safe   from every evil.
So here in this place now   with mind and might   (470)
the champions of God   achieve His wishes
by attempting exploits,   since The Eternal Almighty
wants to bestow on them   a blessèd bounty.

In the city of glory   as rewards for their works
dwellings will be redone   from these fragrant plants
because they uphold   holy teaching
fiercely in their hearts,   love The Lord
day and night,   and with souls surging
choose the beloved   light of faith
over wealth of the world.   There's no joyful hope   (480)
for them living long   in this fleeting life,
thus the moral man   shall earn through his zeal
unending bliss,   a heavenly home
with the loftiest King.   When the end-time comes
on that final day,   followed by Death,
the bloodthirsty warrior   wielding his weapon,
as he snatches each life   and swiftly sends
corruptible bodies   bereft of their souls
to the grip of the ground,   shall linger long there,
covered by dirt,   until the fire comes,   (490)
then massive numbers   from the race of mankind
will be led to a reckoning.   The True-King of Triumph,
The Father of Angels,   the Lord of Legions,
will hold a hearing,   judge with justice,
then all of the men   on Earth will undergo
their resurrection   as The Mighty Ruler,
Prince of Angels,   Savior of Souls,
trumpets an order   over the vast Earth
that by the Lord's might   dismal death
shall halt for the holy.   They shall change nobly,   (500)
gathered in groups,   while this whole world
shaped by sin   is simmering in shame,
kindled on a pyre.   Each person shall become
afraid for his soul   when fire savages
his fleeting treasures,   flame swallows
earthly riches,   greedily grips
the ruddy gold,   and ravenously gobbles
Earth's ornaments.   At the hour of unmasking,
the beautiful and ecstatic   symbol of the bird
shall come into light   for all kinds of men   (510)

163

as God's power   pulls everyone
from the grave to gather   together bone
limbs, trunk   and the spirit of life
before Christ's knee.   A crystalline gem,
The King will gleam   gloriously from His throne
upon the holy ones.   In that terrible time
one who can please   God shall be well.
There the spirit-covers   cleansed of sin
will go glad-heartedly,   returning their souls
to their bone-vessels   as the blaze vaults   (520)
high in the heavens.   Many will be seared
in the frightening fire   where each of all
the righteous and sinful,   the flesh with soul,
shall seek God's glory   from a mouldering grave
while fraught with fear.   Flame will march on;
it will sear away sin.   After they have suffered,
the righteous ones   will be ringed by their acts,
by their own works.   These are like the welcome,
impressive plants   with which the wild bird
wholly surrounds   itself outside   (530)
the nest that abruptly   bursts into flame
and scorches in the sun   along with the bird;
and once fire languishes,   life returns.
So too in this way   members of mankind,
each and everyone,   are cloaked in flesh,
resplendent and restored   so each with their longing
can then incline   the King of Glory
to be merciful to them   at that massive gathering.
Sanctified spirits,   the chaste and chosen
righteous souls,   shall sing a song,   (540)
voice upon voice,   to praise the power
of the Lord in air   sweetly scented,
then ascend to glory   through their good deeds.
The souls of these servants   will be cleansed of sin,
brilliantly refined,   through the blazing flames.
Let none of the race   of mankind reckon
that I sing a song   with deceptive words

164

by writing poetry.   Listen to the prophecy
of the verses of Job.   Moved in his mind
by the Spirit's aura,   he spoke boldly   (550)
with glory and honor.   He gave this speech:
"Worn-out as a warrior,   in my heartfelt thoughts
I do not challenge   that I could choose a bed
of death for my nest   and head out humbled
on a lengthy trip,   covered in clay
while gripped by the ground,   regretting old deeds,
and then after death,   through God's grace
after resurrection,   like the phoenix bird
be allowed to gain   life again
with joy for the Lord   where His beloved legions   (560)
adore their dearest.   I cannot wait
for this life's end,   for joy and light
ever and always.   Delighting the worms,
my decayed corpse   will undergo crumbling
in its mouldering grave;   the God of multitudes
will discharge my soul   after the hour of death,
and wake it to wonder.   Hope in my heart
never fades   for I hold fast
to unending joy   with the Prince of Angels."
So in days of old   a wise elder,   (570)
God's prophet,   sang prudently
of a resurrection   into everlasting life
so that we might grasp   in greater detail
a famous symbol,   the brilliant bird
that foretokens by burning.   After the blazing fire
it gathers all   of the ashes and embers,
and bits of bone,   then the bird always
clutches them with talons   clenched sunward
toward the House of the Lord.   Here they lie
for many years   with the bits reborn,   (580)
wholly renewed,   in that land where no one
is able to threaten   any thrashings.
So through the Lord's power   at the point after death,
just like the beautifully   emblazoned bird

with a distinctive scent   in its holy state,
souls gather   together with their bodies
where the steadfast sun   keeps shining
on those assembled in the gleaming   City of Glory.
High over rooftops   Christ the Healer
is streaming light   upon steadfast souls.   (590)
Beautiful birds,   chosen spirits
brilliantly restored,   celebrating in bliss,
follow Him   to that happy home
forever and ever   where some outcast, wicked
fiend can do   no evil with devilry,
yet they live forever   as a luminous army,
just like the phoenix bird   in brilliant glory
in the peace of the Lord.   The labor of people
shimmers for everyone   in their happy home
as brightly as the sun   before the face   (600)
of the always peaceful   everlasting Lord.
There the crystalline crown,   splendidly set
with precious gemstones,   hovers over the head
of each of the holy   as their heads glow.
Cloaked in majesty,   the amazing diadem
of God graces   each of the faithful
with light in life   where lasting joy
renewed forever   never fades;
they still abide in beauty,   engulfed by glory
with fine ornaments   of the Father of Angels.   (610)
Nothing in that place   will be painful at all:
no strife or want,   no times of struggle,
no hunger or heat,   no horrible thirst,
nor anguish or aging;   the noble King
will grant what is good.   The assembly of souls
praises the Savior there   and celebrates the power
of the King of Heaven   with hymns to The Lord.
The group sublimely   sings its songs
near the high, holy   throne of God.
With blissful angels   the blesséd adore   (620)
their most worthy King   this way in a chorus:

"Peace and prudence   be yours, true God,
and thanks to you,   enthroned in majesty,
for recent gifts,   for all the goodness.
Unmatched, immense,   of commanding strength,
on high and holy,   Father almighty,
Lord of all lords   with the angels above,
Heaven and Earth   together are gorgeously
filled with glory   and our Majesty's majesty.
Defend us, Creator of Origins!   Father almighty,   (630)
you are in the heights   as the guardian of Heaven."
Cleansed of evil,   defenders of fairness
speak in this fashion   in that famous city.
A steadfast company   proclaims His majesty;
in Heaven they sing   hosannas to the Sovereign,
the One for whom   everlasting honor
is His alone.   He had no origin,
no beginning of bliss,   though He was born
here amidst the world   in Middle-earth
in the form of a child.   The fullness of His might   (640)
high over Heaven   still remains holy
with unbroken glory.   Though He had to bear
the ordeal of death   on a wooden cross,
a terrible torment,   on the third day
after His body's ruin   He was resurrected
with the Father's help,   like the newborn phoenix
that wakes at home   once more in ash
to a life of lives   with strengthened limbs.
It signals the greatness   of the Son of God—
like the Savior offering   sustenance to us   (650)
and life without end   through loss of His body,
like this bird with both   its wings weighed down
with a handsome harvest   of succulent and sweet
spices when he wants   to speed away.
As Scripture instructs us,   these are the words
of the voice of the holy,   whose hearts are eager
to head Heavenward   toward merciful God
into joy within joys   where they will offer up

this glorious state   as a gift to the Maker,
the welcome fragrance   of words and works   (660)
in that life of light: "Praise be to Him,
and the miracle of glory,   honor and might
high in the skyward   realm of Heaven
forever and ever.   He is King by right
of Middle-earth   and heavenly hosts,
swathed in glory   in that gleaming city.
We have been allowed   *by the lord of light*
while we are here   *to be made whole*
by doing good deeds   *with joys in Heaven,*
a place where we might   *in the greatest dominion*   (670)
seek then sit   *in the lofty seats,*
live in the bliss   *of light and peace,*
have a home   *of gentle happiness,*
savor good times,   *pleasant and placid,*
see divine victories   *without end,*
and sing His hymns   *in perpetual praise*
while elated with angels.   *Alleluia."*

Translated from anonymous Old English with translated Latin in italics.

168

Lowell's Bedlam

Characters:

Robert Lowell ("Cal"), the poet, Pulitzer Prize laureate, age 32, Boston Brahmin, handsome, with dark curly hair.

Celeste Haydon, nurse, age 28, blond hair under nurse's cap; tries hard to be professional, is attractive, deferential. In one scene, for a few moments, she plays a hallucination Lowell experiences and seems to be his former wife Jean Stafford.

Elizabeth Hardwick, ("Lizzie" or Mrs. Lowell), novelist and critic, age 33, pretty, petite, auburn-haired, with a Southern accent and an assured self-presentation.

Dick Jaffee, fellow patient, a story editor for film, but out of work. Attractive in a rough-hewn way, with a faint Brooklyn accent. He is the play's Narrator, aged 62 when he narrates, aged 34 when he appears in scenes.

Elizabeth Bishop, age 38, short, dark wavy hair, a mixture of reserve and cheerfulness; poet, lesbian, and friend of Lowell. (This role can be doubled by the actor who plays Celeste.)

Time and Place:

Act I, Scenes 1 and 2: September 1949, Pitney Akins mental hospital, New York City. Patient's room.

Scene 3: Recreation room for patients

Act II: Recreation room for patients.

Act I

Scene 1

*A patient's room, Pitney Akins Hospital, New York City, late September 1949. Lighting is expressionistic, undersea, blue-green. Occasional projections of filmy forms like jellyfish or paramecia pass along the walls. Background noises include sighing, muffled thumps, faint groans, an occasional note from a piano or string. At several points during the play characters will repeat a phrase and the gestures going with it, and we understand that this is something happening in Cal's mind, not something belonging to external reality. If possible, the repeated phrases should be recorded for instant playback and amplified. Otherwise the actor does the repeats. Phrases like this are marked * *.*

Jaffee, the Narrator, dressed in bulky-knit sweater and corduroys, enters stage right and stands at the periphery of the room. He wears a soft cloth rain hat, carries an aluminum walking stick, moves haltingly. He stops and looks around, nodding.

Jaffee: Yep, here we are. Or were. This is what our rooms are like, everything dead-on, just like it was. Fanciest little bin in the world. Unless you needed padded walls, and Pitney Akins Hospital wouldn't take customers who were that far gone. Only the semi-cuckoo were admitted, though, sure, they stretched a point for some people. Including Cal Lowell, who was way out on the walnut branch when he came in. Or was it a hickory nut? They're a little harder to crack, but the right nutcracker can do it. Anyway, our hickory-dickory Doc gave him a pass and admitted him. Welcome to the nursery, welcome to Wonderland on north Madison Avenue in mad Manhattan. I guess he figured poets always are a little loonsville even when they're sane, I mean, to the extent that they ever are. Because, if a *bard* believes he's Napoleon or Milton, we just take it for granted, right? Would-be playwrights like myself, we had to toe a stricter line. Though I'm not sure it's so much crazier, when you think about it, to believe you're the equivalent of Eugene

O'Neill or Clifford Odets—which was my situation. Never mind that I couldn't get *arrested* when it came to getting a play staged. I just kept pounding away at the Underwood, tippa-tappa, play after brilliant play, and told myself the producers would see the light eventually. Hard to believe, but they were every bit as crazy as me And it worked for them. I made them honorary members of the Droolers' Club. (*Gestures.*) You don't like it when I make jokes about mental illness, do you? I should be more respectful. No, *you* should be, I don't *have* to. Alumni of the Flight Deck are allowed to say whatever we damn well please. In fact, it's a sign we're well as soon as we're able to make cracks about ... the cracks in our brainpan.

(*Looks around.*) Incredibly amazing how clear things still are, even after thirty years. I don't remember what the hell I did last week, but I can remember *this*. I can remember the intake process, first me, and then two days later Mr. Robert Lowell, Boston Brahmin and Pulitzer Prize-winning poet! Breathing fire and brimstone and determined to save the world from illiterate clods, the *Mayflower* upper crust, and complacent suburbanites. And despite all of it, a soft-hearted sonofabitch. The poor slob kinda grew on you, despite all of it. (*Spot fades as Narrator exits, light comes up on the opening door.*)

Celeste: Now if you'll just come in here, Mr. Lowell, we'll make you comfortable.

Lowell: (*Ironic smile.*) Won't be that easy. This is my second detention. I'm a repeat offender.

Celeste: I beg your pardon? *beg your pardon?*

Lowell: (*Pauses.*) I did time in Baldpate Hospital for two months this past summer. Up in Massachusetts, north of Boston.

Celeste: Oh, I see. I think you'll find the doctors and the... accommodations at Pitney Akins the very best, Mr. Lowell.

Lowell: Sort of boarding school for grown-ups, isn't it, until we get a grip on our subjects. Unfortunately, they didn't teach psychology at St. Marks or at Kenyon College. I didn't even know what manic-depressive symptoms were until I had them. And I still didn't. Until they locked me up. And I locked them out. (*Stands stock still.*)

Celeste: (*Takes his overnight bag, gestures toward a chest of drawers.*) You can put your things in these drawers *in these drawers*.

Lowell: (*Studies her.*) I haven't got much of anything. Nothing much at all. (*Chuckles.*) Not even my mind. And from nothing comes nothing. Nothing, nothing, nothing. Dead. Dead wrong, dead, dead as a log. King Log is dead. Long live the King, and watch your step, little frogs! King Stork is on the way!

Celeste: If you'd like, Mr. Lowell, you can lie down and rest until time to speak to the doctor.

Lowell: That's the first step toward glory, isn't it? Lie down, stretch out, and wait till lightning strikes. (*Laughs nervously.*) It's just that … I never lie, not even down. (*Chuckles.*) I never talk down to anybody. You can ask my mother, I've always been a good boy, thoroughly well behaved, even if it doesn't always get you to Heaven, or even Heaven-Haven. But I tried to be a good boy, always. Though my father wouldn't agree that I did, he thought he'd raised a little hell-raiser. What I didn't know then but now *do* know is that bad boys have their place in the scheme of things. The world would miss the hell out of us! I myself am Hell. Some men stand apart from others. Apart and above. (*Hams.*) Beneath Mr. Milquetoast's mild exterior is a lion, the king of beasts, and his name is Zarathustra! You think I don't know I'm crazy, but yes I do know. It's terribly funny.

Celeste: (*Hesitantly.*) What is terribly funny, Mr. Lowell?

Lowell: Insanity. It's a tragedy chock full of laughs. Chock-a-block. Terribly funny, like poor Tom hamming it up in *King Lear*. Tom is the bright side of Lear, he's the real ruler. (*Laughs hollowly, but with growing conviction.*)

Celeste: I see. May I take your coat? (*Takes it, hangs it in the closet. Takes things down from a shelf.*) Here are some pajamas *some pajamas*. And a bathrobe, and your slippers.

Lowell: I'm fairly used to incarceration, you understand. I also spent some time at the Federal Detention Center on West Street down in Greenwich Village. That was an earlier incarnation. Now I'm reincarcerated here. But this time as a … madman instead of a criminal. They didn't keep me there for long. After a suitable dose of prison life, during which I met several murderers, some of them very polite, they sent me to Connecticut. (*They stare at each other.*) For being a C.O.

Celeste: A C.O.?

Lowell: Conscientious objector. During the war. I don't kill, either. (*They stare at each other.*)

Celeste: Of course not. But this is a hospital, it's not... a penal institution *a penal institution* *a penal institution*. You'll be going home as soon as you're feeling well. Dr. Miller will be here in just a moment.

Lowell: Miller. He a Navy man? My father was. He used to speak of a fellow officer named Miller. My father was a staunch Navy man.

Celeste: Navy? I don't know, the doctor never mentioned it. But I'm sure he wouldn't mind if you asked him. I know his medical degree is from Harvard. Am I wrong to guess that's your alma mater?

Lowell: Not really. (*Two beats.*) If I decide I don't want to see Miller, will you back me up?

Celeste: Mr. Lowell, I—I'm just a nurse here, I don't supervise. I'm sure you'll find Dr. Miller thoroughly professional and a very nice person.

Lowell: I'm detained until he says I can leave. He'll be checking up on me. (*Looks toward the audience.*) This is a two-way mirror, isn't it? You don't have to tell me, I know it is.

Celeste: We don't have mirrors in the rooms, Mr. Lowell. The window is dark now and, as you know, they reflect when they're dark. I forgot to say that, if you brought a hand mirror, we'll have to keep that for you while you're here. Unless it's a round, metal mirror.

Lowell: (*Pointing.*) What about this mirror?

Celeste: I'm sorry? (*A beat.*) There's no mirror. That's a window, Mr. Lowell. We thought you would enjoy the view. Most patients like that, but I can draw the curtains if you'd rather. Mrs. Lowell thought you would want a room with a view *room with a view*.

Lowell: Which Mrs. Lowell? My mother? The Mrs. Lowell I used to be married to? My current wife? Doesn't make much difference, does it? All of them like mirrors a lot. (*Celeste blinks and tries to speak.*) You don't read, do you? I mean you're not bookish. Not many women are. (*Declaims.*) Because if you were, you'd know that writers hold a mirror up to the world. That's also their defense against the world. They hold it up as long as they can; and, because they're not Atlas, not even Charles Atlas (*laughs*), one day, it falls on them. (*Looks over the proscenium. Voice rises.*) Anyway, you're wrong. This one's definitely a mirror. (*Whispers.*) That's me there, no mistake about it. And your doctor is hiding on the other side, I'm sure… (*shouts*) HE CAN LOOK AS MUCH AS HE DAMN WELL PLEASES! LISTEN! I'M NOT

AN ADULTERER! NOT AN ADULTERER! HE WON'T SEE ME DISFIGURE ANYBODY, ANYBODY! I'M NOT A MURDERER. HE WON'T SEE ME BUMP OFF A SINGLE SOUL, NOT ONE! NOT ONE!

Celeste: (*Rapidly*) If you'll just—just remain calm, Mr. Lowell, Doctor Miller will be coming right along. Just try to be CALM!

Blackout. Scuffle noises. Sound of electric buzzing, strobe lights suggesting electroshock.

Scene 2

Light comes slowly up. The setting is daylight-realistic, the only sounds those produced by the actors. Lowell is in the bed, propped up. Seated in a hospital chair near him, wearing an old fur coat, is Elizabeth Hardwick, who affects a brisk optimism.

Lizzie: So, do you think the doctors are doing better here than they did at Baldpate?

Cal: (*Abstracted, dazed, soft-spoken.*) Well, I think so, dear, but then I've only got my own mind to judge with, and that's sort of a fried egg just now.

Lizzie: I know, I know, but, honey, you look better than you ever have, really. We're going to get you well, I promise. (*A beat.*) I spoke to Peter and Frank; and Randall and Allen called. They're all rooting for you; and said they're hoping to see you soon.

Cal: I'm amazed Allen still cares to have a bedlamite as a friend. I feel rotten when I think how I behaved with him and Caroline.

Lizzie: Oh, why do you say that, Cal, he's very loyal. Bedlamite! (*Shakes her head.*) Oh, honey, you're not a bedlamite, you just have an illness, and it *is treatable,* darling. Dr. Miller is very definite about that.

Cal: But during the night here I wake up and see myself, I mean, from the outside, as though I were somebody in a movie, and that lunatic is attacking Allen. I don't think there's any way for him to be loyal to someone who almost killed him. It'll be in the dark here in the dead of the night, and I keep seeing myself holding him outside the window (*extends his hands over the edge of the bed and shakes them*), and I hear myself saying, "I'm going to let you go, Allen, if you don't repent for your adulteries. *Repent, Allen, repent and reform!*" And his eyes bug out and he looks down at the ground thirty feet below him and then at me and he yells like a madman and …

Lizzie: But you were ill, dear, and he knows that. He knows perfectly well what illness is. And drunkenness, too, he's had first-hand experience with it himself. (*Touches her hair and the corner of her mouth with the nail of her little finger.*)

Cal: You don't think he's petrified I'll be sprung from here and do it again?

Lizzie: Of course not. He expects you … to get well; and back in the game again, the same as we all do. Give yourself a few weeks, Cal, and you'll see.

Cal: So is everything all right up there in Red Hook? Don't you … feel a little lonely?

Lizzie: (*Lies.*) Oh, I'm fine. I miss you, Cal, so much, but everything's fine, really, please don't worry about me. It's pretty up there. The leaves are starting to turn a little. I've become quite friendly with Mrs. Philip across the way. We take drives down to get a view of the river. It's just gorgeous—factory chimneys, Satanic mills, and all (*laughs*). I'm not lonely at all, I'm working hard and enjoying the peace and quiet. I just wish we could be together. And we will. I know we will, soon. (*A beat.*) Of course I

176

worry that I'm no help to you, which is why I fall all over myself trying to reassure you with my silly bromides. That's all I want, darling, is to offer some sort of support, if I can. Please tell me how you are.

Cal: Honestly, I don't feel I'm myself? Really? My mind's sort of … there's nothing there. Like a room that used to have furniture in it, and you look for the armchair you always sit in when you read, and it's as though it'd never been there. The desk isn't there, the rug isn't there, the lamp isn't there. Not a thing, nothing there. You feel as though you must have dreamed they were there, but actually there's nothing in the room. At least not at first. And then when you begin to feel there is something there, when it starts to swell and rise up, when the feeling begins to pound and pound in your head and you think you're king of the world, you realize madness is on the way, and just maybe you'll be able to put the brakes on in time and—or maybe you won't catch it and you'll …

Lizzie: (*Interrupts.*) Well, that's a brilliant description of clinical depression and the onset of the manic phase, Cal. But it *will be resolved soon.* (*A beat.*) I've spoken to Dr. Miller, and he says if you feel strong enough, we can bring in your typewriter so that you can get back to your work. I know that will make an enormous difference *an enormous difference*.

Cal: (*Looks up.*) But I loathe the idea of writing right now. No ideas at all, or if I have any it's as though I'm walled off from them. (*A beat.*) When the manic side of the seesaw went up (*extends his arms, lifting the right higher than the left*), I had plenty to say.

Lizzie: That's true, and (*ironic*) you did say it; but you didn't write it down and, um, from what I heard… You may find that you're actually in a better frame of mind *now*, than you were then, to do substantial work. That was just a little… pump-priming.

Cal: It might help if I could speak with a priest.

Lizzie: It might. It might, but, you know, I wonder, honey. So much of what you were saying and doing before you went to Baldpate was about religion and sin and godknows what. So maybe it's better if you didn't reflect on all that for a while and just, you know, rested.

Cal: I'm not that sold on resting, Lizzie. I'd say it was pretty damned convincing, that passage about Him coming not to bring peace but instead a sword. You know, it's the tradition of Christ the King, strong in the battle against the Adversary. Which doesn't do much for his reputation as the Gentle Shepherd, the Prince of Peace, does it?

Lizzie: Well of course he is depicted as making that remark about the sword, *if* we take every word of Scripture as literal and historical. But; looking at it objectively; don't you think; when you divorced Jean; you were demonstrating that; whatever your feelings for ... faith in general; you knew you didn't belong in the Catholic Church? *in the Catholic Church*?

Cal: Just because I didn't belong with Jean doesn't prove I don't belong in the Church.

Lizzie: Well, Cal, maybe they can find a loophole for you, maybe an annulment. They've done that for so many people. We can speak to experts, religious professionals. We'll try to arrange all that later on. When you're back on your feet. But I can tell you this much: *I* feel married to you, if that makes any difference. You tell me a lot of your feelings, but what I feel (*nervous laugh*) should count in the equation, shouldn't it? I don't know. I just loathe seeing you so upset and ... sad. I have high hopes for us, I did from the beginning. Just remember how much fun we had this summer, living in Fred's amusing old house, cooking our own meals, reading your poems aloud, and reading my book reviews aloud, and pouring ourselves whiskies, and getting up at dawn, and mowing the lawn ... uphill in the heat. So much fun. That was less than a month ago. All summer you didn't go to church a single time *a single time*.

Cal: Well, my doctor here is Jewish, so maybe he'll argue me out of Catholicism.

Lizzie: (*She smiles brightly.*) I don't think he will; unless you want him to.

Cal: Part of me wishes he could. Or that I *could* want him to. Thing about it is, I know how to be a Catholic poet but not how to be a secular poet. What on earth would I write about if I were a pagan?

Lizzie: I'm absolutely certain you'll get back in the swing of your writing as soon as you're well, and out of this place. By the way, Fred isn't renting the house in Red Hook to anyone else. He says we can still have it when you're discharged. You'll be able to write there. Or just rest and enjoy yourself. There's more to living than writing poetry *writing poetry*. Surely there is, don't you think?

Cal: (*Three beats.*) What about you? Are you working?

Lizzie: Well, Cal, you know me, I never stop scribbling. Lots of new pages for the novel. And I'm making excellent notes that I know I'll be able to use. After you, it's the most thrilling thing I've experienced. Ever.

Cal: You promised me you weren't putting me in the book.

Lizzie: I did promise. You're not in it. It's as I said, I'm doing a fictional version of that killer we read about when we were living in Iowa City. I want to focus on the moment when he—. Oh, but of course I don't expect you to remember what I'm working on, I mean, with all you have to contend with just now.

Cal: I'm glad you're not putting me in it. Although, as Oscar Wilde said, the only thing worse than being talked about badly was not being talked about at all. The same goes for written about.

Lizzie: (*Two beats.*) I don't know who else is talking or writing about you, Cal, and whether that's a good thing; but I'm not planning to, myself. (*Softly*) I love you, darling. (*Leans forward.*) So much. (*A beat.*) You know I'd do anything for you, you know that. Oh, and, um, do you still want me to keep all this from your mother and father?

Cal: For Christ's sake, don't tell them. I don't want to know they're worried about me, and I certainly don't want them to come down here.

(*Celeste enters.*)

Celeste: Good afternoon, Mrs. Lowell. Dr. Miller expects to see Mr. Lowell shortly, so I'm afraid I'll have to ask you … (*She clasps her hands and then opens them.*)

Lizzie: Oh, certainly, I was just going, I'll be right on my way. (*She stands, goes to Robert, bends down as he reaches up. They hold a kiss for several beats, she kissing him more than he her. Hardwick turns, reaches in her bag for a handkerchief, puts it back, waves as she exits.*)

Celeste: How are we feeling today?

Lowell: Feeling no pain, even without liquor. And that's sort of boring, I'm afraid. I don't suppose anyone here can be bribed to smuggle in a fifth of whisky?

Celeste: Would you like to get up now and put on your robe? Here are your slippers.

Lowell: Any reason you're being so considerate? It's just part of your job, isn't it?

Celeste: I … I'm glad you feel that Pitney Akins has been taking good care of you, Mr. Lowell. I'm *personally* glad *I'm personally glad*.

Lowell: Are you married? Do you have children?

Celeste: Mr. Lowell, whether I'm single or not isn't important. You're scheduled to speak to Dr. Miller now. (*She holds his robe for him. He slips the right arm, then the left, into the sleeves. Then turns to face her. She begins backing away as lights dim and fade to black.*)

Scene 3

The Recreation Room of the clinic. A television plays in the background, perhaps the Milton Berle Show. Against the wall, a water cooler. Lowell and Jaffee are wearing hospital clothes. They shuffle cards and begin playing a game called Russian Bank.

Jaffee: What are you in for?

Lowell: A manic episode.

Jaffee: Depression here, so I guess we make good pair. If we get tired of our roles we can swap. (*Lowell doesn't laugh at his joke, so Jaffee does.*) Wait, hold on. (*Plays a card.*) What line of work you in?

Lowell: I write.

Jaffee: And do you publish what you write?

Lowell: Yes, there are a couple of books. Of poetry. I'm a poet.

Jaffee: Seriously? (*Lowell nods.*) Well then I guess you already passed the qualifying exams for this place a long time ago. (Beat.) A poet! Does it pay?

Lowell: Not much. There was some money when I won the Pulitzer Prize.

Jaffee: You're crapping me, you won that? I shouldn't ask, though. I spoke to a guy yesterday who thinks he's Harry Truman.

Lowell: You can look it up. Robert Lowell, Pulitzer Prize for Poetry, 1946. I'm not here for thinking I won a prize. I'm here for thinking I was the Superman.

Jaffee: But now you know you were really Clark Kent. Who replaced you on *The Daily Planet?*

Lowell: That's good, but what I was talking about was Nietzsche. Jaffee: Never read him, but from what I understand he was the first Nazi.

Lowell: That's a gross oversimplification, but why don't we just drop it. (*Jaffee shrugs, plays a card.*) So what about you, what got you depressed?

Jaffee: Well, to start with, *the* Depression. My father lost his life savings, which made him depressed—he, the great Irving Jaffee, theatrical impresario, friend of the stars of stage and screen, the last big spender from the East—overnight without a thin red cent to his name. No wonder he was depressed. And then he, you know, passed it on to me. Misery loves company, and a son should support his old man, if you can dig that. But I decided to fight it. I got the hell out of Brooklyn and went to Hollywood as soon as I could. Got into films. Worked on quite a few. People say the best work I did was with Robert Siodmak.

Lowell: You wrote screenplays?

Jaffee: Well, it's more like I *rewrote* them. You know how they get all these high-toned novelists to come out there and do scripts? F. Scott Fitzgerald, William Faulkner, all of them out there determined to make a quick buck. Well, you wouldn't believe the fancy crap they turn out. Way too flowery for the movies. So I would read them and toss the highfalutin stuff. I don't know, *you'd* probably call it poetry. But poetry doesn't play in the movies.

Lowell: So you were … kind of a censor.

Jaffe: Um, no, they didn't call me that. Consultant. Script doctor. My mother liked the doctor title. Anyway, I'm not sure it qualified as useful work, but it was a way to pay bills. I have no literary pretensions to amount to anything, really, so I didn't knock the job, somebody's got to do it. (*A beat.*) Actually, I'm lying. I really did want to be the next Eugene O'Neill or Clifford Odets. I had a lot to say, so I thought. I hadn't realized nobody wanted another one of those, I mean, like, one of each was enough. So when paying work came along, I grabbed it. Best decision I ever made. No question about it, none whatsoever. That's the honest truth.

Lowell: Maybe you're protesting too much?

Jaffee: (*Two beats.*) Maybe. That's not to say I didn't like working in film.

Lowell: Fine, but then you got depressed again? (*Drops a card on the floor, bends to pick it up, seems disoriented when upright again. Looks at card and smiles.*)

Jaffee: Right. Do you know why? Back in my wild, dissolute youth I joined the Communist Party. We used to think that revolution was the answer to the Depression. Besides, the girls who joined all believed in free love. Or enough of them to keep the male Commies busy. And undepressed.

Lowell: Oh, you were a Communist, you were that serious?

Jaffee: Serious.… No, actually, for me it was just for the laughs. Workmen of the world unite, you have nothing to lose but your chain-smoking!… Look, I'm Jewish. We had a lot *not* to laugh about after the War, you know, when the whole thing came out.

(*Lowell doesn't understand.*) The camps. The death camps. Even at *The Daily Planet* they have heard about those, right? Communism was supposed to put a stop to bigotry. There wouldn't be any more Fascism. What the hell did we know about Stalin?

Lowell: You must have at least known about the Hitler-Stalin non-aggression pact. (*Jaffee nods and shrugs, holding his palms up.*) But then you eventually did resign from the Party? (*They toss in the cards and stop playing.*)

Jaffee: Sure thing. But … Hollywood isn't in a forgiving mood these days.

Lowell: What are they supposed to be forgiving?

Jaffee: They're purging all the Commies and ex-Commies like myself.

Lowell: Why?

Jaffee: Well, they claim they're being patriotic, making the world safe for democracy and stockbrokers. Making the world safe for Depression. Business is business. God forbid the blessed public should think our great American movie industry is a hotbed for Red propaganda. Bad for box office, and in Hollywood box office is king. The Commies have to go. So they included me out, as Sam Goldwyn used to say.

Lowell: Didn't you tell them you'd resigned your Party membership?

Jaffee: I did, but the truth is, the Party hadn't made a note of it. I was still on the rolls. Didn't make a damn's worth of difference that I hadn't been to a single meeting in Hollywood. Out on my can.

Lowell: So that's why you got depressed.

Jaffee: What do you mean, is that not a big enough reason? I was pretty good at what I did, and suddenly I was told I couldn't do it anymore. Not to mention that the checks stopped coming, and the electric company wasn't all that understanding about the problem. It was déjà vu the second time around: the Depression! Happy days! Down the hatch! (*Three beats.*) And there was more to it. My wife Christine decided she didn't much care for the color red, and it was time to move on to greener, less Communistic pastures. Her old man was an exec at RKO, and she didn't want to be linked (*points thumb at his chest*) to this particular liability. So. (*Gestures. Three beats.*) And yourself? Had a manic episode? (*Laughs.*) Or was it just a bender?

Lowell: I've been on plenty of benders, so I think I can say I know the difference. In some ways, being manic was more enjoyable. For a few days I was omnipotent, I got to play God.

Jaffee: If you want to make enemies, there are easier ways than playing God. (*A beat.*) Now that you're not omnipotent, are you impotent?

Lowell: Matter of fact, yes.

Jaffee: Tough. You married?

Lowell: Yes.

Jaffee: To the wrong woman, sounds like. (*Lowell stands goes to the water cooler. Jaffee follows. They fill cups of water as they continue.*)

Lowell: No, Lizzie's grand. But I don't feel fully divorced from Jean—my first wife—yet.

Jaffee: Why not?

Lowell: I'm a Catholic. Or at least I was one. So in the eyes of the church I'm committing adultery.

Jaffee: Sounds like fun, what's the problem?

Lowell: All right, but jokes aside.

Jaffee: Go back to the first wife then.

Lowell: No, it's over, I don't really love Jean now. Not in the right way.

Jaffee: What happened, she start holding out on you? Was she cheating? (*They move back to the table, sit down. Jaffe idly shuffles and reshuffles the cards.*)

Lowell: No, it began even before we married, actually. She'd come to Boston to meet my parents. It was Christmas night. I suppose I'd had some eggnog. Do you really want to hear this? Okay, it was dark, I made a wrong turn down a blind alley and stepped on the gas rather than the brake. The car had a manic episode, I guess you could say, and smashed against a brick wall. I wasn't hurt much, but Jean was. Her face got busted up. (*Jaffee gapes.*) She had to have four or five operations to rebuild everything. Horribly painful, she went through hell. So every time I looked at her, I felt guilty. And I guess guilt … it was like a mortar and pestle twenty-four hours a day. It pulverized what I should have been thinking. We … I guess we started destroying each other. She … she … she'd get drunk as hell and let me have it with both barrels. It got worse, and eventually she had a nervous breakdown. You won't believe this, but she was *also* hospitalized right here. I keep expecting to see her walking toward me down the hall, every time I turn a corner. It's like being stalked by a ghost, only, she's not dead, she's still alive.

Jaffee: Ri-i-i-ght. But you think you should still be married? Isn't that just guilt? If you don't really love her, why do you think you should be married?

Lowell: Doesn't matter what I think, the church says we *are* married.

Jaffee: So divorce the church.

Lowell: I did, but I don't actually *feel* divorced.

Jaffee: Well, pal, you came to the right place. Couple of more sessions on the hotseat, and you won't remember you ever were married or ever set foot in a church.

Lowell: You think that's what they're doing to us here, lobotomizing us? We're just going to end up like apes, aren't we, chattering and scraping the tops of our knuckles on the floor. Hi-ho, nobody home in the bone dome.

Jaffee: Let's hope so, I sure as hell don't want to keep on with the freak show that was going on in my mind. It was like finishing up what the Nazis didn't get to. I was ready to rub myself out, seriously. Usually, when you're going through some kind of meat-grinder, your pals will bolster your bruised ego and see you through it. But not when they're your co-workers, and there's a blacklist going around. Dirty rats. Overnight, everybody forgot who I was. "Dick Jaffee? Who he?" People are no damn good, right? Just hope and pray your safety and well-being don't ever depend on the conscience of the average guy. Lost nearly every friend I had. Which just added to the depression. Knew I'd rather die than go on feeling the way I was feeling. I couldn't get a job, and I couldn't feel writing anything of my own was worth a tinker's damn. One day I found myself staring at the window of a gun store in downtown L.A. And that's when I came back to the old hometown. At least Ma had relevant experience as to what you do with a depressed family member.

(Stage darkens as Jaffee withdraws, pulling the card table off with him. His words "depressed family member" are echoed twice. A lurid spot slowly comes up on Lowell, standing up, facing stage front. Around him, the undersea lighting, with translucent projections.)

187

Lowell: Don't lie to me. I know what you're doing with that mirror. You're spying, you're collecting evidence, taking down every word. (*The sound of plain chant, perhaps Hildegard von Bingen's for solo woman's voice, begins to be heard softly.*) You're waiting to see me, what, to Do Something Crazy? So that you can lock me up permanently? I've been in detention before, I know your methods. "I think you'll find accommodations at Pitney Akins the very best." Well, I don't find them the very best, and I won't *stand* for it, I won't be treated this way. I'll send a letter to the papers. I'm a Lowell, they'll listen to me. When I became a C.O., they damn well listened. When Henry VIII divorced the church they listened! (*Celeste approaches from the wings*) and I'm not crazy. "Just remember how much fun we had in Red Hook, living in Fred's amusing old house, cooking our own meals and mowing the lawn." Cooking AND mowing, I did all that perfectly well. "Now that you're not omnipotent, are you impotent?" Don't WORRY, I'll be omnipotent again. Long live the KING! (*Sees Celeste.*) Oh, Jean. They didn't tell me you were here. I'm sorry, forgive me!

Celeste: Mr. Lowell?

Lowell: Jean, Jean, listen. Listen: I respect you, and I admire you, but I can't live with you. I know we're still married, or the church believes we are, but I'm sorry I don't feel any love for you now. Though I do ... I do feel ashamed. I'm asking you to forgive me for everything. What I now feel is reverence for you. I want forgiveness for the accident. Those things you said, I don't hold them against you. I'm not angry about that. But now I want you to forgive the divorce. (*He falls on his knees, clasps Celeste's body to his face.*) Forgive me for not marrying you again!

Celeste: (*Shakes her head slowly but then stops and draws herself up to her full height and becomes rigid. She is transformed in Cal's mind and becomes his first wife, who then speaks in a commanding voice with an accent different from Celeste's.*) Forgive you? Forgive you? Oh, so *you're* the person who's suffering and needs comforting! That's ridiculous. You have *no idea* what I've been through. It wasn't enough for you to crash the car and put me through a dozen operations, was it? (*Beat.*) All you saw was my smashed-up face. I was this disgusting patient who had become too unattractive for a poet to love. (*Beat*) And that wasn't enough punishment, oh no, then you had to slough off the damaged goods like a pair of old golf shoes. You miserable ... man! Now you want me to forgive you, so that you can feel better. No! I'll see you in Hell first. I'm never going to forgive you. That's the priest's job. Ah, but you can't go to one now, can you? Not any more. You left the Church, you *silly* fool! Just so you could get a divorce. Well, too bad, there's not going to be any forgiveness for you. You made your bed. Now lie in it.

Lowell: Please, now, Jean, don't say that. Please, don't, please, please forgive me ... (*Falls in a heap on the floor.*)

Celeste: (*In her own voice again.*) Mr. Lowell, Mr. Lowell, I'm going to ask you again to stand up! There's nothing—. Just be calm for a moment, I'll call Dr. Miller *I'll call Dr. Miller* *I'll call Dr. Miller*. (*Tries to pull him upright and fails.*)

Lowell: We need an annulment, Jean! Ask the Monsignor. Get someone to write His Holiness, if you have to! For Christssake, let's be divorced, Jean! DIVORCE ME! DIVORCE ME!

(*Stage goes dark.*)

ACT II

Scene 1

The Recreation Room. Light is dim but otherwise natural. In a corner is a Christmas tree with winking lights.

Narrator: (*Dressed as he was at the beginning of Act I*) You would *think* that Cal would've had to stay longer than I did in the hallowed halls of Pitney Akins. But that's not how it worked out. Combination of two things. His wife was eager to spring him just before Christmas, and she managed to persuade everybody that he was back in commission. If they'd asked me—which they did not—I'd have said he should stick around a while. (*Two beats.*) He left, and I stayed. Here's how it went: Just when things were turning around for me, my father died. The upshot was, my mother collapsed. I asked to be discharged because there was a lot of business crap that needed to be taken care of. The Pitney Akins comintern agreed, I got my discharge papers and all, but the morning I was supposed to go, I couldn't get out of bed. Just lay there like a catatonic sack of potatoes. So they extended the run. I mean, I didn't get out till March, and I was *still* shaky. You might want to say that, uh, a part of me never *did* get out. It's like if you're ever a war refugee in one of these places for more than a few nights, there's a way that, to be honest, you don't ever live on Normal Street again. Ever. The so-called real world's just not as real as it used to be. Surface cracks are patched up, oh yeah, but you can still feel the break underneath, and you know not to put too much pressure on it because things can fall apart at any moment. (*Three beats.*) And here's the weirdest part of all: in a way you sort of *liked* being inside, it was a safe haven? Out there in the deep water were all these sharks waiting for you, be they the government, your profession, your relatives, or your creditors, what have you. Inside, the doctors and nurses babied you, they catered to your every need, treated you like royalty. (*Beat.*) I might've stayed longer except I knew Mother was having to foot the bill. I had to get up off my rear end and face those sharks. Face 'em down. But one part of me just didn't want to. Didn't want to, and the fact is, I never one hundred percent left the place. Not completely. No. (*He takes off the hat, lets the aluminum stick drop, slips off sweater and trousers. Underneath is his hospital uniform. As Lowell enters from the wings, Jaffee joins him at the table and lights come up.*)

Jaffee: It's beginning to look a lot like Christmas. (*He croons*) "O, little town of Bethlehem…"

Lowell: You mean "bedlam," don't you?

Jaffee: Hey that's good! "O little town of Bedlam!" The bard speaks!

Lowell: Glad you like it, but I'm afraid I didn't make it up. That's the origin of the word. "Bedlam" was originally Bethlehem Hospital in London. It was where they locked up mental cases. People pronounced it "Bethlem" and eventually "Bedlam."

Jaffee: You're kidding me.

Lowell: No, I'm not, that's where the term came from.

Jaffee: So Baby Jesus was born in Bedlam. Makes sense when you think about it.

Lowell: Well, the best way to understand the Incarnation theologically is that God took on all human suffering. Of every kind. And I suppose that would have to include madness.

Jaffe: So then, for example, God is a manic-depressive. That makes a lot of sense.

Lowell: Or, to follow your metaphor, He's also schizophrenic.

Jaffe: That makes even more sense. All those mixed signals. You're damned if you do and damned if you don't. Jesus! Why did no one ever explain this to me before? I've got to start reading poetry.

Lowell: I'm sort of surprised you don't already, since you write plays. I suppose you're aware that Marlowe, Shakespeare, Jonson, and Dryden were all poets?

Jaffee: I'm going to shock you and tell you that the only one of those guys I ever read was the Bard himself. Wait, I did read one Marlowe, *The Jew of Malta*. Didn't much care for it.

Lowell: In my view one problem with the contemporary stage is that it doesn't include any poetry. There was still some in O'Neill, but then it petered out.

Jaffee: Well, the theater has to appeal to the public that's actually out there, agreed? Movies pretty much killed off the poetry side of things. And if television takes over as it looks like it's going to, who knows? Bye-bye poetry and bye-bye theater as we know it. Although: Do you know about this new guy who calls himself Tennessee Williams?

Lowell: I've heard of him. He writes about working-class people?

Jaffee: Not exactly. My point was, he puts a little poetry into his stuff. But I'm not sure I like it that much.

Lowell: Then he should put in more. That's the only way the theater is going to get interesting again.

Jaffee: Duly noted. I'll write that statement on a piece of cardboard and tack it up over my writing desk.

Lowell: If you weren't interested in what words can do, why did you want to write plays?

Jaffee: Oh, I was interested, sure. I thought words, or let's say conversation—at least when it's spoken by living, breathing, hungover characters—could lead to social reform. Yeah, I did! No kidding, I really did! I mean, if those words and those characters showed where exactly it was they were hurting. (*Beat.*) And what they didn't understand.

Lowell: Yes, of course. But it's an open question whether literature has any influence on politics. I'm not aware that it's ever been proved.

Jaffee: I think it does have an influence. But if a play gets all poeticky, it ain't gonna influence anybody. Except it might influence people to clear the house after Act I.

Lowell: As they do after Act I of *Antony and Cleopatra?*

Jaffee: Touché. (*Beat.*) Touché. (*Beat.*) I don't know what I'm talking about, my plays never got a chance to influence or not influence anybody. People like social change about as much as they like "poesy."

Lowell: I disagree. They don't realize they're interested until someone shows them they are. That's the problem with writers, currently. They set their aims too low instead of accepting that they should be educating the audience. Everything is just cranked out like an industrial product for the lowest common denominator, without any effort to bring things up to the intelligent par.

Jaffee: Do you know what production costs on Broadway now are? Think about it. Once you've sold your tickets to the six hundred "higher level" clients, where do you get the cash to pay your overhead?

Lowell: That's not the writer's problem. His problem is to write well. Period.

Jaffee: Yep, that's the way a Boston Brahmin like yourself would think. Money isn't a problem.

Lowell: My parents didn't have any money to amount to anything. A little trust fund but no real capital, nothing liquid.

Jaffee: Really? So it was like genteel poverty?

Lowell: Not poverty, but we weren't rich. And I'm still not.

Jaffee: Well, the one thing I got from the Party is the Marxist idea that money stands behind everything. Everything.

Lowell: Yes, and the result of that theory is that you let yourself be discouraged from writing socially significant plays and went to work for Hollywood. Which then blacklisted you. You might want to reconsider the logic of that.

Jaffee: Robert, please don't make me do that. OK? Please don't. They're treating me for depression here and you're not helping. You think I don't realize I've failed? You think—

(*Lizzie enters.*)

Lizzie: Hello, Cal. They just said to come right in. (*They kiss. She looks at Jaffee.*)

Lowell: Elizabeth, this is Dick Jaffee. (*They nod.*)

Jaffee: All right, I'm going to … go back to the room for a while. Nice to meet you.

Lizzie: (*Solicitously*) Yes, very nice to see you. (*Jaffee leaves. They sit down.*) You look very well, darling. Feeling better? Who's your friend?

Lowell: He's a fellow inmate.

Lizzie: Inmate? You mean patient, darling. (*Laughs.*)

Lowell: Yes. He's being treated for depression. A former playwright. He says Hollywood put him on the blacklist. I've come to like him.

Lizzie: The blacklist? Oh, that's terrible. So unfair. Why, is he a Communist?

Lowell: No, but they think he is. He wasn't able to clear his name.

Lizzie: Oh, that's too bad, it's completely unjust. I've heard of other stories like that.... But what about *you*, Cal, are you feeling better?

Lowell: (*Unconvinced*) Yes.

Lizzie: Good. Does Dr. Miller have any plans about your being discharged?

Lowell: He hasn't said. He thinks I'm making progress.

Lizzie: Progress. Yes. Yes, I know you are. You're getting better and the strange thing is …

Lowell: What?

Lizzie: (*Tries to conceal sadness.*) Nothing. I get in these moods, that's all. It's nothing.

Lowell: Nothing. What sort of nothing? There's more than one kind.... Now, Lizzie, I think you have to level with me. What's going on? I know: you hate having a madman for a husband, don't you? You wish you'd never married me, is that it?

Lizzie: Oh, honey, no, not at *all*. I love you so much, darling, more than I can say. But you can imagine how, if you love someone, and he is … having difficulties, it's hard. It's very painful. (*Beat.*) And what if it's my fault? What if I caused it?

Lowell: That's ridiculous. You had nothing to do with it. It's my problem.

Lizzie: In a way, that's comforting and in a way it's not. You're saying I didn't make much of an impact of any kind, I guess.

Lowell: You're twisting what I said. You ... you're what keeps me sane.

Lizzie: I am? You mean that? (*Takes his hands, kisses them.*) I wish I could believe that were true, sweetheart. I don't know, I've just been upset at how long... I admit it, I don't have the virtue of patience. I'm really an awful amateur at that. But I suppose you're getting the best care possible. *You* are the patient person, it's really heroic.

Lowell: That's what patients do. They have no choice. (*They laugh softly.*)

Lizzie: Now, darling, it will be perfectly all right if you don't feel up to it, but—

Lowell: Up to what?

Lizzie: When I was coming in, Elizabeth—Elizabeth Bishop— stepped in the entrance hall right after me. She's come to visit you, darling.

Lowell: Elizabeth is here? Did she wait?

Lizzie: Well, yes, she did. We thought I'd come in first to make sure ... you know, you wanted visitors. Do you?

Lowell: Certainly. I'd love to see Elizabeth. Let's go, let's invite her in now. She shouldn't have to wait.

Lizzie: No, no, you just sit here. They don't like you going out there. Here's a kiss, sweetheart.

Lowell: All right, I'll wait. (*She leaves. He pulls out a handkerchief, wipes his hands and face. Makes an effort to comb his hair with his* *fingers. Stands up, brushes himself off. Sits down. Draws himself up to his full height and looks toward the entrance. Elizabeth Bishop enters.)*

Bishop: Hello, Cal. (*They make their way toward each other and he kisses her on the cheek.*) Lizzie said to tell you she was just going, and … she'll be back later.

Lowell: I'm so glad you came. I wish I'd known.

Bishop: I wasn't sure you wanted a visit. Or if *they* wanted me to come. But they said you were better. (*He nods.*) You look well! I'm really relieved. I mean, it's silly, but I couldn't help worrying. (*A silence, during which he draws himself erect.*) I brought you this. (*Gives him a present, a stuffed toy. He opens it.*)

Lowell: A reindeer! That's wonderful. Thank you. They haven't given me any toys to play with here. This is my first Christmas present.

Bishop: You probably can't tell who it is: it's Rudolf. See, he's got a red nose. Like me when I've had too many whiskeys. (*Laughs*)

Lowell: Rudolf? Oh, you mean that song. That's not a real carol, is it? Just a radio kind of song.

Bishop: (*Nervous*) I couldn't find a real reindeer, this was all they had. The fur felt soft. I'm sorry about the lightbulb nose.

Lowell: No, I prefer it, this is better. Where would Santa be without Rudolf?

Bishop: He'd look out of his igloo, see the pea soup fog, and tell the elves he wasn't going out in *that* for anything. He'd just stay up there at 90 degrees north and get more rest. Just sit around doing nothing and have Mrs. Claus bring him pots of China tea. But then our stockings would be empty, except for a lump of coal. No tangerines, peppermint sticks, and brazil nuts for us!

Lowell: Brazil nuts? Well, I'm not a brazil nut, exactly.

Bishop: Oh, Cal, I didn't mean that. Please don't think I meant *anything* by that. Anyway, the brazil nut is me. I've been reading about Brazil a lot. I'd love to go there.

Lowell: Why?

Bishop: Well, you know me and my weakness for tropical flora and fauna. Miss Moore and I have that addiction in common. Whenever I see a palm tree, I practically faint, I'm so thrilled. Of course that doesn't change my basic bluenose, cod-fishing Yankee temperament. Not for long.

Lowell: Well then you're Rudolfette, the blue-nosed reindeer, right? (*They laugh.*) The Yankee part is the addiction that we have in common, Elizabeth. I don't know why, but the tropics are a blank for me.

Bishop: We should have gone down to Key West together. I'd have made a convert of you. You'd be wearing shorts and sandals and a Hawaiian shirt in nothing flat.

Lowell: I'm sure I would have. I know you were happy in Key West. Why *didn't* we go?

Bishop: Oh, Cal, you're always busy, you're always being a distinguished ambassador for poetry. You were married. And now you're married again.

Lowell: Not to mention currently in a mental institution. Bedlam.

Bishop: Like Ezra Pound.

Lowell: Like Ezra, but not as sane as he is.

Bishop: Well at least you're more reasonable than he is.

Lowell: During my sane moments, maybe.

Bishop: You seem perfectly sane to me. (*A beat.*) I admit I was a little afraid.

Lowell: Oh, you expected to find me in a strait-jacket foaming at the mouth?

Bishop: No, not at all. It's just … well, I think I told you about my mother being in an asylum. When I was a little girl. (*He nods.*) This is awful, but … I never went to see her. Not once. They told me when I was little that it would just upset me and maybe … have … a damaging effect on both of us. And I knew they were right, it *would* have, at least on me. And then later on … I couldn't. I couldn't bring myself to do it. Because she might be just sane enough to tell me I'd been a horrible child because I never visited. The longer I postponed seeing her, the less it seemed possible to go.

Lowell: But that's perfectly understandable and forgivable, Elizabeth.

Bishop: Well, perhaps it is, or maybe not, I don't know. This probably sounds… but anyway, I had the feeling that if I went to see her, I might just end up *staying* there. Because of course I did miss her horribly. So if I went to see her, I'd fix everything, I'd make it all right, by staying. We'd be in there together. Which terrified me. So I never went at all. I think it's the thing in my past I feel most guilty about. And, believe me, there are a hundred *other* things I feel guilty about. I'm really a *terrible* person. (*She laughs.*) As I said, I almost didn't come. I would have been no friend at all and just a coward. Actually, I've been one ever since my mother was taken away.

Lowell: It wasn't your fault. And then, too, it's true, she might have been made worse if she saw you. You know, that she'd forever lost the chance to be your mother and all. I wouldn't feel guilty about that, Elizabeth, not in the least. (*They look at each other feelingly.*) Would you like some water?

Bishop: Oh, yes, that'd be nice. (*They go to the water cooler, fill cups, and toast each other. Drink, then stroll back.*)

Lowell: I'm so glad you came. I have one chum here, but it does get lonely. But maybe it's good for me to be alone and focus on getting well. And that's what I've done.

Bishop: I don't want to pry, but … have you discovered what it was that brought this on?

Lowell: Well, I think it's partly inherited. But the immediate cause was the guilt I had about Jean, which got worse when I married. Until then the divorce didn't affect me much. Suddenly I was a case-hardened sinner.

Bishop: Oh, Cal, I wish you didn't think about it that way.

Lowell: I don't anymore. I've gone over that many times and that's not the way I feel now. I know I'm not Catholic, and I no longer want to be. I don't even want to be a Catholic. And that's the job that I'm faced with now. To find a new direction for my work. And you'll be able to help me do that. You and Lizzie.

Bishop: Will we? How?

Lowell: By the example of your work. You know how much I admire what you do.

Bishop: Oh, Cal, that's absurd, *you're* the great poet, and I'm just … me. You know so much more than I do…. About everything. (*Two beats.*) And just to contradict myself, I've brought you a poem. (*Hands him a folded piece of paper, which he takes and unfolds.*)

Lowell: Thank you, Elizabeth. I'm so glad to have this. Will you read it to me?

Bishop: Oh, for heaven's sake, no! I hate reading my poems aloud! I just wanted to bring you something … as, what, a reminder … you know, that's what we really are, we're writers. Silly of me, but "it's the thought that counts." I'll take it back, you have plenty to read. (*Tries to take back the poem.*)

Lowell: No, please, Elizabeth, I want to hear you read it. Please. (*Gives it to her*).

Bishop: Oh, dear. Well, I read so badly. (*Clears her throat.*) It's called, the title is "Mate."

Lowell: "Inmate"?

Bishop: No, "Mate," m, a, t, e.

Lowell: "Mate"? As in "match"? Or do you mean the way the British call their pals "mates"?

Bishop: (*A little vexed*) However you like to think of it. I partly based the poem on the game of chess. You know, at the end of the game they say "mate." It's not a good title, this is only a draft, I'll probably change it. (*A beat.*) Oh, Cal, do I really have to read this? I don't know what possessed me to bring it.

Lowell: Please do, Elizabeth, as a special favor.

Bishop: (*Nods, clears throat, reads in an embarrassed, halting way.*)

Mate

If he found no white pieces, the black couldn't see
To manoeuvre, becalmed in ambiguous fog

With a chessboard and pawns who've turned aimless
    and gray.
The conscript contending on both sides helps neither.

Why regret that the starting-gate slot fate assigned
Was the White Knight's quixotic, extravagant quest?
Once you claim it as your own invention, the role
Will solidify, courage be galvanized, strong

As the muscular stallion's sleek neck. When a lance
As intent as a heron takes aim at your chest,
You'll rely on your mount's alert caracoles, which
Can elude most offensives. Aware that a thrust

Inspires its own counterthrust, those who attack
Will prepare for an equal, contrary reaction.
So the quester at ease in Andorra today
Must tomorrow decide: will he stop or ride on?

(*Coughs*) There. As I said, it's only a draft, there's a lot I need to change.

Lowell: (Takes poem from her hands) It's magnificent, Elizabeth. You're not like anybody else. This is completely you. I want to read it again. The black and white chessmen: that's about race, isn't it?

Bishop: Oh dear, I don't think so. I didn't mean race, that didn't occur to me. It's more … the idea that you have to live with both light and darkness in your experience, that they're somehow … reciprocal. You know, that there can't be a game without both. I know that doesn't make much sense. I felt I understood what I was saying when I wrote it, but now I'm not so sure. I'll work on it, it takes me forever to finish the least little thing.

Lowell: Oh, no, it's clear, I just needed a little more time. To reread and follow what you were getting at. I just needed some more time. I'm delighted to have the poem. You don't believe me, but it's what I've said before: I admire you more than any other American poet now writing. You're the way out, you've broken the strangle-hold, Randall thinks so, we all do.

Bishop: Oh, Cal, don't be ridiculous. If you keep talking that way, they're not going to let you go. (*Touched.*) Anyway, it's sweet of you to say that, so, thanks so much, really. (*They gaze at each other.*) But now, to change the subject, I spoke to Elizabeth briefly out in Reception, and she tells me she's taken an apartment in town, so that she can visit you every day. It's good that you have each other, that you're not alone. That's something to be grateful for. (*A beat.*) By the way: I knew a long time ago that Lizzie was going to be the one, that you were going to end up together.

Lowell: What do you mean?

Bishop: Well, remember the Poetry Weekend at Bard College that Ted Weiss organized?

Lowell: Of course. You were there and Bill Williams and Lizzie and lots of people.

Bishop: Yes. What you probably *don't* remember is that, the second night, at the party, you—not to mention a lot of other people—had a few too many.

Lowell: Hmmm. I'm sure I did. I don't recall much about it, though.

Bishop: So Lizzie and I thought we should help you get back to your room. You sort of leaned on both of us (*mimes this*) as we walked you back. By the time we got there, you could barely walk at all, but we managed by a sort of jiu-jitsu maneuver (*flips her arms*) to fling you on the bed. (*Beat.*) And then you started to snore. Lizzie said, "I suppose we should take his shoes off." Which we did! One broken taboo deserves another, so then she said, "Maybe his clothes, too." To be honest, we weren't all that sober ourselves! (*She mimes reeling around.*) So we got busy, and off they came! And Lizzie took a long look at you and said, "Why, he's an *Adonis!*" And I knew right then what was going to happen. And I was right. Because you *were* an Adonis. (*They both laugh.*)

Lowell: Before or after he was gored to death? But now, why weren't you affected by that glorious prospect?

Bishop: Oh, well, I'm immune, I'm "Mariana in her moated grange."

Lowell: That's not the best Tennyson, Elizabeth. How does it go, let's see: *"I am very dreary, He will not come,"she said; she wept, "I am aweary, aweary, Oh God that I were dead."*

Bishop: Oh, but I'm not taking on responsibility for the whole poem, just the "moated grange" part

Lowell: No, of course not. You're not weary or dreary or anything like that. And … Elizabeth, let's make a promise, a solemn promise to each other that, even if we wish we were dead, we will never, that we won't even *think* of …

Bishop: Oh, of throwing ourselves in the moat? Certainly. I can make that bargain. I solemnly promise I will never do that. I will not become a self-executioner, even if it turns out I deserve it.

Lowell: And I won't either. (*They hold hands.*) You do promise?

Bishop: I do. And do you?

Lowell: I do. (*They gaze into each other's eyes.*)

Lowell: (*He fastens on to her arm.*) Oh, Elizabeth, I think in many ways it would have been so much more—

Bishop: (*Apprehensive, she tries to extricate herself.*) Cal, you are so dear, but Lizzie said that I mustn't keep you too long, and

I shan't. I'm so reassured. I can see you're nearly well, it's just wonderful.

(*Lizzie enters, stares at them.*)

Lizzie: Cal? (*They step apart. She approaches.*) Am I interrupting? (*They shake their heads guiltily.*) Cal, I've been speaking with Dr. Miller, and his opinion is—

Bishop: Oh, I really must go, I've kept you too long.

Lizzie: ... he says that you'll be well enough to leave before Christmas. Isn't that terrific? (*Cooler.*) Elizabeth, you don't have to go, why don't you stay a while longer.

Bishop: No, I'm afraid I do, I have an appointment. I can see that Cal is doing fine, and that's really all I wanted to know! So I can be on my way now with my overly solicitous worries settled. (*To him*) It's so reassuring to know that you're going to be yourself very soon. (*She begins backing away.*) *you're going to be yourself very soon* *to be yourself very soon* *very soon*.

Lights fade to black. "Jingle Bells" plays. A little red light and a little blue light dance around in the dark and then exit.

Lights come up and the older Jaffee is center stage in his regular clothes. As he begins to speak, Lowell enters silently from stage left and stands behind him. Then the women characters, one by one, beginning with Celeste, then Lizzie, then Bishop, slowly enter from stage left and come to stand next to him. They each remain there beside him for a minute each, and then slowly exit stage right. (Which of course involves a costume change for Celeste if the role is doubled.)

Jaffee: And the Bard of Bedlam did get his honorable discharge soon after that. I staged a little graduation party for him. I didn't make other friends while I was there so when he left I had time to myself, time to think about the man. I did admire him and sympathized with the situation he was in. And I came to the conclusion that he was some kind of martyr for, you know, the *arty* side of writing. Not that he made a distinction between writing and living his own day-to-day life. Writing was living and living was writing. Which meant you had to draft your planetary existence as honestly as you knew how and hope you had some kind of originality. Otherwise the, call it, the *poem* of your life would be junk. And if you went crazy, your writing also went there with you. You didn't lie about it. You owned up to the facts and made the best of them. (*Three beats.*) That's what he communicated to me. And it was something like, uh, a medical vocation for him. I think he and I were, each in our way, both trying to be the doctor for each other. Not the same way Dr. Miller was, something else. I was helping him edit his life-poem, and he was doctoring my life-script by telling me I should take myself a little more seriously, that I was a clown, okay, but a serious clown. It really felt that way, and I know saying it may mean I wasn't one-hundred-percent cured, but … it was what it was, and yes I am a seriously embarrassed clown.

About a month after he left, I got singed [*sic*], sealed, and delivered as cured, but that didn't mean re-entry was easy. The movie business was off limits, so I got into journalism. And I got to write about all kinds of interesting things. What things? Well, like the Rosenbergs being switched on like electric light bulbs, the hydrogen bomb test, Korea, Eisenhower's golf game, UFOs, you name it. It was a living, and I got to put in a few opinions of my own. Eventually the blacklist was lifted, people forgot about it. But I couldn't bring myself to go back to the industry that had given me the royal shaft, and anyway by then who would know me from Adam's off ox? Hollywood's totally based on the idea of "What have you done for me lately?" Two years offstage and you no longer exist. But you know, it was just as well.

I never saw Lowell again, but I read his books, most of them. Wait, I did see him on TV when got the media coverage for his anti-Vietnam-war activism. He had changed a lot. His hair was white and he wore it long, so, to tell you the truth, he looked crazier than he did when he was in here. OK, but it was the Electric Flower Power era and everybody tried to look and act as bonkers as possible. Welcome to Luna Park. It was around then the institutions like this one got the bright idea to begin releasing people who'd been inside for just about forever. It was like there was a new definition of who was insane and who wasn't. If you could walk a quarter mile without throwing yourself on the pavement and rolling around screaming, you were de-certified. They just opened the doors and sent all the warm bodies out there on their own. Great for some of them, not so great for others. Lot of them are still out on the streets, ranting their poetry to all and sundry. But it doesn't do any harm. If somebody will go out there with a recorder—who knows?—they may find the next Pulitzer Prize winner.

I'm also aware Lowell had his marital problems, a two-time loser or winner, however you want to look at it. The Catholic Church may be right and divorce is habit-forming. But at least the theological agony of it all stopped being the issue for him. I don't know what he ended up believing, but it seemed to be enough. Christmas and Easter, that's usually sufficient, just like Yom Kippur and Passover or whatever your chosen annual moment of ritual seriousness or joy is. It's when people turn into fanatics that you've got a problem, when they unleash their dogs on the other guy, lock him up, torture him, push him up against a wall, lynch him, shoot him, bomb him, put him in an oven, et cetera. Bedlam is child's play compared to that. Nowhere near as awful. In fact, it's the best solution I can think of. What I mean is, let all of us well-meaning screwballs *out* of Moonworld, and bring those rats *in* to take our place. They need help bad. Maybe a doctor could do something for them. I wish like hell somebody, somewhere, some time, could. God, I wish that.

Lowell turns and exits stage right, followed by Jaffee. Stage goes dark and we hear Lowell's voice call out with longing, "Elizabeth!"

CURTAIN

"My Mother's Hands":
Indigenous and Black Poets from Brazil

Translated and with an introduction by Tiffany Higgins

I write this note on the banks of a river in the Amazon. The city where I am living at the moment, Belém in Pará state in Brazil, recently received the Amazon Summit (Cúpula da Amazônia), hosted by President Luiz Inácio Lula da Silva. First, the Amazon Dialogues occurred, three days of self-organized conversations among the Amazon's diverse peoples—not just Indigenous, but also quilombola (AfroBrazilian maroon descendants), ribeirinho (riverine), and peasant peoples. These conversations and demonstrations included demands for a moratorium on petroleum drilling, which the Brazilian government is poised to begin at the Amazon River's mouth.

Two days later, these same peoples were barred from entry to the Amazon Summit (Cúpula da Amazônia), negotiations between presidents of eight countries of the Amazon. It didn't escape the notice of the excluded peoples that all the fruitful interchanges they'd had seemed to have no apparent impact on the executive-level conversations. (Painfully, Cacique (Chief) Raoni of the Kayapó people, in his nineties the elder statesman of Indigenous politics, was turned away from the presidents' negotiations room.) The Belém Declaration, the document issued from the executive conversations, seemed to have arrived prepackaged from Brasilia, critics observed, noting the refusal of the Brazilian government to set a year for zero deforestation, or to rule out regional petroleum development.

This underlines how voices of Indigenous and traditional peoples, including Afrodescendant peoples, continue to be excluded from regional, national, and international conversations, with policies and language imposed on them from above. The south of Brazil imposes economic priorities on Brazil's north, largely populated by Black and brown and Indigenous peoples, often with grave results.

Though in the realm of Brazilian literature there have been some advances in recent years, there are continued inequities in representation and access in Brazilian national publishing.

Plainly put, it is a matter of singular urgency that more voices from Brazil's North and Amazon be heard—on their own terms. It is with the intent of contributing to efforts to reverse the direction of cultural valorization that I present, in this selection of poems, an Indigenous poet from the Amazon and two AfroBrazilian poets from Salvador, Bahia.

Márcia Wayna Kambeba is a poet of the Indigenous Omágua-Kambeba people, located in the Brazilian and Peruvian Amazon, with a smaller population in Ecuador. She is a photographer, performer, and educator with a master's in Geography, currently getting her doctorate in Linguistics. Her poetry is filled with enchanted spiritual entities, from the curupira, a forest guardian in the form of a boy with flaming red hair and his feet turned backward, to the mapinguary, a hairy giant with just one eye, and its mouth near the navel. She evokes these beings, implying the extent to which the forest is not an inanimate, nature-only space, but an animate one filled with plants, trees, and animals, and spirits who are not objects of regard but creators of the generative sacred.

Kambeba's poetry depicts Kambeba and other Indigenous cultures and their values of care of their forest-river homes, and how these values gave way to the European-originating settlers' entirely diffcrent, largely destructive manner of treating the environment in which they arrived.

Historically, living along the Amazon River, the Omágua-Kambeba people were highly impacted by Portuguese colonial raids in search of slaves, compelling the native people to migrate as they fled. As Márcia writes, in the past they were forbidden to use their language, and so the Kambeba language itself (from the Tupi linguistic trunk) has been a precious and precarious gift to keep and transmit, along with the interethnic Tupi, also known as nheengatu.

As a response, the poet integrates words both from the Tupi and Kambeba languages into her poetry, a political and artistic stance asking readers to encounter cultural differences via Indigenous language. In the 17th and 18th centuries, the Omágua-Kambeba people flattened the cranium, which according to the poet, was a cultural survival technique in response to Portuguese raids targeting peoples they thought to be practicing ritual cannibalism. Her people, she told me, at that time decided to be "cabeça-chata"—literally, having a flattened head—in order to distinguish themselves from other peoples. The poet also uses cabeça-chata to refer to the Omágua-Kambeba people's identity, to my ear, proudly implying all the historical travails that they've survived.

Both Alex Simões and Livia Natália reside in the city of Salvador in Bahia state in Brazil's Northeast. During what Brazilian historiographers designate as the Sugar Cycle, Bahia was one of the earliest and most significant areas of Portuguese colonial settlement in Brazil, bringing Africans to labor as slaves on sugar plantations. This cruel history is present in the background of both poets' works in and around the city of Salvador, redolent with muggy sea air.

Livia Natália's poetry departs from the Portuguese history of sea crossings and shipwrecks, turning the associated literary tradition on its head, as she figures Black fishermen, thus remaking the space of the transatlantic slave trade to emphasize Black protagonism and heroic Black bodies in relationship to the sea. Her experience in the Ketu Candomblé tradition strongly influences her writing. She dedicates her book *Água Negra e Outras Águas* to Osun, who in Candomblé is the goddess of freshwater rivers, and the themes of waters and of divine orixás flow throughout her poetry. Her poetry also critiques machismo and state violence against Black bodies. In an infamous incident, Lívia's poem "Quadrilha," which describes the grief of a woman whose lover was killed by Brazil's Military Police, was censored in Bahia in 2016. Copies of the poem, which had been displayed publicly on billboards as part of the Poetry in the Streets project in Ilhéus, were ordered to be removed.

Poet and performer Alex Simoes' 2015 book, *contrassonetos*, from which the poems here are drawn, transformed the sonnet form radically with his content exploring what it means to be "black, poor, queer" in the city of Salvador, Bahia. He critiques the unequal distribution of wealth, based in colonial, race-based patterns of large landowners (latifundiários), which continues to influence inequalities in Bahia and beyond. While tracing the physical presence of these inequities in Salvador's built environment, he sings the praises of a Black feminine divine, Black women, and trans bodies. Insisting on joy, he weaves romance and desire through the day to day life of the city, with linguistic playfulness, arch tones, and wordplay, praising Black creative remakings.

Belém do Pará, Brazil,
August 2023

Ritual Indígena

Iapã iapuraxi o ritual!
Vamos dançar o ritual!

Em noite de yaci-tua,
O pajé convoca a nação,
Tambores ecoam na aldeia,
Começa a celebração.

Dentro da Uka sagrada,
O pajé inala o tawari,
E no transe evoca os seres da mata,
Vem o mapyritua, a curupira e o mapinguari.

A metamorfose anuncia,
A presença do sobrenatural,
Na sua forma se vê a magia,
Hora awa, hora animal.

O que era um culto sagrado,
Guardado como ouro ancestral,
O branco achou que era pecado,
Invadiu meu ser espiritual.

Deixei de ser filha de Euaracy,
A cruz se tornou meu sinal,
Proibiram minha dança dizendo:
Não existe mais o teu ritual.

Indigenous Ritual

Iapã iapuraxi o ritual!
Let us dance the ritual!

On a full moon night, yaci-tua
The pajé convokes the nation
Drums echo in the village
Continuing the celebration

In the sacred Uka
The pajé inhales the tawari
In a trance evokes the enchanted forest beings
Here comes curupira, forest guardian with the flaming hair,
Mapyritua the sloth, and the giant one-eyed Mapinguari.

The metamorphosis announces
The supernatural presence
In its form you see the magic
Now human, now animal.

What once was a sacred rite
Safeguarded like ancestral gold
The white man judged a sin
Invading my spiritual core.

I stopped being the daughter of Euaracy
The cross became the sign I wore
They prohibited my dance, saying:
Your ritual exists no more.

Translator's notes:

Curupira—forest guardian who takes the form of a boy with flaming red hair and his feet turned backward

Euaracy—sun goddess

Mapinguary—a huge, human-like, hairy creature that lives in the Amazon rainforest, described sometimes as having just one eye on its forehead, and a mouth in place of its navel

mapyritua—sloth

pajé—shaman

tawari—derived from *Tabebuia serratifolia,* a tree in the family of Pau d'arco, the bark of which has medicinal qualities

uka—in this case, a collective building

Yaci—moon goddess

yaci-tua—full moon

Márcia Wayna Kambeba

Os filhos das águas do Solimões

A água é a mãe que sustenta,
A vida que nasce como flor
Alimenta a planta e o ser vivente,
É estrada por onde anda o pescador.

Na enchente, vem veloz e furiosa,
Derrubando ribanceiras, destruindo a plantação,
Afeta a vida do indígena e ribeirinho,
é um ciclo, que se renova a cada estação.

Na vazante o rio quase some.
A praia começa a surgir,
A água, agora bem calminha,
Não tem forças para a roça destruir.

Nas margens de um rio em formação,
Vive um povo que a água fez nascer,
Em um parto de dor e emoção,
Na várzea, o Kambeba escolheu pra viver.

Mas em um contato fatal,
Com um povo mais socializado,
Fez dos herdeiros das águas,
Um povo desaldeado,

Tomando seu solo sagrado,
Sem dor, piedade ou compaixão,
Os Kambeba foram escravizados,
Apresentados a "civilização".
Exploraram a sua força,
Forjando uma falsa proteção.

Children of the Waters of the Solimões River

The water is the mother who sustains
The life that is born like a flower
She nourishes plants and living beings
She is the street where the fisherfolk walk

In the flood season, she comes swift and furious
Bringing down riverbanks and plantings
Affecting Indigenous and ribeirinho lives
A cycle renewed in each of the four river seasons.

In the season of ebbing waters, the river almost disappears
And natural beaches begin to emerge
The water, now quite calm
Lacks the strength to destroy gardens.

On the edges of the fluctuating river
Live a people whom the water
Birthed in exultation and pain
The Kambeba chose to live on the floodplain.

But deadly contact
With a people of Progress
Made the inheritors of the waters
A villageless people

Their sacred soil taken
Without conscience, pity, or compassion,
The Kambeba were enslaved
Presented to "civilization"
Their strength exploited
Forging a false protection.

Translator's notes:

villageless—In the colonial period, after Portuguese trips raiding Indigenous peoples for slaves, one of the Portuguese policies was to induce Indigenous peoples to give up their remote villages (aldeias) to settle in missions or towns, giving up Indigenous clothing, language, worship, and other cultural practices. Many Indigenous peoples thus ended up "desaldeado," or "villageless," with a larger connotation of grave cultural loss.

ribeirinho—Ribeirinhos are traditional riverbank peoples, not identified as distinctly Indigenous, who maintain fishing, small-scale farming, and collection of seeds and fruits from the standing forest.

Natureza em chama

Na terra sagrada
Que Tupã criou
Do seio materno
Se ouve o clamor
Da mãe natureza
Sofrendo de dor.

O fogo ardente
Ao longe se vê
Queimando a mata
Sem quê, nem porquê
As folhas se torcem
Querendo viver.

No solo desnudo
Os restos mortais
Do verde da vida
E dos animais
Queimados, sofridos
Em cinzas reais.

Dos gritos agudos
Se ouve o clamor
Do fruto ardendo
Na chama, no calor
Ceifado, perdido
O fogo o calou.

Dos olhos tristes
Uma lágrima cai
O lamento de dor
Com o vento se vai

Varrendo o chão
Varrendo o chão!

Nature in Flames

On the sacred earth
Tupã created
From the maternal breast
That sustains
Mother Nature is heard
Crying out in pain.

The searing fire
From a distance is seen
Burning the forest
For no apparent reason
The leaves twist
Wishing to live.

On the bare soil
The mortal remains
Of the green of life—
And the animals
Burned, suffering
In real ashes.

In sharp shrieks
You hear the scream
Of fruit burning
In flames and heat
Lost harvest
That the fire silenced.

From sad eyes
A tear falls
A lament of pain
Carried by the wind
Sweeping the ground
Sweeping the ground!

Translator's note:

Tupã—a creator god

Márcia Wayna Kambeba

O choro da terra

Quando em mim a vida se fez
Te moldei e te formei,
Fui cuidando, te alimentei,
Na velhice te abriguei.

Tu em resposta me adubavas,
Consumia o que precisava,
Não tinha plástico, nem poluente,
Convivia em paz com tua gente.

Mas eu vi o progresso chegar,
Aos poucos comecei a sangrar,
Retalhada por fronteiras,
Fui alvo de luta e dor,
Poluída e enfraquecida estou.

Seguro o peso do mundo,
Abrigo plantas e animais,
Eu sou a herança que Maíra te deu.
E nessa luta pela vida,
O choro não é só meu.
Pela vida e biodiversidade,
Não faz maldade, pensa no filho teu.

The Cry of the Earth

When life made itself inside me
I shaped and formed you
Cared for you, formed you
In old age I gave you shelter.

In turn you fertilized me
Consumed only what you needed
Plastics and chemicals didn't exist
You dwelled with your people in peace.

But then I saw progress arrive
Little by little I began to bleed
Chopped by borders
I became the target of strife and pain
Now I'm polluted and weakened.

I hold up the weight of the world
Shelter plants and animals
I am the heritage that Maíra granted you.
And in this struggle for life
The cry for biodiversity
Is not only mine
But also your child's—
Don't be cruel.

Translator's note:

    Maíra—the fire goddess who created the Tembé Indigenous people.

Mãe natureza

Mãe natureza, tua força o machado cortou.
Terra mãe que em seu seio nos alimentou.
Água sagrada o lixo a contaminou.
O grito dos pássaros o fogo calou.

Olha só o tamanduá! Foi pra cidade,
não viu o sinal vermelho
e o carro o atropelou.
Ficou para traz dele
só o urubu se lembrou.

E o que será do amanhã?
Alguém já se perguntou?
Natureza e homem
uma relação de união,
mas, esse elo se quebrou.

E o "indígena" se pergunta:
sem mata, água, terra,
pra onde eu vou?
Se até meu solo sagrado
o "progresso" tomou.

É preciso prestar atenção!
E vestir a camisa da conservação
para não beber e comer
com sabor de poluição!

Mother Nature

Mother Nature, the axe slashed your strength.
Mother Earth, who fed us with your breast.
Sacred water: trash polluted you.
Birds' cries: the fires muted you.

Just look at the anteater! It went to the city
didn't see the red light
and a car hit it
far from its terrain.
Only the vulture
remembered its remains.

And what will become of tomorrow?
Has anyone stopped to explain?

Nature and humans are one whole
But this bond was broken.

And the Indigenous people wonder:
Without forest, water,
earth, where will I go?
If "progress" has taken
even my sacred soil.

We must pay attention!
And make haste
To conserve if we're not to drink
And eat pollution's taste!

As mãos de minha mãe

As mãos de minha mãe são imensas
e seguram seu corpo minúsculo
como as chagas de cristo lhes se sustentam a santidade.

Nos dedos vincados de veias grossas,
na curva que se enruga no mais preto das dobras
as mãos de minha mãe perfazem os caminhos de meu mundo.

Se os búzios cantam nas palmas singradas de rotas negras
é para predizer maresias e ondas dolentes em meu caminho.

As mãos de minha mãe, cada vez mais idosas,
guardam, em suas linhas, o segredo de nosso destino,
elas se cruzam no ventre da espera, e nasce
sempre feliz, sempre feminino.

My Mother's Hands

The hands of my mother are immense
and hold up her minuscule body
as Christ's wounds support his sanctity.

In her fingers marked by thick veins,
in the curve that wrinkles in the blackest of folds
my mother's hands lay down the paths of my world.

If the sacred shells sing in the palms
sailed by black routes,
it's to foretell sea-scent surges
woeful waves on my path.

The hands of my mother, older each day,
safeguard in their lines the secret to our destiny
they cross the waiting womb and are born
forever happy, forever woman.

Versos escritos à beira do dia

A Ruy Espinheira Filho

Na exata hora em que o silêncio dorme
palavras passeiam na escuridão do quarto.
À orla da cama desenham estrelas decaídas
que se desprendem de um confuso céu,
e, presas ao chão,
ainda procuram seu perdido hálito celeste.

Repousam enquanto os gestos ensaiam,
em outros mundos,
sua existência onírica e impossível.

Um mundo inteiro suspenso,
apenas,
pela carne triste do sono.

No entanto,
as palavras,
como flores delicadas,
aguardam o despertar da primavera,
para devorar o ar lúgubre,
com seu cheiro violento
e inesperado.

Verses Written on the Shore of Day

At the exact hour when silence falls asleep
words passed through the room's darkness.

Fallen stars, breaking loose from a confused sky
draw themselves on the shore of the bed

and, captives on earth
still search
for their lost celestial breath.

They rest while in other worlds
gestures rehearse
the stars' impossible, oneiric existence.

A whole world suspended
by only sleep's sad flesh.

Yet words like delicate flowers
await spring's awakening

to devour the sluggish air
with their violent
and surprising scent.

Enterrado Vivo

O corpo do morto tem uma presença indecisa
que remói o mundo entorno
com dentes de ruído fragoroso.

O corpo morto devora o mundo sobrante
como se mordesse a uma maçã:
dela tirando o grânulo fino de cada espera.

O morto, que passeia carregado
como uma criança rediviva
traz nas mãos,
que lhe vão cruzadas sobre o estômago,
o signo claro de sua fome sem fruto.

Buried Alive

The corpse has an indecisive presence
that grinds the world around it
with teeth that roar.

The dead body devours what remains of the world
as if it were biting an apple,
removing the fine grain of each delay.

The corpse, passing by carried
like a revived child,
carries in its hands
crossed over its stomach
the clear sign of its fruitless hunger.

Canção do Silêncio

Um carnaval me atravessa violento,
meus ouvidos apenas digerem algo do que se ouviu,
numa oficina lenta de mastigar palavras.
Minhas gengivas sangram mudas,
tanto colorido de pura sofreguidão
é como a morte nos descampados da primavera imensa.

Para além da flor em seu perfume,
há a vespa e o áspero do seu ferrão.
Meu grito de dor e calma,
este mesmo que vaza grosso de meus olhos,
imita a voz das cigarras.

Amigo,
aprenda agora
que a cigarra não morre cantando.

Jamais.

Dentro dela vive uma ferida sem remédio,
ela abriga no seu ventre
um corte nascido de dentro,
que dilacera as entranhas.

No seu ventre moram medos insondáveis.
E um corte que sangra alto.

Toda cigarra,
como eu,
morre gritando!

Song of Silence

A carnival passes through me violently.
My ears barely digest what was heard
in the slow work shop where words are chewed.
My gums bleed mutely
colored with pure voraciousness—
like death in the wastelands of immense spring.

Beyond the flower of your perfume,
there's the wasp and its rough stinger.
My cry of pain and calm,
the same one that leaks thickly from my eyes,
imitates the voice of the cicadas.

Friend, you should learn now
that the cicada doesn't die singing.
Never.

Inside her lives a wound with no cure
that opens in the womb
a cut born within
that shreds the guts.

In your womb live unfathomable fears.
And a cut that bleeds fiercely.
Every cicada, like me,
dies screaming!

Soneto à Ladeira da Montanha

o nome era Barão Homem de Melo.
só que, nesta cidade, trocam os nomes,
não só das ruas, mas também dos homens.
ficou ladeira da montanha, belo

belo projeto de intersecção
entre as cidades: a alta e a baixa,
em todos os sentidos que se encaixa
a terra da axéglobalização

aqui passamos todos, mas as putas
ficam, assim como suas histórias,
filhos e, principalmente, os abortos

aqui e só aqui a mãe das putas
cuida dos filhos da cidade, os mortos
e os vivos têm Mãe Preta, nossa glória.

Sonnet of the Ladeira da Montanha

*In Salvador, Bahia, steep alleys (ladeiras) connect the city's high and low
sections*

the name of the street was Baron Homem de Mello.
but in this city names get changed
not only of streets, but of men.
it became Ladeira da Montanha

beautiful project of the intersection
between cities: the high and the low
all the meanings that our land of
AxéGlobalization encloses.

here everyone passes through, but the whores
remain along with their stories,
children, and especially the aborted.

here and only here: Our Mother of the Whores.
she cares for the city's children, the dead
and the living who share a Black Mother: our glory.

eu canto pras paredes

o preconceito é uma parede enorme
contra a qual desde sempre me empurraram
mas se tentaram e não me executaram
é que aprendi bem cedo que não dorme

o apontado: preto bicha pobre
no paredão cresceu e ficou forte
ainda com a dor que o véu da morte
bem do seu lado alguns amigos cobre

e é por eles que não me vitimo
nem quero mais derrubar a parede
apenas canto para além de um íntimo

desejo reforçar rizoma e rede
cheia de nós, que não estou só, sou vivo.
picho a parede: meu verso afirmativo.

I sing through walls

prejudice is an enormous wall
against which they've forever pushed
me. but if they tried and didn't execute me,
it's because I learned early on who's targeted

doesn't sleep: black poor queer
grew up on the big wall and got strong
still with pain that the veil of death
of friends at his side collects

and for them I don't victimize
me, nor wish any longer to break down the wall
I merely sing beyond to my intimate

I desire to weave rhizome and web all
full of us, so I'm not alone I'm alive.
I spray-paint the wall: my verse affirmative.

Alex Simões

Soneto para a Rua da Forca

eu não quero morrer com medo, nem viver
achando que pisar na merda é natural
medo de andar na rua medo etcetera e tal
com medo de morrer de medo de morrer

medo de atravessar a rua e muito medo
de quem anda nas ruas de quem vive nelas
medo de quem do lixo vive, elas por elas
só peido vem de quem come feijão azedo

ou vai ou racha, aqui, nesta cidade escrota
feita pra andar de carro e com vidro blindado
enquanto se pensar que adiantando o seu lado

no cada um por si, se desviando do esgoto,
longe do odor da urbe, que é só mijo e cu,
"quero morrer olhando o infinito azul".

sonnet for Gallows Street

Rua da Forca, Salvador, Bahia

I want neither to die with fear nor to live
believing it's normal to step through shit
fear of walking on the street, miscellaneous fears
with fear of dying of the fear of dying

fear of crossing the street, and there it starts:
fear of those who walk the streets and live on them
fear of those who live on garbage & roll carts—
from those who eat sour feijão come only farts.

either leave or laugh, here in this bullshit city,
made for cars with bulletproof glass
while you imagine that pushing your crap—

every man for himself, avoiding the open sewage,
far from the urban stench—is only piss and ass:
"I want to die looking at the infinite blue."

pátria zinha

*poema em coautoria com Reinofy Duarte

Fui parido pelo ventre desta pátria
Dos irmãos que sentem dores pela história
Em que anseiam por ter um dia de glória
No solo tão gentil da terra mátria.

Mas somos os herdeiros de uma xátria
Que se instalou no centro da memória,
Deixando no poder a velha escória,
A pátria bem pode se chamar látria,

Bem como de larápios os seus filhos,
Ao menos os que dela bom proveito
Tiram de um tal jeitinho que, sem jeito,

Deixam os que ainda insistem em andar nos trilhos.
Ordem pros pobres, progresso pros ricos,
Mandam os civis, porém sob os milicos.

little baby country

co-written with Reinofy Duarte
"order and progress": the motto on the Brazilian flag

I was birthed in this nation's belly:
two brothers who feel history's pangs
anxious to have their day of glory
on the so-gentle soil of the mother country.

but we're inheritors of armed brahmans
who installed themselves in the center of memory
leaving in power the old guard scum
a country you could call BigAgArchy

sons and fathers pickpockets
at least those who've found a way to profit
off-the-books & underhand take such advantage

they leave in the dust those who insist
on working honestly, with class.
order for the poor, progress for the rich.
civilians command, but under military brass.

Alex Simões

bursite, tradição e tá lento, o individual

doem-me os ombros, tantos são os pesos.
línguas mortas e vivas misturadas,
a plêiade no peito embaralhada,
os esquecidos como contrapeso.

mil vozes confundidas no desejo
de ter consigo a minha entrelaçada
e o medo de parar na encruzilhada,
entre rimas ideias e solfejos.

a folha em branco amarelada está.
há sempre um risco de perder-se, há
sempre um mesmo fantasma em breve assomo.

o mundo derretendo-se em milênios:
poetas trôpegos, prestos boêmios,
eu e você cantando velhos nomos.

tradition, bursitis, and the (slow) individual talent

with so much weight my shoulders ache
dead and living tongues all jumbled
the pleiades disassembled in my chest
the forgotten ones as counterweight

a thousand voices confused in the desire
to have yours and mine interlaced
the fear of stopping at the crossing
between ideal rhymes and do-re-mi.

the sheaf is white toward yellowing.
always the risk to lose oneself
always the same ghost I'll soon face.

the world is melting down millennia.
unsteady poets, expert drinkers
you and I chanting our odes to Apollo.

de perguntas e poetas

a Marcus Vinícius Rodrigues e Állex Leilla

não se pergunta nada a um poeta
que é por definição das Evasivas
amigo, assim como Musas e Divas
lhe rodeiam a cabeceira, cometas.

com um poeta nunca se intrometa
que a sua cabeça à beça a si se esquiva
e no esquivar-se iguala-se à sua Diva
e fica mal ferir a quem com seta

fere, mas só com amor e com rodeios.
e nisso é que consiste o não indagar
àquele que ignora qualquer freio

ou direção. não tente lhe roubar
porque ele vem vazio. quem mesmo sabe
por que será que nele tudo cabe?

of poets and questions

ask nothing of the poet
who by definition is one of the Evasives.
friend, just like Muses and Divas,
comets turn around his bedside.

never meddle with a poet
or your head will learn to duck—
and, in diving, be equal to your Diva.
it never works out to injure one who wounds

with arrows of love and circumlocution.
and this is what it means to not question
the guy who ignores any limit

or directions. don't bother to rob
him for he arrives empty. who really knows
how everything seems to fit within him?

Alex Simões

[fechai os olhos para a Poesia]

fechai os olhos para a Poesia,
colocai-a em cálices de vinho,
derramai ao longo do caminho
o poema nosso de cada dia.

afastai vossa dor da ironia,
imprimi a beleza em pergaminhos,
deletai toda a dor de ser sozinho
mas também relatai toda alegria.

ficai de joelhos para a Poesia
e pedi, sem pudor, ao firmamento
que não vos seja vão cada momento

de busca, na palavra, da harmonia.
mas não deixeis que a vida vos esqueça,
nem que as traças vos subam às cabeças.

[close your eyes for poetry]

close your eyes for poetry,
gather her in chalices of wine
spill it out along the path
and give us our daily poem.

put away your ironic pain
print beauty on parchment
delete the pain of loneliness
but be sure to relate your happiness.

fall on your knees for Poetry
and shamelessly beg the firmament:
may it not be in vain, each moment

of searching—in the Word—for harmony.
oh may you not let life forget you,
nor let bookworms climb to your head.

cozinha íntima

para Marcus Vinícius Rodrigues

tem um poema aqui dentro
que esqueci de lhe mostrar
espere só um momento
que vou lá dentro buscar

ele está em andamento
faz favor de não contar
pra ninguém do fazimento
pro bolo não desandar

peraí, que eu volto já
enquanto isso, o rebento,
todo acontecimento

vem quando tem de chegar
meu poema tem fermento
e a lua, pó de solar

intimate kitchen

I've got a poem inside here
I forgot to show you
wait just a moment
while I go inside to find it

it's on its way, in the oven
do me a favor please
tell no one how it's made
so the cake won't fall or separate

hold on, I'll be back soon
meanwhile, shoots & saplings
everything happening

arrives when it's meant to
my poem's got yeast
and the moon, dust from the sun

Robert Kelly

Leucothea

Goddess of Sea Spray

Canto I

He wept a road
in front of him

followed
where his sorrow led

But why am I grieving?
I am no crusader,
avenger, or missionary even.

I'm just a self —if that—
in a gloom of world,
this war world is a sad place.

But there was no battling,
no triremes on the middle sea,
only sharkless shallows,
jet-free clouds,

the azimuth
must mean something,
clean, clear,
if you can spell it
it must be real.

Canto II

But which way *is* up
out of the doldrums of desire?

She answered
his silence, saying
With you and you
it's all about going—
Crusaders, explorers,
exiles, emigrants,
refugees, invaders,
all about going,
migration, vacation,

all about being gone
from where it found you
when it set the world
in its exact
order for the hour of your birth,

go, going, gone

your mind is music

the measure
is a skip
and a hop.

But he quarreled
you said nothing about desire

her answer a little
sweetened the silence

A skip and a hop
leap
and still be here,

desire is always
about somewhere else,

a skip and a hop
and mind the music.

Canto III

Are we the same when we speak
as when we are silent?

And what does it mean,
to be safe,
clamshell, handclap
of slamming door?

On the fringes of sleep
these questions vexed,
and was she near enough
to answer him?

One more question.
Ohimè, he moaned
as if in opera,
and remember Spanish *pregunta*
and wondered about that too.

And then she answered.

Canto IV

At the back of your mind
there is a crystal chandelier,

it's been there since childhood,
your aunt's house, remember?

Its thousand faceted lights
shine and shimmer, you think
you're remembering something,
you call it memory, you value it,
rightly,
       but what it is, what they
all are, are the crystals gleaming,
even when the lights are off.

That is the tragedy: no two
people remember the same thing
precisely, no two people
mean exactly the same word
when they speak it.
And that is the glory of language too,
mother of all poetry.

Canto V

Long song
I loved
when I was young
but now be swift,
music, not much time,
Learn to whistle again,
he thought, a song
no longer than a breath,
faster, faster, get it said,
get it sung, no time no time!
But then she whispered
right in his left ear
circular breathing, *u-khor*,
clarinet, basset horn, gyaling.
Sing as long as you live.

Canto VI

But don't I become
another when I talk?

Doesn't the word
estrange me from myself,

word spoken or written
or gouged in a marble wall?

Or is the self that says
the real one, the saint-
in-training, the aged choirboy?

And this silent me
a fading echo, a shambles
of leftovers, shadow
of what once, once had been said?

She smiled then and said:

And you're still here,
your knees by the timid fire
in the old franklin stove,
a cup of coffee at your elbow,
your only fear you'll knock it over,
would you rather be in mid-air
hang-gliding over Rio?

He shuddered and closed his eyes for once.

Canto VII

It's not what it was,
it has no trees in it

or on this rock three
tall trees dying
while the sea gives life all round

and I am always complaining
he thought
                                      but she soothed
(yes, sometimes she's soothing)
not complaining, just explaining
how in this case the ship
does not fit the water

                                                    but how can that be
he doubted, the water
accepts all our gifts, mistakes,
even some trireme lost three
thousand years ago off Malta
safe in the sea's embrace

Don't be so romantic, she chided
(yes, back to her usual chiding self)
you were born yesterday
and so was whatever you see,
three thousand years ago?
yes, in a way, but that's tomorrow—

any history you can think
really hasn't happened yet.

Canto VIII

Forcing the issue
is what it means
he thinks, and thinking
is half-way to a meaning
too, force it, force it
he thinks and then he thinks
she isn't listening.

But she always is.
That is the real issue,
the presence unending,
only the notice ever fails,

the presence never.

The surf is speaking
and he does hear that,
naturally tries
to put words on that,
fails, thanks
heaven for his failure

and listens on.
I am just what you hear
it says, and I am enough.

He lay back
and wished that she would
say something to him, in him—
as if she ever stopped!

Canto IX

When she walks
her feet don't touch the floor.
When she swims
her skin stays soft and dry.
When she flies
she never leaves the ground.
When you gaze at her face
she closes your eyes.

He found that carved
on ancient stone,
not in Greece or Israel
but in the trees past his back yard.
He stares at the words now,
hopes he got the translation right.

Canto X

At least it wasn't in Greek,
no chance to show off
his scholarly chops,
it was in his own unknown
native language, words
any child knows, words
nobody understands.

Fly the sky
it said
but don't leave home,
insult the sea
no longer with your ships—
white sails are right
but the hulls are wrong.

So he sat down to think it out

and suddenly he felt
her breath on the back of his neck,
her breath felt like more words:

Some things are not
to think about
but to do. So do!

He felt her breath again,
it made him shiver

and he was sky.

Canto XI

It is morning, child.
You can open the wooden box
and take your words out
one by one,
careful, the way
the dove picks seed.

Listen to the female
cardinal, she taps
her feet on the rail
as she picks, chews,
takes more in.
Rhythm, she makes rhythm.

                                 Your words

come in neat compartments,
always more than you need,
just find the right ones.

And now a bird flies
up onto the roof,
you'd rather go out
and watch it, watch them
all, watch it all happen,
but first your box,
seek, find, pick, speak.

He wrote all that down
soon as he woke up,
hurried to show it to her,
o, she said, I read that already,
long ago, while you were sleeping.

Canto XII

Say the truth
before you know it—
that is the only way

to save reality from memory,
some old book you read once,
your mind on something else.

That famous Girl Next Door,
the price of corn.

He paused then in his listening,
wondered which girl,
why corn, doesn't even like it much
except polenta, tortillas, yes,
process my food for me,
stand at the window
show me your face—

then she spoke again,
her voice almost angry:

if you have to think,
think of a blue flower.

Canto XIII

Blue flower
what is that?
And then he knew

if remembering
can be called knowing.

The blue hydrangea!
His favorite flower!

But there was history in the way. When he was a child, there
was a huge blue hydrangea bush in the little garden behind the
ivy-vined brick house. He didn't like those flowers—too big, too
showy, too fluffy, puffed out and frilly, like one of his older aunts.
He liked the roses better, and even more, the pansies purple and
frail in the window box on the garage. And most of all the pussy-
willow beside the gate to the alley, not just florescence to look
at but soft rare furry thing to please his fingers. But then the
family moved away, to a house with none of the above, and then
he grew up and lived for years in a building—from no window
in his apartment could he see even a blade of grass, much less
a flower or a tree. Then he moved to the country where all the
above could thrive. Joy. And then he began to remember the blue
hydrangea, *die blaue Hortensie* the German poets he was reading
called it. He began to miss it, he planted hydrangea bushes, later
still to a house with a bush there already, but these hydrangeas
were white, or pink at best. For blue hydrangeas, he was told by
those who know, you need the sea. Your first flowers were when
you lived in the sea wind, the outwash plain of Long Island by
the Atlantic, they explained, up here no such atmosphere. If you
want blue, you have to add a whole chemistry set of stuff to the
earth, wait, hope, and maybe. By now, the blue hydrangea (the
one he couldn't grow near him, the one that lives gleaming by

the sea of memory) had become his favorite flower. And then one year his new wife took him to her island. And there they were, blue, blue and rich. She had seen them in the Himalayas (how could that have been? No sea for hundreds of miles … a hillside blue with mystery, not far from Darjeeling), blue as the sea two blocks away. And here he was, with her, and with his favorite flower.

He stopped thinking—
was it really thinking?—
and asked the voice
is that what you mean,
the blue flower?

It rained at dawn
she said,
now the sea-mist
is full of sun
and people walk up the hill—
isn't that enough to know?

Canto XIV

Is it dew
or was he able,
wet glisten
on the leaf,

could he make weather
all by his no-self
as his teachers taught

or was it rain,
morning drizzle
while he snored—

did he snore?
So much he doesn't know,
he needs her to tell him that

Some days he sits in the park
and watches children play
and wonders, wonders
what play is, how do we learn it.
He tries to remember
his own, was it his own?
don't we have to learn to play,
only from others? Otherwise …
and then he thinks *other wise*

knows wisdom comes from them.
They make the weather too.

Canto XV

Will she ever speak again
or will she ever stop speaking,
will wisdom ever leave him alone
with some dumb sensuous fact,
or will it come save him from it,

her words release him
her presence binds him,
compels him

he doesn't know what he wants
and that makes him who he is

not gender but *genius*
he hears her whisper

mist charged with sunlight
but no sun
we need images, images!
picture a smile slowly fading away

but leaving something like love behind.

Canto XVI: *Queruloso*

He thinks: what does solemn mean,
ritual, prayer, praise for something
worth all that.
He snarls at his childhood—
the only organ needed
is the brain,
not some church pipes
bleating the Intermezzo
from *Cavalleria Rusticana*
while we shuffle up for Communion,
fact, they did that at our church
where now they say Mass in Igbo.
No telling. But Language surely
better than the organ groan. Moan.
But where was I?

Long days, frightening nights.

No, she said, none of the above.
You've flunked your morning quiz
which was not about cultural opinions
and taste and all that *doxa*
but about sheer knowing,
you know, look out the fucking window.

Canto XVII

So he had sailed into contradiction,
had lost his glory along the way,
was dumb as his brother
and he had no brother.

Her voice was impatient,
how long it had taken him
to get to recognize
all his judgments and opinions
just get in his way.

And so she sang
imitating the irritating
plink plunk of a guitar
"There is a palm tree
on an island
but not this island.
There is a palace
in the sky but not this sky.
Say what you like,
words will wrap around you
like a solemn toga
or a sexy sarong or whatever garb
Saint Morning
chooses for you.
Now dance with me,
motionless, silent
while the words preach
the gospel to your legs—
it takes a long time
to learn to dance,
especially to dance with me."

Canto XVIII

I can't find the right word

Wait, she'll come
to your table
be nice to the waitress
friendly not flirty

or flirt just a little
to show that you care

then she'll say something,
the word you read.

But at the end of Act II
where the opera breaks off
Moses cries out in despair
Wort, Wort das felt mir!
which means Word, Word
that I lack, but literally
says Word that fails me,
word that takes
itself away from me,

how can he stand there
on the edge of the Boston stage
and sing that, groaning
complaining and blaming
God for not speaking?
I was there, I saw the whole thing,
how could the city not break,
the sea roar in and drown
such blasphemy?

                    Easy, easy,
did you really think that?

Almost, almost, I was shocked,
the horror Schoenberg must have felt
as he let his Moses yammer thus.

Are you like Moses
in your subdued islandish way,
are you blaming
the very Silence
from which you were born?

Never, never, but sometimes I fear,
fear the word will not come,
will swish away from my table
with an angry twist

So you'll be like Moses again,
this time the one in Exodus,
where he sees only the back
of God passing him by,

you're left with the hinder
parts of the word—
hearken, the silence breaks.

Canto XIX

More like an essay than a song
but essays mean something
or try to at least
and I'm not so sure about this

I do my best

You know the old cavil—
when your best is not good enough,
you call for help then
and that's where I come in.

But who are you, really?

My name is half my power,
the other half is what I know—
that's the half I share with you,
or with thee if you prefer,
solemn nowadays, the old
second-person singular, familiar,
but now used only in poetry and prayer,
I'm teasing you, being playful,
can't you feel the song in all that?

Try to smile as the word
sways towards you again
having forgiven
or forgotten your blasphemy—
you're not the only troublemaker here.

Sway of her substance,
smile of her sound—
if that isn't a song, what is?

Canto XX

What did you say your name was again?

Did I ever say?
Today you can call me Nora
your governess before the War
taught you to love women
and hold on tight
taught you a little French,
taught you loss by leaving.

And that was you or you are she?

We're talking names,
not identity.
I can say Nora
and your eyes will roll,
you'll reach out to clutch me—
I'll slip away of course,
leave if you're lucky
a word on the tip of your tongue

and who said anything
about who I actually am?

Now say what comes to mind.

Canto XXI

Anonymous answers
kept arriving—
what could he do
but try to make use of them
one by one, fitting the word
to some question he'd find
to feed them.

                              Who tells me
these things, he thought,
these things I think?

More answers than questions
it seems, and yet, and yet
think of the mountain range
where questions are born,
Spine Ridge and Mount Occiput
and the dangerous Gonad Hills,
and the way even the eyes look
at everyone asking Is it you,
is it you?
                          At least she sounded
amused when she answered,
this time straight from her to him
just her voice to his lips.

So he heard himself say
Now it is clear, an answer
always comes before its question,
a question is Time clearing its throat
before an answer flashes in your sky.

Cuttyhunk Island
July 2022

Letters to Maximus, from *V*

A Later Note on
Letter #15

I have taken to writing my list of things to do in walnut ink, with a
    fountain pen.
It doesn't make me better, but slower, and less in control.

The ink does what it will.

No ideas but in coffee cups,
no song but the mourning dove's coo.

128 past the old drive in,
  red rock,
   ye olde exit 13

"View" : fr the Orontes
fr where Typhoon

The serpent on the rock at Cressy's,
the men all rising out of the water:
Jim, after swimming with the fish he'd let go
or Joe, in stories told about years gone by
or Tiger, driving piles and dredging channels
or my own brother, pulling lobster traps and
cleaning squid

The stories they tell, bending the truth,
the Rhumbline, hugging the curves,
the high-tide line changing every day.

And the rock they stand on,
the rocks
smoothed and black with algae,
or rough-cut quarry rocks,
or carefully carved curbstones
along old main streets

The Young Ladies
Independent Society
of East Gloucester

the young women
of East Gloucester

the young of Gloucester

East Gloucester,
independent of the young
who are rising from the flames—

The women, the men, the young
have declared independence.
The Shire is independent of the flames,
of men, of women, of serving.

Our children have declared independence
of man and woman, of love with kisses,

Our children kiss the flames.

I

patriotism, the fourth of July
or the third, or the eighth, this year,
with fireworks in the fog and
a laser show on the boulevard,
patriotism, the flag

II

Pulling papers, running for mayor,
or city council, or school committee,
and this is what we want: engagement,
involvement, voices, action.
                And still—

this feeling like it's all too much,
not an addition, but a subtraction,
                a way of quieting,
                of displacing,
                of taking up space,
muddying waters

III

the head of the
Department of Health
six months on the job, staff quitting,
unstable, unrest,
        trying now
        for a different office

the boys on the boats
won't learn her name

Bk ii chapter 37

1.   The inland side of Washington St between
the rotary and Carl's, the furthest I have lived from water,
in between the house in Annisquam,
my father's office on Middle Street,
the church on Pleasant Street where we held his funeral,
Lanesville, Lanesville! the secrets I can't yet tell,
the beach in Magnolia, the woods by Dead Man's Cave,
    roads and paths hidden by new growth

and this is a life, the habits we make and break,
the places we walk, and walk past,
the places past, our own mythologies, the foundations
we build our selves on, the bridges we burn.
There are places we go for ceremony, places
for comfort, places we don't go.
Jumping in the canal on a hot school day,
swimming off a dock in Lobster Cove,
years at Flat Rocks, a teenage sunrise at Long Beach.

A moonlit quarry off of Barker Ave,
its monsters hiding in shadow

below the low-tide mark,
barnacle-grip, seaweed-sway
and above it, rock walls to scurry over,
formations in the woods,

and inland, moraine trail,
Whale's Jaw,
Spiritual Power

nobody knows
the whole story

Peloria: dog sleeping under the privet,
newspaper boy bit, bloody leg, skin-teeth,
privet berry smashed into dark ink, finger-stained.
Maximus. Maximus! My mother, terrorized
by all of you, all of you maximi, your jaws,
your fingers, your hands and your words.
From Annisquam, to Lanesville, downtown,
at the deli counter at the IGA, meaty fingers, salami.
Your words, your stories, your ideas—
my own grandfather meeting you, being you,
all Maximus, all maximi,
as if you knew birth, knew the pain of having Maximus
map it out for you

and my own children, my own Peloria,
smashing our globe

In the Face of a Chinese View of the City

This bar that is my office, this public office,

this public life, glad-handing the regulars.

Gravelly voiced women, devastated to have missed his funeral,

sing, sweet-sounding falsetto along with the house music.

The owner, the publican, complaining about tax breaks

for a competing venue, while he spends Tuesdays

perfecting nip pin bowling on an empty bar.

This fall's ballot filling up, candidates

upset about unpaved private roads,

softball fields turned into schools,

affordable housing anywhere.

The gravelly-voice turns and asks the empty bar

"Is this a tape somebody made?"

Everyone an authority, an expert on what they know.

They cup their hands in the incoming tide and say

This? This is the ocean.

June 26, 2023

Whortleberry (bilberry, cowberry)
ripe right now, and with the rain
the woods are full of mushrooms.
Between the moons, the greenheads are out.
Obadiah Brun went to Plymouth in 1642,
then Gloucester in 1643.
Next year will still be 400+.

Summer traffic, cars
from out of town parking
along Eastern Point Road,
tickets glaring in the sun.
The guard at Eastern Point
directing traffic
away from the breakwater

Τὰ Περι Του Ωκεανού

The marshes of Tanais, its stories, histories,
like the shell deposits off of Wheeler's Point.
More than what is written, than what learned men say.
White-washed, white houses, white faces
yelling at cars to slow down. Sewing circles,
guards at Lighthouse Beach, settlements
a stone's throw from where white-hairs
rent the upstairs of the Wonasquam Village Hall.

the woman
at the table beside me
googling why she can't order bud light

this island
a stepping stone, a struggle,
a hold out, a shame

the room nearly empty,
this poem,

same

Jul 26, 2023

After the Perfect Storm
a few years' drought, a movie
here or there, Wicked Tuna, CODA

and now the serpent's everywhere,
and a cake at the rotary celebrating
Gloucester's 400

and the kids are asking
how 1642 adds up to now.
Real estate math.

At the museum, Hopper and Davis
(a decade difference there too)
cover the walls.

The cannons at Stage Fort Park
have been upgraded, amended,
made more suitable for guests.

What will the city be like
once the party's over?

Jul 26, 2023

Moses at the laundromat,
face red, hair white. Blue?

The old men of Gloucester,
the walkers, the men on the street,

the nameless, the nicknamed,
the people we love, the lost.

A note left in a cookbook
giving thanks for a couch, an ear,

a warm place to stay.
On East Main St

the house I. drank himself out of,
before roles reversed,

when it was all right.

the feet, the walking,

up and down streets,

beating paths.

My mail's a mess.

These days

the men walking home from AA

are more regular

than the mail.

people want delivery

and it comes with boxes, drivers, vans,

gig workers from out-of-town.

It takes days, no, weeks

for the letters I write

to make the post.

Ruth, I promise, it's coming.

the Masonic side of the dance pavillion
Jose Canseco of the Caribbean Sea
    I be influencing them to freestyle
    they be influencing me to write

Jul 30 (Sunday) 2023

the shape of a stitch
the turn of a hem

Jul 30th 2023

the hill behind Our Lady
the harbor, beyond

446 commercial vessels in 2018, the Lannon sailing between

Younger than 400 years
older than its settlement
and still struggling between
old and new

The changes we make,
the changes made to us.
Flattening the sails.
Pawl-post politics,

no turning back.

Chronicles

1

You struck up this idea,
this poem, these poems
and made myth of it all—
Maximus (I don't even know
where he bought his bread)
the rock   the bull

rosa rugosa growing
at water's edge,
the song she put
in each of our mouths

2

Taurus,
merry bull, Merry's bull
the flourish, the bravado
with which Maximus
declares‑ ‑

Once you list the gods
and the historians,
the comings and goings,
the who's who,

the tracks, the paths,
the people of note,
once the stories worth telling
are told, is it possible
that somewhere in the shadows
       or under your nose
something else is happening?

in the hills of Bayview
in a house of empty rooms
Vivian Dedekian lies in bed
and knits, waiting to join
her sisters in death.

ten pound, five pound,
salt, and hog

3rd letter on Georges, unwritten

[In the time since this started I have changed
so much has changed   this thing where a man
can be a master of a thing has changed
the thing has changed   the man has changed
you'd been at it a dozen years   half that for me
I imagine you there in that fort apartment
and the fort has changed even my kitchen table has changed
and the captains have changed, fishing has changed
but that feeling you haven't been able to write,
choosing which wall to be up against]

298

Amanda Cook

The Gulf of Maine

To be sure, to be so sure
of this thing, of going, of taking,
of launching into the unknown
and trusting, trusting
in one's own rightness,
in rightness at all

       we set out to sea and
       if we make it back
       we kiss the land
       like it is divine

       there are ships in the harbor
       and pleasure boats and such
       still I know men
       who are desperate to leave the shore
       men too affected by gravity
       men who can't stand their own weight
       on dry land

       and that's different than striving,
       than discovering, than
       going into the unknown
       for glory, or pride, or place

       it is different than leisure

       I know men
       who let their boats rot

into early graves

We on this island
tilting at turbines
What are we
in relation to it all?
Hopper's houses still stand.
The Babsons hold reunions
on the edge of Dogtown.
Ringo Tarr—

Additional "Phoenician" notes

             shorebird
songbird   birds of a feather

from Gloucester to Maui,
missing in Lahaina

So this is what we have come to:

poems, into poems, into song

Joseph Torra

Letters To Tao,

Forget Tao / & you are out of the trap
  —Wei Yingwu

Dear Tao,

I'd like to call you by your real name. But it won't be your real name. This morning out the window the evergreen branches swayed. I couldn't see what moved them, but it goes by the name of wind. Last night wind whipped rain against the house and rattled the eaves, waking me from sleep. Wind blows like breath through a flute. Sounds of sadness, joy, restraint, force, pleasure, rage, regret, change, stability, weakness, strength. Sounds swell and subside. Earth sings through myriad holes.

Dear Tao,

Yesterday I forgot you. That's the point. But how I forget you makes all the difference. When I forget to forget you, I quarrel with this and that. This and that can prevent me from forgetting you. Words and names do that. Without them, we can't communicate, yet in naming this and that, mind and tongue get twisted into images that are not the real you. Each of us has our own this and that. Arguing one against the other seems pointless. Birds don't point to this and that. They move without personal agenda. Today I'll try to remember the way birds don't speak of this and that so I can forget.

Dear Tao,

It's said everything arises from nothingness. That you are everywhere in everything. You have no beginning and no end.

But if everything arises from nothingness, nothingness must be the beginning. If everything is renewal and decay, mustn't one be the beginning and one the end? Or are you simply indifferent? Without body? Without form? Then how forms form from the formless? How begin from unbeginning? Perhaps I should mind my own business. Let my mind wander without complications. There is nothing where thoughts have been. There is something where they are not. This is known as the void which is infinite. It cannot be emptied or measured. Everything arises and returns from it. Maybe I should mind my own business.

Dear Tao,

Whenever I read one of your texts, I scratch my head, thinking, "Ah, if it were only this easy." I should be adaptable, but I'm assertive which causes obstructions. I want to be water finding its way through cracks. Like water encountering an island midstream changing shape to go around. If I could divide myself in two, and meet myself on the other side, I could dwell in nowhere and rest in nothing.

Dear Tao,

When ancients wrote about ancients, did ancients of the ancients have ancients? We measure time, but time is part of this and that. If the glass is empty, it can contain anything. If we remain empty like the empty glass, imagine what we could contain? Perhaps clocks are not correct. Perhaps it is not 8:57 AM but an empty glass of time waiting to be filled. Summer is here. The birds alive and singing. Somewhere it is cold, animals are hungry—the glass is not empty, and grass not green. How much time to open a mind? How much time to change a season? In ancient times were this and that different from this and that now? Or do mysterious workings have nothing to do with past, present, and future?

Dear Tao,

Some days I lack humility. I talk too much. Lose my temper. Let the ways of the world disrupt me. I grow excitable. Commit errors. My blood pressure rises. I'm ashamed of my behavior but have no control over it. Nature isn't perfectly balanced. When there are violent storms, the river tosses wildly. Trees blow, limbs break and fall. Animals and birds duck and hide. The next day the weather is calm. Animals and birds reappear. The surface of the river a mirror. These are workings of yin and yang. Best resign myself to what can't be avoided and accept things I can do nothing about.

Dear Tao,

I wasted many years expending reckless energy, consuming alcohol, and drugs, seeking pleasure, acknowledgement, and praise. My excessive, wayward behavior flew to the four points of the compass. Refusing to acknowledge my faults, ignorant of nourishing the mind and body, I failed to breathe with the sky and earth. Now, in old age, my body spent, is it too late to cultivate original simplicity and attain non-doing?

Dear Tao,

It's been said, leave your thoughts in places you don't visit. How can I leave my thoughts some place if I don't go there? And everywhere I go thoughts follow me. Places I have been carry memories. I try to dissolve negative thoughts, but new ones replace them. I see my own failings but cannot accept them. Maybe it's wrong to attach to negative thoughts but ok to accommodate them. Sometimes I think it's easy to understand you but difficult to believe in you. Or maybe it's easy to believe in you but difficult to act according to your principles. All this thinking tangles the mind. What should I do? What should I leave alone?

Dear Tao,

It's said don't limit learning to what you understand. The more I try to understand you, the less I do. It's not good to try and find reasons for everything. Not everything has a reason. Best keep attachments at a minimum. Knowledge is easily used as a tool for haggling. Useful things can be used. This I know. But what use the useless? If only I could avoid wasting mental energy. It's impossible to lose the mind. The harder I try, the more it intrudes. You don't help a strained, overworked horse by making it work harder. Best return it to pasture.

Dear Tao,

Today at the ocean a man walked by and said life is good. A strong wind blew onshore, turning the water murky. Sometimes nature is not still and clear. Gulls huddled along the shore, unwilling to take on the rough surf. Off on the horizon sat a thin cloud formation. Seas, birds, clouds, and wind are named. More than I can say for you.

Dear Tao,

This morning fluffy frosted clouds drifted across the sky. Chickadees darted in every direction. Chestnut tree leaves shifted in the breeze. Suddenly, a sparrow flew frantically onto the porch bouncing off a window, landed on the floor, springing up when a large hawk swooped in, lunged after it, missed, rearing back on its wings, charged again. In a flash-second the sparrow escaped. The hawk flew away in the opposite direction, defeated. One bird's luck is another bird's hunger.

Dear Tao,

Sometimes I doubt you. I doubt myself. Perhaps I am a fool tracking you down. Clouds morph continually. Life and death are inevitable. Seasons change. Calm water today is turbulent tomorrow. Long or short, large or small, hot and cold are relative. Desire, anger, envy, are natural human traits and cannot be eliminated. The mind won't be stilled, and the universe can't surrender to it. It's easy to separate text from sermon. I don't believe that Lao Tzu left the Tao Te Ching in the hands of a gatekeeper and disappeared into the wilderness. An immortal is the one who cooks my breakfast at the diner. He doesn't break yokes or burn the toast.

Dear Tao,

I'm best when I think least. When I leave the books on the shelf. When I don't force myself to consider the pattern on the surface of water, or the implication of birdsong, or amorphous shapes clouds make drifting across the sky. What do they have to do with me? Some nights I wake from sleep to restless, racing thoughts. The brain is a vicious machine. Some mornings I wake refreshed to a calm heart. If I waste time thinking too much, I miss the truth. Words and concepts confuse and contradict. Maybe I should mind my own business.

Dear Tao,

It's said that you are the foundation of existence but cannot be understood by rational thinking. I find myself forgetting you on a regular basis. Days pass without my giving you a thought. Sometimes I worry, have I lost touch? I haven't opened one book recently with your name on it. Haven't written in my notebooks. This my first letter in weeks. Isn't it what I have been working towards? Then why am I writing you again? To let you know that I have not forgotten to forget you. Sometime soon, I will remove a book of yours from the shelf, open it to find you are not there.

Joseph Torra

Poems from *By This River*

the river a mirror
fogged in at the far side

lone goose afloat
in reflection of boats

wrapped in
winter dry dock

~~~~~~

above the river
moon round—

a car accelerates
in the distance

I've forgotten
the time—

look around—nothing
besides this place—

to set out to
emerge to return

overcast sky
the river still—

old cemetery
back to 1600s

engravings on
stones worn,

an entire family
here—deer tracks

between woods
and salt marsh—

cold eastern breeze
these feet carry me

~~~~~~

no sun three days
gray blanket,
drizzle on and off
ducks and geese
got their game on—
raindrop—how
big of you to
hold all this

wind numbs the ears
sunrays stripe dark clouds

incoming tide
swells the creek

cattails across
the salt marsh sway

~~~~~~

fierce wind blows
ice chunks in waves
against the shore,
the creek frozen
to the bridge—
in the sky forms
come and go
no need a mover
to make it happen

wind gusts and rain
in and out of sleep

the house shakes and rattles
trash barrels overturn

restless dreams
unsettle the mind

thoughts awhirl on
way to blue heaven

~~~~~

emerging and returning
snow turns to fog—
shrouds the landscape,

evergreens
forever green
summer or winter—

rushing water
doesn't reflect,
who knows its end?

sun and moon
opposite sky—

two white swans
cruise the river's edge—

yield a method
of the way

~~~~~~

under morning star
turkeys gobble
from tree roosts—
merge forever
with earth's roots

morning star
in chestnut tree

ducks and geese
call from the river

heat exhaust
from chimney tops

a truck speeds off
this oldest new day

~~~~~

light incense
make bed

green moon
in western sky

tea on porch
alone in dark

await first glow
above the river

dead leaves
don't try or
say anything

stirred by wind
they act with-
out acting

~~~~~~

the marsh creek swells—
empties with the tide

same every day—
never the same

what departs returns—
no limit to distance

deer in headlights
bounds across the road

chased by coyote
—another

—vanish
blink of an eye—

as we humans
desperate

for our place
in the world—

~~~~~~

morning birdsong—
an owl's hoot,

a woodpecker
drums a tree—

sun lights pink
ice crystals

across the lawn—
unfurling

10,000 years
dead leaves stir

underbrush and briar
loosen muscles,

skunk cabbage
breaks through—

birds sing a
new tune—

air cool, wet,
tastes of mud,

flies swarm
fresh coyote dung

sun over shoulders—
shadow long

~~~~~~

doves perform
their mating ritual
on the railing,
puff up—
as if filled
with air and
wild grace—the
continuum aflutter

whitecaps on the river—
gulls waver in gusty wind

a rotted tree limb
cracks and drops

who dares stop
and look?

~~~~~~

morning clouds
don't seem to move

though birds alive and well,
faint breeze stirs leaves

easy to see—
hard to believe

whitecaps on the river
no boats in sight

air heavy with moisture
but no rain—

lone gull struggles
against wind pockets

busy ants scurry
this way and that

eyes shut I see
no beginning or end

~~~~~

summer not yet over—
morning breeze
through window green
branch brushes against—

flesh exposed,
first upper body
then bottom—

I am the river
illuminated—
flowing smoothly
on a cool breath
of a leaf

mornings cooler now
squirrels work horse chestnuts

clouds speak of change
children grown and gone
how young they were—
and August just another month …

drought has killed the grass
there'll be no mushrooms
come autumn without rain

~~~~~~

temperature dropping
air drying out

squirrels active with
heightened urgency—

the sky, a different
shade of blue—

watch the seasons
never linger long

dark clouds turn,
cast green hues—

sound of wind
against waves

look deep
into sorrow—

wanting to let go
but not yet

~~~~~~

Joseph Torra

After Wang Wei

well along in life,
quite a way—
I found my home
by this river

moving with the spirit
learning late a few things
one needs to know—

alone, I follow the river
on foot, watching
clouds rise and pass

come the day
I'll go off—
meet an old friend,
talk and laugh—
never to return

322

Cheryl Clark Vermuelen

Autobiography Reaches for Mother

The coast is no longer

a closet of snow with a long arm

where the body used to be

gnawing at the unfinished

shape of everywhere

protecting silences as she

beset by furious gems

beneath her coat

has dropped something along the way

who I am who is not me

Cheryl Clark Vermuelen

Out of Mistake

The composer depicts a cityscape
some shit of promenade to the lake
a loaded apple tree & fisherman

one of the places mistake comes from.

On a later train stakes open, cores
thrown, commodities blown,
one train door opens to another.

Then glue the trains. Not a tongue wagging:

the man's a secret. A group of them
called a secretary. In shorthand
the glyphs roam for miles in the Loop.

One dictator has a phone to each ear,
brokering, shipyards hopping,

then the vanishing acts.

Cheryl Clark Vermuelen

Humming in the Accidental

Gram but not Mom mothered
with hums. A cardinal sighting
could interrupt it. Cardinal, look!

Humming I too relax my mothering,
though the crows demand a response.
My children know this & follow suit–

vocal folds to syrinx. We let our accidents
meet, loosen our forms, instruments lapped
into a hum mothering another hum a lake

would love. In small vibrations sailing
through contingencies and toxicities
on glugs and glances, savoring and

sorting non-negotiables, mine, theirs.
Institutions do not love us. Our lips
birded. We can build a house in a hum.

Cheryl Clark Vermuelen

The Other Rows of Seats Repeat FED FED FED

Janine, I'm pregnant and flying and my belly is a boat that undulates
        and jerks while I wait for my snacks next to a lap dog
    surprisingly chill, not even sniffing at a nut or a cracker.
        I'm eyeing the basket, wishing for swifter snacks.
  Maybe the dog has been sedated
                                and I'll feed myself

    patience. Waterlogged, I pee a lot
  so I settle on an aisle seat for the first time
where I can't see any rivers. Two human-head boulders
obstruct the clouds, three in the other direction. Passengers
        head downstream through the narrow aisle. In our seats
            we tuck in our boredoms and our hands lie hospitable.
                        Except for the couple's foot rubs going on

in my periphery. We just need to enter the river, I said to my friend
on the phone last night. Now I imagine us floating on plump inner
        tubes
with a keg attached to be people we aren't, all the while
        counting the loons, swallows, and stubs of beach.
    I close my eyes for another river:
the current of noticed, spied, recorded, summoned, we say, it'll
keep us alert—afloat. For your river, I'll wait
and for what we'll both ferret out.
O listener! The buoyancy!
        I am nowhere near you as I am nearing you. If your inner tube
                ever punctures—squeak onto mine so I can carry you.

Cheryl Clark Vermuelen

My Buying Self Goes to the Library

after the Boston Public Library, circa 2015–16

On the first floor the long tables are gone!—
replaced with computer carrels. A tad lost
like a fruitfly on gristle, I bet, though, there's less
screaming across full-family-sized tables
causing a guard to tap someone's shoulder
for saying *stop looking at me, dick* or *bitch.*
Usually one of those. Then the longest pause.

The guards may no longer tap. A touch could
explode inside a cubicle. Most are typing
big plans, or so it looks, thickly inventive jams
bursting row after row from that faux privacy.
Goodbye, long tables, with your scrumptious spread
of offerings—my book near yours next to others
left to relish as the shared dignity of appetizers.

Yet I'll return. And when buying books only feeds
my buying self, I'll go on borrowing. Poetry is in
non-fiction. Hmm. On the first floor is the new.
Next up the mezzanine.

For Marsden Hartley

One morning your name appeared.

What would you like for breakfast?
Have you showered yet? Will you swim?

How was working at the Maine shoe factory
after your family moved to Ohio?

Then Cleveland Art Institute on a scholarship?
Transcendentalism? The spirit?

And how did you imagine your mother
after she died? Childhood was vast with terror

and surprise, you said. You trudged alone
soluble in grim, painting to move through

the broken in a play that danger frets.
Is this where I show?

On the Atlantic coast again, the brined
boulders look draped in muscled skin.

Your cobalt astringent, your colors portly
unless a plate of pale fish like washed-up

soldiers, a cold family of them; for years
I've bumbled the word, putting soil in soilders.

Marsden, my grump with undying
inner drive, who will pay us for our powers?

Our hearts? Like locksmiths for the land.

Cheryl Clark Vermuelen

Goths at a Cemetery

It's dark, 9 or 10 p.m., we were far into the woods
   when the cops arrived. I was down in the tomb
        hiding liquor and a candelabra,
my nylons ripped into the best spider webs.

Hearing far-off stadium cheers, they asked,
        guns slung to their sides
     Why aren't you at the football game?

We hid our disgust. Recalling now, I goth nothing more
               than our whiteness
  in the middle of the night in those dark woods
       —those guns just slung to their sides

Cheryl Clark Vermuelen

TVintimacy

Falling for Pretenders' Chrissie Hynde
           on the cover of my brother's *Spin* progressed
    when she wore that red bath sponge on her head
        at the VH1 Fashion Awards, what a bright pouf!   How sad
          it would have been if I had missed the
  provocateur's love—that progressive music.
      My gangliness may have never recovered.
    I scissored my legs along with hers. She sang
    I'm gonna make you notice me, luring us
        to the height of her grand vessel
         exfoliating all the drab norms   we could.

Cheryl Clark Vermuelen

The Ground below Our Feet

A man ran outside and ran back in.
That was a small jog.
A neighbor walks her dog as she thinks
about race and reconciliation in nations
around the world. A long walk.
I've been thinking of a former student
who shot himself last November.
He parked in a forest-preserve parking lot,
locked the car. The obituary says little more.
He barely did any work for my class, a few essays.
Often didn't show up. In our last interaction
in my office, which seemed even smaller than it was,
he had said things like *wrong crowd* and shook my hand
after he decided to withdraw. Was he already aware
of the depth of his withdrawing? What would've
brought him back to himself? A return that is crucial,
not selfish. He had plans for a fresh start.
When I ask our school counselor whether his family
would want his beautiful essay about loving to play
the ukulele, she offers to see me. Boys are more likely than
girls to use guns, I remember, from my fifth-grade speech
on teenage suicide—sublimating before I knew the theory.
What does all of this have to do with race?
We had talked about coming from Bogotá, arriving in
the U.S. when he was five or six to live in Connecticut
which seems brutal in my imagining. Winter is coming.
My sons are sleeping. It's Giving Tuesday.
Would he have imagined my crying for him? Did I?

Cheryl Clark Vermuelen

Trust: A Predicament

In the snow the crosshatched tire treads
are in a quiet flurry like an asterisk—

like a scarfed word. I lower my chin
into my chest and talk freely into my scarf.

What I say to myself is ghastly.
I pass a house slapped with green.

In this new land no one brings us bread
and my tongue is not enough. No grouse

flies fully from my head.
If we mention to ourselves what we will learn

what we will learn will run ahead of us
and never let us in.

Cheryl Clark Vermuelen

Turning into a Mother

What milk I had was theirs.

Too soon they could name my flaws,
how I languished in them.

I helped them spell, sounding out
one vowel loosening into another
in a diphthong, say, in fault.

Do you feel your shape of your mouth
changing?

My Grandparents Meet Duchamp

When I make the replica Duchamp picking corn with my
grandparents, they say *welcome!* and give him an ordinary
glass of water (knew nothing of the bride). Duchamp asks,
why war? The linens and the ladies are swaddling a baby or a
wounded arm. Gram says she wrecked her arm pulling up the
carpet and Gramp jokes that she must be feeling better since
she's back to giving him, he pauses, *trouble.* Regardless, *shit* is in
the air. Her chore as a child was to bring the slop bucket to
the pigsty, feeding the hogs that frightened her so with their
vicious rooting. When Duchamp turns up with a readymade of
a child with a slop bucket, she doesn't like it: turns right around
and goes into the kitchen to fix dinner. Whole decades are
simmering in there; I like to stick my finger in them. When the
grandmaster, an old man, plays chess across from a naked young
woman, I am baffled—grossed out and engrossed are eating the
same sandwich, and I think she has nice tits. Gramp must've
rubbed off on me, or episodes of *Benny Hill* and *Hee Haw.* Even
that's only half the story: I insert my relatives into narratives of
famous artists, and when I would ask my Gram for her stories,
she'd say, *why do you want to know? We were so poor.* Even more,
Duchamp is she and she is he or so explored. Everywhere we
go we sing with our mouths as steering wheels but with better
horns. Duchamp transforms into another face, photographed,
conversing with several of himself, and shirks anyone but his
mistress: the chess piece. He declaims, *professionalism is the death
of art,* but he is a businessman no doubt, curating shows and
selling his and others' art while the Arensbergs bankroll. He
shares a recipe with Gram about cooking shock. Prescient, she
hangs a flag of her sanitary napkins enameled with silhouettes
of the first woman President.

Cheryl Clark Vermuelen

The Refusal of Time

after William Kentridge's five-channel video installation

A massive silhouette parade crawls through a loop

of places   a body-twirling booty-shaking grand procession

as a stoutish man stands by encyclopedia pages whizzing by

his chest hair is drawn as if giggled out in pencil   flirting

with the self   his arms swinging   swallowing whole sentences

hello there   gesture   a quick splash of a silk ribbon on film

then erasure   it could be quiet   until the cycle returns

the shadow-drilling machine   trudging drudgery   its metronomic

pump   measures avalanches   notates a tragedy that'll be

shaken off in this mighty horizontal   this joyous cavalcade heaving

in my periphery   now in dunce hats   they're drumming   one on

megaphone   another trumpeting and   heading this way   again

did someone win?   is that a tuba or a man?   hippopotamus?

a paper doll dancing on a map carrying an atlas?   paper confetti

floats by   charcoal's blown off the page   its Brownian motion practice black hole or incognito   Move around!   fear resurfaces

its convulsive archive colonizers charlatans   the sick charters

are we prime for motion? lumbering like an old lung?   i'm in

the darkness my whiteness bathes or intrudes   paper rock skin

galaxy in a fingerprint   an index-finger string a time zone

in the hand's procession now   a brief film fills in people's features

silently   who else is hiding in there?   see the masking

tape on the floor where chairs go   will something come rushing

out of the ground?   never ready just begin never done just going

ever eponymous never done you will not finish you will always be in

the middle of something a mess of scraps on the floor the curators

have allowed   you will not finish   you will always be in the middle

Cheryl Clark Vermuelen

The Mental Health Association Thrift Shop

I burst out crying after selling the fabric flowers
right out of the vase that had been carefully arranged
by someone more exhausted than me, someone at
wit's end. Slip up and say crazy and I'd get reprimanded.
I had to tell her no one was playing tricks on her.
The customer only wanted the flowers. To her, the
empty vase hung around like a threat to her efforts.

One employee saw bugs and bugs in garbage bags
of donations, but I couldn't tell her counselor
there'd never be. Who knew what was in those bags?
One lady who lost all affect hardly spoke
but she could work the register, pressing buttons
as if adding up cavities or a death, a steady regiment.

In the break room, the employees would compare
the volume of their hallucinations. One said, "Know when
you hear the voice-overs of a character's thoughts on TV?
It's that loud." One day the furniture cashier fled
from the store, so I yelled out to her in the parking lot.
"I needed some air," she said. My own exhaustion
spoke only to itself, I remember you, alone, in this dull
town. One day, I went to the mall for a makeover
so someone would touch my face. Her warm hand
steadied on my cheek as she applied the eyeshadow.
One night, I wanted a raccoon rushing up the tree
to recognize me, groceries in hand. Exhaustion had me
make rubbings of the linoleum floor, charcoal in all
my fingernails, how I'd come to know the pattern:
exhaustion making the making sound like it made me.
Making, you exhausted me. *Move slowly. No one is
chasing you. No one has foundlings in their pockets.*

I want to call you by your name, Donna. You saw me
break down that day though I got in trouble
for breaking down that day
in front of the "mental health consumers."
(I said it—the new job's jargon I hated.)
I never believed my boss. She was pressing
that the consumers needed to know
that someone was in control, since they were not.
Across from her I sat nodding
(wish this meant sleeping) but just nodding yes,
next time I'd run to the bathroom to hide it.
That day, Donna, you handed me a handwritten letter
saying, "At that moment I felt the closest to you."
Then you may have written to the President,
as you always did with each new President,
you told me, to share your thoughts.

Cheryl Clark Vermuelen

Online Shopping

Any beachfront sojourn is a bit out of my league.
My mind goes in and out of places. For my not knowing

how to heal cloth, a woman years ago berated me.
This one needs a bit of a stitch, she'd say and glare at me.

Now I'm looking at apparel and get so tired, so glazed
that the rate at which I'm consuming cannot match

the rate at which I'm uncertain this is consumption.
I didn't buy a thing, I couldn't get my specialness

to sink in, to stick; it stunk some. All the while peril keeps
an eye on *near* and *far* until they touch with aplomb

and now is never found. I have walls in my eyes. Malls
too. One summer my friend's job was to be a storefront

mannequin, a stiff shift. It's better, now, when we don't see
everyone shopping, but these grumbling delivery trucks

keep coming when I'm homebound, convalescing,
feeling my eyes and their chambers and membranes

knowing that their conjunctiva is known more for its –itis.
This whole body exudes an ache, a bodyitis, an oblivion that

my pets get and thankfully keep to themselves. No app can
translate their language. I need vitamins, not painkillers,

and a cheerleader delivering an exclamation mark to my door.
Here you go! A delivery is a good distance. I close the door.

339

Any tiny epiphanies are just little ellipses … or passwords,
codes for our security punched in. Later I'll circle any overkill

in what I've said. I don't even have a bitch front
that could help. A batwing to go along.

Cheryl Clark Vermuelen

The Protest at the City's Tree Lighting Ceremony

Boston, 2014

I show up at the protest because I cannot.
It takes a few blocks for *I* to weave into *we*.

Once cut, the tree wears those lit teeth.
There are steel barricades around the tree.

Block by block we are shouting,
demanding *Eric Garner, Michael Brown.*
Shut this racist system down!

To be immersed in full belief, letting it
reverberate in my white body.

Struck we repeat what bears repeating:
Black Lives Matter. A family is gathered
at their window ten floors up.
Two grownups, two kids, huddled together.
I want to blow them a kiss—
allow free passage of the love
also emanating from these streets.

We walk en masse and the roads widen
and criss-cross, multiplying, yes, it seems
that we are headed to the interstate
to block it. Police in riot gear are filing out
of three city buses, shields for eons,
a tactical upper hand—they all know the plan
and the chokehold—but we are snaking fast
and my friend and I, deciding risk, swerve out,

asking each other, What will you do
next? What can we carry?

Cheryl Clark Vermuelen

By the Airport

Planes undo the quiet
perform their ascent
as a gruff muffled tuba
moving through me in
lockstep with commerce
about to hatch another
airline engine ah the line
a definite trajectory not
a stroll or meander but
a cloud plow on to another
propulsive opp along the
horizontal *fortissimo* over
the Atlantic. Consider its
orchestrated pleasurable
music priming the brain
suffusing the soul with
their treble and bass
a whistle ring to turn
into lines and filter out
the flutter of a handout
the wind mines (a girl
reads for class) or the
growl of a truck com-
pcting. When two planes
glide into a steady *uh*
I'm on the bus and the air-
conditioning vents suck up
the sound my inner hair
cells were dancing to

Cheryl Clark Vermuelen

For a Good Time

In city bathrooms stall-door
advertisements never took off
but the dryers with their plaques
were prime braggadocio
about their not being wasteful.
What else can we save?
Once I rubbed my hands
and arms under the blow
turning it on, maybe, five times.
I was cold and haunted by
the condition of the toilet,
plus other discomforts. And I
liked being alone. For a good laugh
at Shay's Pub in Harvard Square
above the slot of the condom
dispenser see scrawled
"For Refund Insert Baby Here."
I've never left that joke alone.

Cheryl Clark Vermuelen

Mother :: Words are Hotel Beds

By noon my husband and children are on the road
to the Northeast Kingdom. I'm green and already
writing their absence. I'll be queening, sipping
absinthe while bathing—if I remember the plan.
Relax my form for morpho butterflies and forsythia
and all else mating and budding. A tub full of
emeralds awaits me. My husband calls—The boys
are jumping across two queen beds, leaping from
consonant to vowel and back again. They made it
in good time, he says jiggling in the bed, then,
this town está muriendo poco a poco, the eulogy
not meant for them, vacationing, to hear, yet from
our dog now gone, they know about dying little by little.
They'll go to the arcade; if all else fails, flashing lights.
Go to the woods, I say. I am home and a guest
to these words that have their own trajectory.
My mother must have thought of me in her absence.

Interview with John Kinsella

CA: Can you talk a little bit about your childhood and upbringing and discuss how this influenced your poetry?

JK: My mother was a poet, though she plays it down now when I say this. But she was, and she had some local 'success', and it was a serious part of her life. She went on to be a literature teacher with a great love of the Romantics in particular, and was a reader (and teacher) of Judith Wright from quite early on. She has always been supportive, and in fact financed me for a year when I was very young to pretty well just write. She was a school teacher, divorced and so on, so didn't have a lot of spare cash, but she did it nonetheless. After my parents separated when I was about six, my father went 'up north' to work on the mines and later managed a very large farm in the mid-West. He also lived in Karratha and Carnarvon with his new family for years, and these places became 'access visit' sites for me, and strongly affected my ways of seeing. But probably the major influence was my Uncle's and Auntie's farm, Wheatlands, north-east of York, where we spent much time. The rural orientation of my work comes out of this, along with living and high schooling in Geraldton, in the mid-West of Western Australia, where my mother was a teacher. The whole coastal-hinterland-inland nexus, the rural and town liminality, and the social tensions around often conflicting communities profoundly affected my poetry and life views. I very strongly came to see and understand that I was living on stolen Aboriginal country, and my love of the land itself and the fact that I had no rights of access caused a kind of disjunction that led me to language to find a way through. I am still trying to, and ultimately know I won't find any answers. But I can find ways of processing human and environmental rights issues through poems, and of using them as activist tools. My brother and I had and still have a profound respect and also interactive relationship with the natural world, and this extends into my family life now. I have discussed much of this in my memoir *Displaced: a rural life,* which also extends modes of living into other places I have lived such as Ohio/USA, Cambridge/England, and West Cork/Ireland. But childhood is a complex thing, isn't it? — I was criminally bullied at school, and the nickname 'Dictionary' was not a kind one. I was interested in chemistry and physics, in nature and writing, and pretty well everything. Being interested seemed to be my driver. I was a fairly 'removed' kind of child, I think, and spent a lot of time making, inventing and creating things. I was close to my mother and, being part of a blending of families for many years, experienced other ways of seeing and perceiving. All of this is the stuff of poetry — when you stare into the compound eyes of a beetle, you see many aspects of your own life reflected! It all seems pretty surreal looking back on it now.

CA: You have discussed how your poems "work as subsets of each other". How does your use of different poetic forms relate to your various social and political preoccupations?

JK: Yes, I still believe and follow this poetics. There's not only overlap between all my different modes of writing and activism, but they share 'objects' in common whole making common usage and also different usage. It's a subsetting without hierarchies and hopefully breaking binaries, so there's an active undoing of their own conditions of making/ collecting/deployment and acting. So when I deploy a particular form, say a villanelle, the 'contents' have to be in dialogue (often in protest) against the constituent parts of that form linguistically, historically, and even culturally. Western poetic forms (at least) are often orientated around modes of class, gender and cultural control, and the most effective poems in these forms, at least from an activist point of view, are the ones that digress or introduce flaws into the code. So I make use of form to undo hierarchies, to contest the status quo which is inevitably embodied in the 'proper approach'. The villanelle is a powerful model for contesting Western pastoral, for disrupting the control mechanisms of human-nature binaries, through its history, its repetitions, its use of the same lines to mean different things. Language is unstable, and villanelles for all their formal restraint can generatively project instability of meaning into activist modes of intervention.

CA: You make many broadly intertextual gestures in your poetry, often to works from different eras. For example, here you mention Ovid's *Metamorphosis* and you have a cycle of poems writing back to, or in dialogue with, Emily Bronte. How does this intertextuality relate to your present concerns?

JK: The language I have to hand is strongly affected by literary language—I have been reading since I was three and it's part of how I understand the world. I write subsets of those sets. But I am also wrestling with the texts that have shown me ways of responding to the world, and I feel a need to reprocess them to say something 'new', to make them relevant in an unjust world. They inevitably do this in different ways in themselves, but not in the particular ways I experience and in the communal ways I wish to function. I have a far-left take on 'the word', as I do in all things, in which a pacifist vegan anarchist mode means things like property don't 'exist', materials are held in common (with respect to cultural materials that cannot be held in common outside their particular communities), and animal rights have to be considered alongside human rights. So, I am working on a 'new version' of Ovid's *Metamorphoses,* but it's a dramatic diversion from the original, and it reconsiders transformations in the contexts of environmental damage, degradation of human rights, the denial of animal rights ... and as a rejection of the policing of gender and identity rights. These aren't zeitgeist issues for me, but core issues of being that I have been writing about and around for many decades. This process of dialoguing with 'classical' texts is something I call 'templating', and there is an act of overlay and departure, but there's also an attempt to redress critical culture around 'famous texts' that have arisen out of conservative curatorial practice. The whole notion of a 'Western civilisation' I find disturbing, and it has become weaponised by the right to create an aesthetic and political hierarchy. As someone who rejects aesthetics and favours a poetics of interaction, it's inevitable I want to interact with 'high points' of aesthetic traditions. Of course, with someone like Emily Brontë, whose poems I carry with me everywhere and have done for decades, I believe so much of this is already implicit in the work, for all her probably 'conservative' outward politics — within the texts themselves are their undoings. The poems themselves see in ways the 'citizen' might not.

CA: You are often addressing the boundaries between the human and the non-human. How porous are these boundaries? Can we really ever cross over, or is it best to stand back and leave the nonhuman in its otherness?

JK: I believe the non-human has a right to complete autonomy and agency. I also believe humans have a responsibility to understand 'other life' so they can respect it. That said, I believe in non-invasive forms of understanding—I am horrified by, say, deep sea exploration that utilises bright lights in dark places to 'explore', damaging the vision of numerous creatures. I am horrified by the collecting and containment of 'specimens', and I feel the same way about zoos and animal husbandry. Humans do not need to be everywhere and go everywhere. We have imaginations and they are powerful and useful. Non-invasive forms of understanding sounds like a paradox, but it's a resolvable one. Empathy is a major factor. The different cultural co-ordinating around animals means there's no prescriptive 'answer', but most if not all cultures have their modes of interacting with animals while respecting the intactness of animals. Often when the relationship is totemic, there's a respect for the difference that is shared specifically. As a person who believes a mouse has as much right to live as a human, it's inevitable I will make certain life choices that prioritise the autonomy and agency of a mouse, while at the same time seeking to understand 'being mouse' so that I can better establish such distance or relationship. And at times of 'mouse plague', this is complex! But we always succeed through persistence, and the human and animals can co-exist without harm to each other. Sounds like a stretch, but given 'mouse plagues' are often the result of human activity, part of this living in proximity whilst respecting agency, is to act in informed and non-intrusive/damaging ways in the first place. I really believe mutual aid is possible between humans and non-human life as much as it's possible between humans. I know this will sound 'far out' in some ways, but I have spent a life living like this and documenting it in poetry, critical work, journals and fiction, and believe it's possible.

CA: You are known for your numerous poetry collaborations and you also mention your work with Kwame Dawes and also ruminations on self-collaboration. Could you say a little about your collaboration with Charmaine Papertalk Green and working with an Australian Aboriginal poet?

JK: It's really important to me, almost the most relevant thing I do—working with other poets. Jeanine Leane brilliantly wrote that what Charmaine and I share is more 'yarning' than collaborating (she contests the term in the context), and I'd agree with that. All these collaborations are dialogues … exchanges. Charmaine and I write from very different positions—she writes as a traditional owner-custodian, and I write as someone with colonial/settler background. My family escaped from British oppression in Ireland mid-nineteenth century to become part of the colonial impetus themselves. This tension is at the core of the whole ongoing colonial machinery that is 'Australia', and Charmaine and I try to discuss what we feel is wrong and how it might be addressed through our different life and cultural experiences. It is an ongoing dialogue, and one I feel privileged to be part of. For me, it's about respecting Indigenous knowledge while being willing to learn from it where it's appropriate to do so.

CA: One of the most powerful moments for me is your Bulldozer poem where you read in front of the destruction taking place in the frame behind you. It's available on YouTube. Could you say a little more about this moment, and also about "creativity-activism"?

JK: That was written as part of the campaign to try and stop the Roe 8 highway development in Western Australia. Many people from all over worked together to bring an end to this disgraceful destruction of unique Beeliar wetlands and bushland, but not before terrible damage was inflicted. A poem has to be an intervention for me, and that poem was written to take to the bulldozers themselves. There's a connect with an early experience I had as an activist trying to help stop the destruction of bush around Murdoch University back in the early '80s when I yelled poems at bulldozers and one driver actually stopped, got down and listened. It didn't stop the destruction, but the bulldozers were temporarily stopped (or one of them was). That early experience showed me the power of language and action if brought together. The familiar protest chanting has its unifying effects, and might impart a basic message, but it relies on the thrust of people ... a poem can be a 'force' in itself, as people seek to unravel the language. I have certainly found this across a life of trying to use poetry to intervene in eco-destruction. Violence solves nothing, and makes for more violence, and as a pacifist I believe there are other methods of changing people's minds ... or showing them other possible ways of doing things ... and poetry can be a big part of this.

CA: If poetry is political, do you also connect to ideas of the aesthetically satisfying in your writing?

JK: Poetry is political but there's also a politics in rejecting aesthetics. I reject it/them because I think they create hierarchies. My book *Shades of the Sublime & Beautiful* is an attempt to wrestle with this/these issues. It was strange reading a critic here and there trying to impose the aesthetic framework on the book that the poems themselves were trying to/were intended to refuse.

CA: Your poetry is increasingly a cross-art or interart activity. Has this changed your sense of your relationship to words? I'm thinking here of your photo-poetry cycles and the *Graphology* volumes.

JK: I can no longer separate the word from 'art' images. They have morphed for me. Looking back, I think it was always this way. When I was a kid I 'published' a local newspaper/writing sheet (one of Tracy's brothers did something similar), and the 'decoration' was very entangled with the words—almost rhizomic. I did a lot of painting, drawing and making, and was constantly writing 'books' (whole sci fi and fantasy novels long since lost), and these were often scrawled over. My brother is an artist, and I respond to his work (many of my covers feature his work), and my maternal grandfather was a signwriter-artist. That merging of word and visuals was the mainstay of his life, and it deeply affected me. I wrote an elegy about this morphing in which I say:

> Often
> I watched him at work
> but my thoughts were always
> a long way off—it wasn't the font
> or sell of words that gripped me,
> but how to escape what was written.

I have been working hard on photo-poem cycles for the last few years, though I actually did my first ones back in my early 20s. There are traces of these in poems (sans photos which are in a library archive) collected in *The Ascension of Sheep,* the first volume of my *Australian Collected Poems.* Similarly, painting was pivotal in my practice from childhood on, and in my early 20s it was visual art that I saw as inextricably linked to my being a poet. Some of that early work is still around, and the cover of my book *Doppler Effect* reproduces one of the paintings that survives. *Graphology* was always about writing, marking, signing, palimpsest, rewriting, drafting, typology, fonts, and orthography, and also about an anti-ekphrastic/ekphrastic tension. One of the series

351

of artworks connected with text I began in my early 20s was around Dante's *Divine Comedy,* and in a new and separate way I went back to colour drawings (with vegan pencils and materials) some years ago to 'illustrate' (there's a whole politics around this!) in a *Graphology* context (I have done a number of versions of the *Comedy*). Last year an exhibition of some of those *Graphology* 'illustrations' was held in Wheatbelt, Western Australia, which was exciting and interesting for me as part of the private/public dynamic of active and activist poem-making.

CA: You see yourself as an activist poet. How do ideas of the lyrical and the reflective connect to activism in your work?

JK: I think all poetry is a conversation between the lyrical and the rhetorical—in a 'concrete poem' as much as a short or long-line stanza poem. I am really interested in classical rhetoric, and often apply its precepts to my writing. But the song, the lyrical impetus, is still how I remember and relate to the world. The 'weighting' of that conversation in an activist context to favour one approach or the other depends on the need of the moment. Sometimes rhetoric and its modes has to be weighted because the details are so direct, but for suggestion and evocation (often before the crisis moment), the lyric gets the weighting.

CA: You have a famous blog, Mutually Said: Poets Vegan Anarchist Pacifist with your partner poet Tracy Ryan. How does this function as part of your creative and political practice?

JK: The sharing really matters. We believe in community, and that means two of us and all of us as well. The blog has an activist focus, and is a way of getting things said and out there rapidly. If I write an activist poem, it's supposed to do something. It goes out to try and redress a wrong or acknowledge something. Many of the concerns we have are ongoing, and there's never a 'resolution' because the threat by invasive forces (mining companies, logging companies, developers) and from specific conservative or right-wing groups is frequently ongoing. It is a particularly generative space because of the intersectional nature of our concerns and the blog's ability to convey respect for diverse yet connected concerns through being read across years. It's a safe space, a space of peace, and a space of resistance.

CA: Would you say that capitalism has attempted to marginalise poetry?

JK: Yes! And ultimately to destroy it. It needs to be opposed in all viable ways!

CA: I know you have discussed your insomnia, and I remember talking to Harold Bloom about his insomnia. Could you say something about this and its influence on your writing?

JK: Yes, Harold was a deeply committed insomniac. I went to his place once and he'd been working since before 4 AM. We clicked on that (as well as other) level/s! For me, it has defined my physical and mental life. These days, I try to sleep, even if I fail, but for much of my life I just went with it and that produced, well, *irregular* results. I am disturbed by even the slightest external noise when I sleep, and that makes it complex, but it also allows me to tune in to nightbirds and night animals in ways I otherwise wouldn't. It creates a kinship with darkness. But in the most obvious ways, decades of insomnia have meant a lot of reading and a lot of writing I might not otherwise have done. It also meant chaos and collapse back in my addiction days, and I still deal with the consequences of that after almost 28 years of sobriety. But I think it also makes you process information differently—kind of slant or offbeat. This is neither better nor worse than other ways, just different. No doubt plenty is lost, and it certainly adds a level of obsessiveness to the way one works, but it also has its own clarities in the moments when others are sleeping. These days, insomnia is still a torment, but I've learnt almost to rest along with it … let it be what it will be, and inevitably that being resolves into poetry.

John Kinsella

What I Have Said Before Differently

Across four decades of publishing poetry I have tried to say many things, but many things differently. There have been a set of core concerns that have 'directed' my poetics, and they revolve around the environment and rights issues. I am a long-term vegan anarchist pacifist, and this necessarily marks my poetics. I have written a number of critical poetics books that contemplate an activist poetics and they in themselves have become extensions of that *ars poetica* and *raison d'être*. However, over these decades I have tried to augment and diversify my approaches to these issues, and to how I go about 'making' poems. In fact, poetry, visual art and music, are increasingly fused and in conversation. I have a 'life series'/cycle of poems entitled 'Graphology Poem,' which pivot around the act of writing, and this cycle takes on many different visualisations—at present, within the *Graphology* spatiality, I am predominantly working in 'experimental' photo and poem-text cycles/conversations, one of which are in evidence here. This also intertexts with my glasshouse/metamorphosis works.

All of my poems work as subsets of each other. When I was doing a version of *The Argonautica,* I was also writing a verse novel of the sea and the littoral (with cross-referencing between the works), *Cellnight,* and now I am working on a series of poems around glasshouses and also a version of Ovid's *Metamorphoses* (I made the first inroads into this well over a decade ago), and these intertext with each other as well as the *Graphology* series.

Like most of my engagements with 'classical' texts, *Metamorphosis* is at a tangent to the original, and goes almost completely in its own directions, but the impetus of it certainly comes out of the original text. The key motif at this 'stage'/phase is the glasshouse (pluralised in the poems), and the ironies of that mode to create environments that function quasi-independently of the conditions without. Obviously, that becomes a metaphor for climate change, but also for many modes of change positive as well as negative. I am also doing a series of *Graphology* drawing poems/illustrations to the cycles, just as I did with the *Divine Comedy* and more recently have been doing with *Finnegans Wake.* All entangled, conversing, and diverging. And what I have said before, I say differently to hopefully open new possibilities for creativity-activism. It's about an energy of commitment and opening different angles of engagement.

Another thread orientates around experimental film, and like many of my book-length poetry works, it started a long while back to gain momentum later. It's been a long-term interest, and my way of viewing and experiencing necessarily changes over time … in some ways, each poem, often based on short films, encapsulates a relationship to specific times and places. Finally, another life-thread: a conversation (since I was seventeen) with the poems of Emily Brontë. I have written a book of these prior (which will appear in the third volume of my *Australian Collected Poems*), and the urge to keep this often 'slant' dialogue going hasn't let up.

I've never seen poetry as a static entity. For me, it has to do something in its moment. Further, I don't separate it off as a genre from my other writing (stories, novels, plays, criticism etc.), and each in its turn hybridises with and around poetry to make things anew (I hope). The act of reading is as vital as the act of writing, the act of speaking as vital as the act of thinking. It's all interactive.

Another important part of my practice is collaboration. In some ways, it divides more off from my 'personal' writing than my personal modes of writing divide off from each other, but there is necessarily (and willingly) overlap. But I tend to write away from an interest when collaborating in an attempt to discover new ways of doing things. I learn from collaboration—I always hope new ways of seeing through exchange with another poet will make things I have been unable to see or see less clearly become more evident, active. I have a very close (across the distance) interaction with Kwame Dawes that has led to the publication of five books, most recently *UnHistory*. This long-term poetry dialogue has become part of my personal psychogeography, and also part of my process for understanding and relating to the world at large. It feels essential, and really gets to the core of poetry for me—to exist with purpose. Collaboration isn't just a swapping, it's an immersion. I am always prepared, I think, to 'leave myself' to engage with this. And here, in the photo-poem cycle, there's a kind of 'self-collaboration' going on (which I have written about in the Australian journal *Rabbit*).

In my recent long poem in four parts, *Metaphysics,* I present a pacifist consideration of the war in the Ukraine, and war in general, and try to consider acts of colonial brutality in that context. Not as a commentary, but an attempt at a pacifist intervention, to say that there is another way beyond bloodshed to deal with tyranny. I understand that this might seem 'easy' to say *outside* a conflict zone, but it's one I believe emphatically and to the point of potentially interposing my physical self between conflicting parties and reacting to neither. A poem can do that, and should do that. Rather than being an aid to conflict, wrong or 'right', it should be a staunch, a thwarting and a quelling of conflict.

This very document becomes an extension of the practice of *Metaphysics,* which is ultimately a lament, a keening for loss, all loss. And that loss necessarily involves the natural world and much animal life as well, and damages and even kills part of the biosphere itself. This implicates us all in a variety of ways. Imposing ways. As does the colonial occupation of Indigenous lands, as does the abuse of refugees and 'irregular' migrants by wealthy, more powerful countries.

I am talking about the pro-active non-violent intersectionality of poetry, and a commitment by poets to creating more intensely effective ways of making 'languages' of repair and reconstruction. These are rarely easy languages to form, and often take some time to be understood, but they can have an effect, and even before being understood can act as immediate interventions through their surprise and (potential) veracity.

The place I most often write is the stolen/unceded Ballardong (on the 'edges' of Whadjuk and Yued) Noongar country I live on, though we have lived many places around the world. At present, I am writing from Tübingen, Germany, where we are living for a year, and my focus is very much on the vulnerability of an ostensibly protected forest system (the Schönbuch Nature Park) that is in fact open to 95 percent incursion for 'natural forestry'. I have observed the passive-aggressive stance of this mode, and it's certainly far more about serving human desires than the health of the forest itself and the biosphere. So, inevitably, I write this in the context of comparing the trauma of forests where I come from—prey to loggers, mining companies and leisurists and land developers—with the traumas of forests here. A comparative 'model' builds across the poems.

In the same way, I have observed and written out of Ohio, Britain, southwest Ireland and other places. Nothing is separate, and all speaks to each other in different (necessarily complex) ways. This idea of multiple presences (in physical, spiritual and conceptual modes) I have termed 'polysituatedness' (and have written a book about this idea), which relates further to my notion of 'international regionalism' (also considered at length in my critical/poetics books).

One of the things that has brought me back to Tübingen again and again has been the poetry of Hölderlin, and maybe even the ghost of Hölderlin itself. He is omnipresent, not only for me but many others who believe in poetry here. I have students here who almost obsess over him (I do, too). The Hölderlin Tower (Hölderlinturm) is a focus not only for scholars and readers of Hörderlin, but almost a spiritual poetic centre. And I have seen his ghost and it kissed me! Honestly!

In many ways, my concerns have been what one might call 'rural', as I have spent much of my life in rural areas, but I am also interested in the false binary of the rural and urban. I am interested in peripheries, liminality, and how categorising never actually works. There are always anomalies, always exceptions, and these instances are often quite telling in various ways. My poetry seeks to understand these. I am also interested in the failings of official derogations of language in expressing the specificities and difference of diverse personalities/ identities/peoples/conditions. For me, language is never static and never bound to a dictionary, a lexicon. It's an active field that might literally change mid-conversation over, near, or inside, say, a glasshouse, or in a field, or walking down a street.

I tend to work in narratives that are both textually evidenced and also, strangely, somewhat hermetic while they are being woven together. Over time, I hope things become evident, but there are often many working parts. Sometimes an external event or a close-to-home situation (such as my father being gravely ill far away in Western Australia, which has had a profound effect on me) act as a gravitational force on my work, and whatever I am working on draws language in a particular direction of contemplation, distress or redress, but even then it happens in conversations with many other factors. If I make a poem, everything comes into play: it concentrates, but it also proliferates connection. And what I have said before, I try to say differently, adapting and responding to the time and place in the most appropriate way I can.

Coda

Other than writing and activism, the primary work modes of my life have either been rural labour (when younger) and researching/teaching. I am at present teaching among other things, writing environmental activism. I am hoping the participants/students/activists will develop

357

interactive modes of writing their environmental concerns such that they are adaptable, pragmatic and deeply committed. I find that hybrid forms involving reportage, poetry, criticism, flash fiction, memoir and even theatre/performance are both exciting for them and also practical. I always write examples of what I mean, and the other day in considering the issues of remediation of brownfield sites I wrote a prose poem/flash fiction/commentary by way of illustration, and also to serve the issue in itself. I had one participant come up at the end of the meeting asking if they could really work in that mode, and I assured them it was as legitimate an approach as any other.

Over recent weeks we had approached many issues slant, including watersheds and drainage via transcendentalism or via Robert Penn Warren's poem 'Watershed', and the fate of the oceans via Craig Santos Perez's, Felicity Plunkett's and David Baker's poetry, nuclear testing in the Pacific via Hone Tuwhare's poem 'No Ordinary Sun', and gardening via early Persian poetry. I say all this by way of presenting that piece I wrote to show how a case study of a brownfield site (in this case the old power station on the river in Perth/Boorloo, Western Australia), can open up a discussion about land health, colonialism, capital (greed), animal rights, and issues around remediation. Here's the text, and in the spirit of cross-conversation within a *body of work*, it serves as a conclusion to this essay, but not *closure* which the ongoing, *in medias res* nature of my practice will not or maybe cannot sustain:

Under the Gleaming Surface: brownsiting

Where the power station had sucked up the river and fed the city's occupants with oil and coal-fired power, the land ached and the river's chemistry fluctuated. Eventually it was closed down, the ground struggling to cope with the toxic residues. Asbestos was the garnish to the 'complications' of the soil, the blunt end of remediation. And then bloated with government incentives designed to serve 'development', the mega-rich linked arms to 'revitalise' a 'difficult' part of the city. That eyesore, that blight. But it went wrong—a fallout. The rich blokes no longer loved each other. The site gives off its aura of damage and sadness, and the land yearns for its people. A desire to convert into a 'vision' for the future, into a focal point for business, means the site will not find its way back into a natural condition. How can it be? asks the egret, lamenting the soil that will have to be removed, deeply. Better a transplant than a death, says the magpie, imagining new trees and cleanish run-off into the reeds along the river's edge. Wetlands. So much is possible if they let it return to something closer to its original state, the magpie adds. Egret says, It can't return. Both are reminded of the prevalence of old waste disposal sites around the region, the opening of disturbed ground. They wonder if the human poor along with birds, animals and plants, will suffer the most, regardless. The paradox of a colonial history of toxicity. At the latest conference of birds, they have looked to intervene, to feather the nests of change, but there are whispers that 'environmental control' might intervene to restore a more 'natural balance'. Meaning a culling of birds. *The more things change the more they remain the same,* said one migratory wader, or so they've translated the translation. There was a heavy smog inversion layer over the city when I heard this, which might have interfered with the transference. I notice that the flocks of corellas are much smaller, and are even willing to retreat to the old power station, hoping to avoid the culls. They remind us: the oppressive buildings are 'heritage protected', but we aren't.

John Kinsella

European Green Lizard in Botanical Gardens, Tübingen

The labels on the plants facing
        off across the path whose pavers
make a jigsaw between hardiness zones

blur with the dash of a European
        green lizard. Across the minutiae
of curve, knowing its body

wraps green around the grey
        and its stomach rises above
its head and its tail. Nothing

is on the level, and this lizard
        is part of a local community,
I read—that has set up shop,

rewriting geographies local
        and global, stony and sandy,
dry and damp, pinnate and ovate.

John Kinsella

Getting to Know Oaks in the Realm of Industrialism

'*Looking ahead but based on tradition*'
   German Forestry
   https://www.forstwirtschaft-in-deutschland.de/index.php?id=60&L=1

I am getting to know oaks—
well, *some* oaks—their manners
and characteristics, if not

their concerns. But some of those
concerns are obvious,
and I am fairly sure I understand.

Oaks seem transducive, especially
in a forest that's 'managed',
and never as safe as its 'protectors'

make out. The human factor
is declared as an intimacy
with oak, but the oaks seem

to be saying, There's something
extra human that's being missed.
Bees high up in a tall oak

are transforming a split
to anneal as inner sanctum.
They aren't *spilling out,*

but working air paths
as human walkers below
weave around each other.

361

Second-guessing, knowing
from experience, inherently
aware. I can't help building

a transformative, comparative
model. I am limited in ways
this oak and these oaks aren't.

The bees have found their own
way, built their own hive,
operate as independently

of humans as they can.
They are saying this, and so
are the oaks. As one voice,

and as separate voices. *They*
are aware of the whole
forest, and that awareness

tells them plenty that doesn't
fit with 'management plans'.
Doesn't fit with reworkings

of 'traditions' to enforce
new exploitations. *Transformative*
is agreement, even collusion,

between tree and bee.
Metamorphosis is a long-term
discussion about futurism—

surviving myriad visions
of the future destabilising
from root to wing, eye to crown.

They are outside the glass-
houses, oaks and bees.
How much can I know of both?

John Kinsella

Local Forest Walk Sestina

I am constantly trying to find new pathways,
to determine different approaches and evoke new rituals,
to find alternative ways down town or under the forest's leaves
that appeared after we arrived, changing the style of a forest's art,
to show leaves shaped like the past even as they shadow a crop
of oats skirting its overhang, or shake with approaching machinery.

And it's inside the forest I am most circumspect about machinery,
of the threat to surroundings and reshaping of pathways,
even more than when I walk between the divided crop
to find my way towards the forest, or to smaller towns; rituals
bound together by criss-crosses and towers, by the art
of contradiction ('nature lovers'/ hunters) under a cycle of leaves.

I am awaiting the deciduous turning point of an entire forest's
    leaves
but as it will be staggered I can't find the median, and know
    machinery
will force a path through oak, beech and pines and conduct its sick
    art
of destruction, laying de-barked logs in stacks along the pathways
with red and blue numbers on their smooth cut ends, a ritual
of capital and 'sustainability' that still turns the forest into a crop.

I can't understand a forest without thinking outside this crop
configuration—I see it as an organism in itself whose leaves
are flags of community and not exclusions, whose rituals
are both private and shared among other species, whose machinery
is organic and spiritual and whose overt and hidden pathways
are an expression of interaction and symbiosis that is the dynamism
    of art.

I also think of the various forests I've studied in art or even depicted
    in art
and realise how far they are from the moment of passing through—
    to crop
an image, to select a mood, to wait for the right light to suggest
    pathways
through to some human doubt. The mental uses we put forests
    to—leaves
as memory, trunks as aspiration, roots as origins, all forms of
    machinery
to state our essential relationship to what we put at risk—rituals

of symbolism morphed into spiritual growth while denying the life
    rituals
of the non-human as well as the human, the complexity of growth-
    art
and soil and hydrology, of an essential organic machinery
of the planet. So many contracting forests around the world, so
    many crops
edging up to replace them. Or their rocky foundations plucked
    from beneath leaves
so their leaves fall whether deciduous or not — a whitewash of
    pathways.

I walk anxious of hearing machinery outside the mechanisms and
    rituals
of the forest itself whose pathways shift with the momentum and
    art
of animals, anxious of the crops that reach inwards, birds splendid
    as leaves.

John Kinsella

Out of the Glasshouse Refuge I Emerged

Effete is not a flower trumpet.
But happily enraged I scale

the edifice—world without
moderate conditions within,

these plans for narrative gambits
against an easily shattered

backdrop, screens of reason.
Heat applied in panes. Capture. Sink.

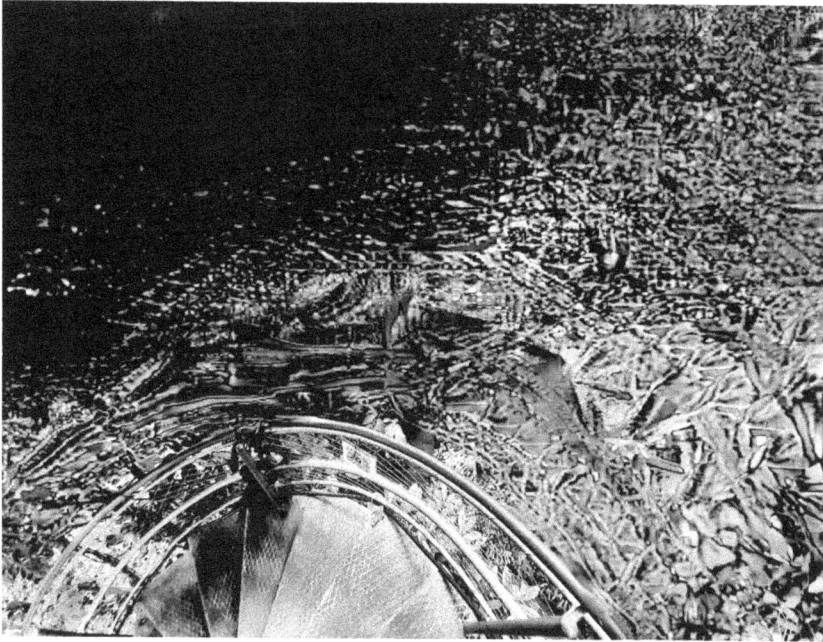

I decline a vertiginous headiness—
ascending jags and steps away

from productivity. Molecular-
marker of foundry, a casting

into vocabulary expanded
to breaking point, leaf plosives

(umbrella, rustle, fan and droop)
and rivulets, nozzle dispersals.

A memoir of emergences that will
never grow the same or adapt less.

Bell tongues thrust from aggregate—
fuzzy, sans palette cleansing

patois, a rudiment of lore:
how to remove sharp words

and sing those atlas xeno-spikes
around tech constellations,

around *rumours of incomers*
who will take it all away.

Store under glass to chime
local interest, draw all in. Observe.

Zones don't hold while display
sways an expectant public.

It propagates as reportage
and demands for offensives.

Musical emanations, 'collapsing
buildings', interference

of unfamiliar roots. Though this
doesn't mean that they can live together,

can't be co-opted by analogy. Pillage
or plants choices. Birds. Insects. Dispersals.

Each encounter with melt
will leave less irony to summer.

De-architecture. Sluice. War
reports. A lack of REM sleep

makes for dangerous botanists.
The labels aren't mass produced.

Two dimensional glassblowers,
tropical framers, alpine sliders,

arid concreters. Every time I watered
the garden for my grandparents

I rose, sank, transpired. Epithets
and eulogies. Germinal cities, visited.

John Kinsella

Drone-mimeo-avian-spoliation-surveillance

> *... We've taken the land from them, we were cutting down roosting and
> nesting trees.... The airspace was the only place that was for the birds.*
> —Gisela Kaplan (ABC news)

Drone-mimeo-avian-spoliation-surveillance,
    deciphering our bird desiring
we delete birds while taking their pictures,

which doesn't serve the requirements
    for ambiguity in the art we make
to fulfill ourselves or sell on the art market.

Drone-mimeo-avian-spoliation-surveillance
    is a honing of eye-hand co-ordination
like developing 'twitch' response

in violent video gaming. *Down below*
    sweeps by in such cascading
and free-flowing spans—a wing

span parody that lulls us into flight-
    dream scenarios, bird's eye view more
    than a bird's eye edited with resolution.
Drone-mimeo-avian-spoliation-surveillance.

John Kinsella

Blue Sky Eclipse

Darkening all my summer skies
Shutting out my sun
    —Emily Brontë

A dozen crows flying northwest
after harsh easterlies have broken down

a fan spinning blue shadows from shade and heat

startled, bronzewings thresh a pocket
of trapped air between silver shed and house

startled, I reverse my progress, breaking
a daily pattern when the UV
has dropped to safer indexing

another flight of crows, jagged
but tracing them same path:
they are the light I follow
and go where the sun can't

a fan whirring shade out of blue shadow and heat;

I am not going to co-opt a koan
to this purpose

listen to the ways a sun
might be shut out of an equation;

how else can I bring sunrise to sunset
and prove 'productive'?—

gratitude one seed among

many being processed
by a bronzewing pigeon
somewhere nearby—

hear its echoing coo;

the solitary wasp is on either side
of the sky's

late blue eclipse.

John Kinsella

Seed Rain Reiteration

I needed not its breathing
To bring such thoughts to me
  —Emily Brontë

It's blown for days,
and last night
trees split
like seed pods.

People get antsy
if you repeat yourself.
I do. We need to.

It rained crisp indented pod-halves
and it rained hard acacia seeds
into morning and now.

Everywhere
seeds are
perfect entries
more perfect
than small burrows
creatures make.

Those vicious easterlies.
The burning winds.
And it is terribly
beautiful.

And this is why
we obsess
over cosmology.

John Kinsella

Symbiosis

In going away I can't share
with the valley sustaining me.

This is my loss, not its loss. This
is no superstition, but if it were,

so what. I will carry descriptions
of rock, plant, seed and erosion

that don't need me though
I have affected them. Lopsided

equation. Denying the supernatural,
maybe I am losing something. I should

record things in different ways
so the pictures become less clear.

We are going away and what's here
stays here. The crow is speaking now,

so particular. I can't say that crows
we hear where we're going won't be saying

the same thing, but it seems unlikely.
Dragonflies might fly differently, slightly.

John Kinsella

Le voyage dans la lune (Paris)

Bullet in the eye of the moon.
Strong-arming the shell of Saturn
we fooled them into thinking *trapdoor!*
Involving solidity, a smile into the sea
of a collapsed orrery, the hubris
of a gas giant. Remember the swinging
street on which we tried to catch
no one's attention, hoping to rock
in silence. Star is the drone of aspiration,
the jargon of mis-en-scene futurism.
Don't forget movement, the lack
of Lycra. That's congress—same
old sign of glitter, rainfall characterisation.
Why would they abjure and abuse an insect?
Insects mean more insects,
the curling sleep of Nostradamus.
Trophy. Collector. Subsets of expansionism.
Labor omnia vincit—again, the pastoral
underpinnings you writhe against,
killing jar celebration, we brag
under musky skies, worshipping space,
statements, the guile of translating silence.

John Kinsella

Three Very Short Films via the 'Original Cinématographe': *Lumière et compagnie:* (1995) David Lynch, Helma Sanders-Brahms, Spike Lee

1. David Lynch (53 seconds)

You've seen the police arrive in darkness.
You've woken to the door coming down
and the tactical response group
lifting us from our beds. Across
the lawn, silent then loud, the cameras
running into darkness at dawn.
Sleep tries to hold, listening to windows
and manholes, listening to aliens
in the window seat. Test subject
tests subjects to gaze in and out
of analysis, for future invasions.
Preservative. Bottled naked woman.
        (*Why?*) Forensics.
At the door with sad news
of the future: foretelling and fore-
boding a hard day's reconnaissance.
This world of hats off. Indoors
keeping outdoors out.

2. Helma Sanders-Brahms (48 seconds)

Hommage A Louis Cochet …

Lush as waterfall lighting
to glean a nymph euphoria
where workers wonder
about rights under the hot
glare reflection of Schumann
to direct the spill cascade
tumble tune-flow cataract
gush—outpouring refraction
of moments you want to
recall from earlier but can't
defend as more than indulgence;
light blows out transpiring
        apotheosis, electricity.
I was electrocuted at the switch
(screwdriver, and power accidentally
turned back on) just below my grandfather's
        great curved fish tank
(a hand-painted backdrop
swelled by the glass)—
thrown across the room in a shower
of sparks as the sharks
compensated. My grandfather
could paint water scenes
lush or minimalist. A trade.

3. Spike Lee (53 seconds)

We come into speech
amazed when a soundtrack
doesn't synchronise, ingesting
all noises that pluralise
a world we are held in,
paused in our pram.
Is saying 'Dadda'
what's required
of the moment?—
a way of opening
the door, of finding
a way into the day?
Those beautiful utterances,
those sounds of the body,
to be replaced, transformed
into agreements. Maybe
 'Da' is enough, 'Da'
is all that needs be said.
A sound of falling,
a code for rising.

Emeryville Mudflats: *Junkopia* (1981) by Chris Marker, Frank Simeone and John Chapman

Kangaroo reflector dazzle in eye of
seaside exotica or someone's lonely
truism on flats to sway a determined
breeze while the wader probes ooze for
heavy metal new worlds. Sized by salt
and decaying skyline, flourishing forms
gift and drift industrial global melt
detritus to view from highway. Drive-by.
Arriving at shores clad in armour the long
legged thin bird-soul whispers feathers
to jags of whistling bottles. Scouring the
'wastes' for bits and pieces to inhabit
a house torn between pragmatics and
aesthetics. So many decades after the
reminder of rehabilitation. The site.
Expression. The flipped fighter ace, flags
of the rift, a Holiday Inn forlorn as a
fixed observer. Ritual flare tide totems of
longitude wind chimes facing first flight
lace-wing finned fish-face scale portrait
weft and weave nail whisper and hubcap
compass-lament driftwood as waves of
Butchertown simmer marshlands to
visualise those intertidal creatures' un-
emerging, and threatening to consume
underlife, to drive off fiddler crabs and
salt grass, or call for redress, to undo the
forms by parts and reflections or Robber
Baron residues: sea-train skeleton of
marooned leviathan, shadow-scale zoo
warnings, and spectres reformulating
hope as fact threatens this wave motion.

ESSAYS AND REVIEWS

Jennifer Bartlett. *The Sustaining Air: The Life of Larry Eigner.* Modern and Contemporary Poetics Series, University of Alabama Press. 198 pages, with photographs. $39.95.

Ellen McGrath Smith

The material, intellectual, and creative lives of poets with disabilities have been sparsely documented—especially of those living before the Americans with Disabilities Act and the flowering in this century of disability culture's contributions to the literary landscape. For over a decade, poet and disability rights activist Jennifer Bartlett carved out time from her numerous other endeavors to piece together a life story for the twentieth-century American poet Larry Eigner, whose work was embraced by the San Francisco Renaissance poets of the 1950s, the New American Poets associated with the signal 1960 anthology edited by Donald Allen, and later, by the L=A=N=G=U=A=G=E poetry movement of the 1970s and '80s. The new biography, which George Hart in his foreword to the book calls "the first complete portrait of one of the twentieth century's true poetic innovators," gives readers a digestible yet comprehensive understanding of Eigner's development as a writer, as well as of the barriers he faced as an individual with cerebral palsy in an inaccessible world.

In her preface to *The Sustaining Air: The Life of Larry Eigner,* Bartlett explains that it was her encounter with the posthumous four-volume *The Collected Poems of Larry Eigner,* edited by Curtis Faville and Robert Grenier (Stanford University Press, 2010), that sealed her resolve to write the biography. The poet Charles Bernstein put her in contact with Grenier, who from 1979 to 1989 had lived with and helped to care for Eigner in Berkeley, California. Given that Eigner was not a narrative or confessional poet like many mid-to-late-century mainstream American poets, Bartlett "chose to build his life directly out of his own words and those of the people who wrote to him," using his creative writing, interviews, and correspondence, the latter of which was especially copious during the first fifty-one years of his life, when he lived in comparative isolation in his family home in Swampscott, Massachusetts—on Boston's North Shore—most of the time under the care of his mother, Bessie.

As Bartlett asserts in her preface, "Larry Eigner and I have three things in common: We are poets, we have cerebral palsy, and we have an

385

unwavering passion for Charles Olson." I organize this review around these three commonalities, albeit in a different order and combination than given in Bartlett's assertion.

A Poetics of the Open Field

The second time I encountered Larry Eigner's work was when, as a contributor to *Beauty Is a Verb: The New Poetry of Disability* (Cinco Puntos, 2011), I also became acquainted with Bartlett and her work. What is common in both of their poetry is the suspension and movement of fragments and white space across and over the page, which enacts "composition by field," a poetics based on Olson's seminal 1950 essay "Projective Verse." Early in his writing career, Eigner was in touch Robert Duncan, Denise Levertov, Robert Creeley, and other Black Mountain poets, all of them orbiting a poetic tendency that, as Olson's seminal essay urges, privileged an organic, embodied composition guided by breath.

The biography, which begins with a timeline by George Hart, consists of short chronological chapters progressing from Eigner's earliest years, when he was on the margins of mainstream educational opportunities, attending hospital-based, residential, or homeschooling programs at different points in his K–12 years. He was fortunate to belong to a family of some means and to have parents, especially his mother, who encouraged him in his love of written language. A signal moment emphasized in the biography was the young Eigner's bar mitzvah, when a relative (prompted by his mother) gifted him with a Royal manual typewriter, which would be his preferred instrument for composition throughout his life.

Each chapter is headed with an epigraph from Eigner's opus, and specific poems are introduced within the biographical narrative. Bartlett is meticulous in documenting Eigner's coming of age as a poet. As was the case for many writers of that generation, Eigner's first encounter with poetry came through Robert Louis Stevenson's *A Child's Garden of Verses*. He wrote mostly formal poetry as a youth, publishing a few poems in student/youth publications and completing a full chapbook manuscript by his early teens. After finishing at a residential middle school at the top of his class and known as a poet whose work was published by the school, he participated in a Swampscott homeschooling curriculum during high school. Following high school, taking University of Chicago correspondence courses led him to become curious about free verse. Bartlett attends closely to this awakening, establishing Eigner as a constant reader who devoured books on a range of topics and had the sort of invested craft questions one expects from college undergraduates, or more likely, graduate students. With limited opportunities to circulate outside of his home, correspondence and reading material delivered by U.S. post were crucial to his growth as a serious writer.

The poet Cid Corman, a supportive correspondent throughout Eigner's life even after Corman established a permanent residence in Japan, was Eigner's earliest mentor. A fellow Massachusetts native, Corman hosted a local radio show called *This Is Poetry* that Eigner's brother, Richard, turned him on to. From the mass of correspondence, Bartlett teases out the ways in which Corman's reading suggestions and feedback on drafts were an extensive and effective way of leading Eigner to answer his own questions about free verse and its possibilities. Among the reading suggestions, which included writers like Marianne Moore and Arthur Rimbaud, Corman encouraged Eigner to read the work of E. E. Cummings, which pointed him in the direction of departing from the left-hand margin (though he was wary of the *veneer* of innovation that Cummings' work presented and would go on to articulate for himself a more holistic use of form as an extension of content). The Black Mountain poets would further bring this out in Eigner's work. Eigner's long acquaintance with Robert Creeley also stemmed from Corman's radio show, where Creeley gave his first public reading.

It should be said that this biography is more for the literary-minded than it is for a general reader. Bartlett "builds" Eigner's life first and foremost as a poet herself. She is able to identify subtle but key moments when Eigner consciously implements stylistic changes to his work, along with what influenced those choices and how he articulated his evolving poetics in his craft talks/writings and correspondence with a community of poets committed to furthering what modernism began without stagnating inside the parameters set by Williams, Eliot, and Pound. Like Charles Olson, he was intent on breaking new ground. Though Eigner rarely interacted with Olson, who for a time lived in nearby Gloucester, Massachusetts, and centered *The Maximus Poems* around this fishing town, his poetics was deeply influenced by what he saw as the "organic movement" and "less controlled" quality of *Maximus 1–10*, which was published in 1953, when Eigner was twenty-six—the same year that Robert and Penelope Creeley's Divers Press published Eigner's first adult collection, the chapbook *From the Sustaining Air*. Creeley had been a supportive editor of Eigner's poems, retyping at least one of them to demonstrate to Eigner the "possible, infinite variations" in the line. He also reinforced Eigner's growing sense of the line break and white space as forms of punctuation. Ultimately, Eigner would write that, for him, "immediacy and force have to take precedence over clarity in a poem," a guiding principle that, Bartlett emphasizes, was rooted in Olson's poetics.

In terms of Eigner's poetry, all roads, for Bartlett, lead to Olson: "His [Eigner's] poems would eventually become the exemplar of Olson's philosophy." In between him and the older poet he referred to as "The Pro," Eigner's interactions with poets closer to his age resulted in publications, readings, and artistic collaborations. Once he moved to the Berkeley area, where his brother Richard lived with his wife, he would get around a good deal more; an attraction of the Bay Area was that it was the home of the Independent Living movement as well as other disability rights initiatives, including the nearly month-long occupation of the San Francisco federal building demanding that the U.S. Secretary of Health, Education, and Welfare enact Section 504 of the Rehabilitation Act of 1973, a successful action that took place just a year before Eigner made the move to the opposite coast. Living away from the family home—first in a group home then in a house his family purchased for him and his caregivers (Grenier and his wife) to live in—reduced Eigner's overall output, in terms of both poems and correspondence—but he gave many more public readings and enjoyed frequent face-to-face exchanges with other poets.

His arrival in the Bay Area also coincided with the critical massing of innovative poets associated with the L=A=N=G=U=A=G=E movement, whose eponymous poetics journal launched in 1978 with the publication of Eigner's essay "Approaching Things / Some Calculus / How figure it / Of Everyday Life Experience." Bartlett notes that Ron Silliman, in a letter to Bruce Andrews, identified Eigner as "the first man to isolate words/phrases/perceptions in such a way as to force the attention onto them, not to the context." While "first man" claims regarding a practice as old and widespread as poetry should be taken with a grain of salt, the claim should nonetheless be seen as a testimony to the degree to which these poets and critics saw Eigner as an important precursor to their projects, as Olson was to Eigner's. Silliman's 1987 collection of essays *The New Sentence* is regarded as an important text for understanding this movement toward poetries that both center language as material and de-center the writing self; further, *In the American Tree: Language Realism Poetry* (National Poetry Foundation, 1986), which Silliman edited to be a wide sampling of the poetry coming out of this community, is dedicated to Eigner. In retrospect, I first knew Eigner's name through my reading of criticism and craft essays related to language-oriented poetry. In other words, I first encountered Eigner as an important name in twentieth-century postmodern American poetry.

In that first context, I had no idea that Eigner had cerebral palsy. Given the era in which he came of age, a time of abysmal ignorance and injustice regarding disability, I'm sure Eigner would have liked it that way.

A "Wild" Left Side

The effects of cerebral palsy differ among those with this neurological condition caused by traumatic brain injury *in utero,* during birth, or in early childhood. Bartlett makes it clear in her preface that she sees Eigner's life story through a disability justice lens, while also acknowledging that Eigner had good reason to resist attempts to foreground his disabled identity in ways that he feared would diminish his literary efforts and accomplishments. She points out how internalized ableism led to Eigner's reluctance to socialize with other persons with disabilities, particularly during a time period when a condition frequently manifesting as spasticity and slurred speech led people to make negative assumptions about the intelligence or stability of individuals with cerebral palsy. Bartlett doesn't neglect to mention important background on early twentieth-century eugenics in the U.S. It was in full swing when Eigner was born, in 1927, and people like Eigner (and Bartlett) were frequently segregated into institutions, where neglect and abuse were common. Bartlett also recognizes that Eigner's family, unlike many families at this time, had the means to keep him out of such places and to provide for his intellectual and writerly development—even if their hope was that he might parlay his interests into writing greeting card verse. It was Eigner brother Richard's idea, which Eigner precociously took to heart, for him to be a "man of letters."

Bartlett demonstrates that, although Eigner did not want to identify or be identified primarily as "disabled," he was nonetheless animated by some of the concepts commonly discussed today, as is seen in his wariness of being used for "inspiration porn" when approached to be the subject of a documentary. After Creeley had sent a copy of Eigner's 1953 chapbook to the aging modernist poet William Carlos Williams, Williams wrote to Creeley what Eigner's friends saw as praise of his style. But Eigner bristled at Williams' comment that reading the work evoked a sense of "relaxation in the face of the world—of which indeed he [Eigner] seems scarcely conscious that it exists." When the passage was to be used to promote Eigner's work, that portion was struck out at his insistence.

The family lived near the shore, but access to the closest beach was poor for Eigner due to the terrain. The bigger the young Eigner got, the less able his mother was to take him after he outgrew the straw carriage they used to transport him him there. Wheelchairs weren't sophisticated or commonplace during Eigner's childhood, though when he relocated to the West Coast at midlife, he gradually adjusted to a power chair that he used to get around in the relatively accessible Berkeley area. For much of his adult life, however, he worked in a glass-enclosed front room of the Swampscott home. As Bartlett shows through several examples of poems (all rendered in a typewriter front to capture the Eigner's compositional process), even though he couldn't readily get to the beach, his poems abound in references to the weather, to nature—to what he observed from his workspace. "References" is not the right word for what became his treatment of his surroundings; rather, he chose words and phrases that seemed at once to embody raw, immediate perceptions and to themselves claim existence in the world of the page—not as representations or symbols or metaphors, but as matter. Over time, he came to eschew adjectives and adverbs; he avoided building up the kind of argument that, once recognized by a reader, risked dissolving the thing-ness of the words on the page.

In addition to impacting his speech, which was difficult to understand, Eigner's cerebral palsy manifested in what he referred to as his "wild" left side. In an interview with Marian Kindel published in 1982, Eigner said, "My left side was wild; arms and legs, until a few weeks after my 35th birthday in '62. I had cryosurgery that tamed and numbed it." Bartlett gives her readers room to consider what that might have to do with his movement away from the left margin, much as she gives them space to consider how muscular spasticity might have to do with the fragmentation of Eigner's syntax. All of these dots are there for the student of Eigner's poetry to connect, but she is also careful not to reduce Eigner's poetic choices and style to the facticity of his body. It's a fine line to keep to. One way that she maintains it is by framing some of the atypical aspects of his embodiment as "tools" instead of seizing on an essentialist correspondence between Eigner's CP traits and aspects of his style. For instance, in naming Olson as Eigner's paramount influence, she observes that Olson's embodied life—as a 6' 7" "giant" who dealt with alcoholism, emphysema, and thyroid issues—was also likely a factor in his poetics—a poetics of breath, of wandering. "It was through their conditions that both poets used their bodies as poetic tools to create new form," Bartlett says, reminding us that all bodies, normative and nonnormative, play into the making of art, literary or otherwise. It is all about an openness to what happens that remains open and searching, like a thought not yet embalmed into belief—a mindset that would seem to be enforced in the following lines from Eigner's poem, "The Fine Life," used to open Chapter 15 of *The Sustaining Air*:

> when you search the
>
> spontaneous thing
>
> objects
>
> the belief
>
> shuts the air

Black Lazarus: Etheridge Knight, 1931–1991: an Appreciation and Memoir

Mark Pawlak

> *I died in Korea from a shrapnel wound, and narcotics resurrected me. I died in 1960 from a prison sentence and poetry brought me back to life.*
> —Etheridge Knight

Denise Levertov and Etheridge Knight, among post-WW II American poets, exerted the most influence on my early development as a writer. Denise as mentor; Etheridge as the poet whose work I tried most to emulate. They were the reference points by which I fixed my bearings as I sought to discover my way to become a poet. Levertov was for me the exemplar of the written literary tradition in poetry, in which I was then schooling myself under her tutelage; in Etheridge Knight, I found an outstanding practitioner of the oral tradition.

Denise taught me just about everything I know about the craft of poetry. She guided and encouraged me. I learned from her how to fashion language, how to live and work productively as a poet, how to function as a "poet in the world." But I found that her own poems, accomplishments which I was in awe of, and which informed, instructed, enriched my life, did not however serve me as models as I searched for my own unique voice. Our backgrounds, education, and experiences were too different. What her poems could not afford me as examples to follow, Etheridge's poems did.

It's fair to ask what a young white man, whose grandparents were immigrants from Poland, could think he had in common with an older black man, whose ancestors were brought here in chains from Africa and forced to live in servility for generations? I was born into a working class family and grew up in public housing in the northern industrial city of Buffalo, while Etheridge Knight was born into a poor, rural black family in Mississippi and grew up partly in Indianapolis. I went to college on a scholarship, obtaining my degree from a prestigious institution of higher learning, which allowed me to avoid the military draft during the Vietnam War; Etheridge in contrast, enlisted and serving in Korean, where he was wounded, later to become a junkie, addicted to the drugs administered to him for relief of his pain.

I was a late convert to poetry, which I read intensively and wrote for the first time behind the gray walls of the Massachusetts Institute of Technology. He first studied and wrote poetry behind the walls of the Indiana State Prison, serving time for armed robbery. But despite these differences, I intuited from Etheridge's poems that we shared one common bond: each of us came to the making of poems, the written literary tradition of the middle and upper classes, from a social underclass and culture where oral traditions held sway.

I grew up in a household largely absent of books. What, in my childhood, substituted for the fairy tales of Hans Christian Anderson and the Brothers Grimm, for the illustrated stories of Beatrice Potter, for *A Child's Garden of Verses,* were the stories told me by my mother and grandmother about life in the Old Country, the passage in steerage to America, the discrimination my immigrant forebears suffered while they struggled to find work and make a new life in this country.

In high school, and later college, I read the anthologized classics of American literature. The survey courses I was obliged to take were designed to inoculate me with the germ of "American" culture. But at the time I proved immune to it largely because I could not find a semblance of myself, or of life in America as I knew it, reflected in what I read; and English literature, which I was also required to study, seemed even more remote. Years later, when Denise Levertov encouraged me to make poems out of what I knew best, I set to writing about my cultural heritage as a third generation Polish-American, about life in the public housing project where I grew up, about what I had observed in neighborhoods where the men folk worked in steel mills, auto factories and railroad yards, while their wives kept house and minded their broods of unruly kids.

Etheridge Knight provided me a model of how as a poet I might successfully bridge the two traditions: the predominantly oral one that was my inheritance and the written literary one that I strove to become accomplished in. I particularly admired him for writing vernacular poems, in which the language was not the American idiom of the college educated, but the speech of poor and working people. The language of his poems was analogous to that which I had heard spoken on street corners and in barrooms, in housing project courtyards and neighbors' kitchens, at funeral parlor wakes and union picnics. His poems served me as an admonition to listen attentively to the speech of my own people: my immediate family, relatives, neighbors; to observe their lives and environment; to make poems out of their struggles, small triumphs, frustrations, and aspirations.

I first encountered Etheridge Knight's poems in 1969. At the time, I was working long hours in an MIT laboratory to complete research for my physics thesis, while also studying poetry with Denise Levertov, who was the Institute's writer-in- residence. Among the duties of her position, Denise hosted several poetry readings on campus. These were the first readings I ever attended, given by contemporary poets she admired, among them Galway Kinnell.

An imposing, broad-shouldered man with chiseled features, Kennell stood, I remember, before the audience in a large room at the MIT student center and recited his poems from memory. This impressed the hell out of me at the time. Midway through his program, he introduced a selection of poems by Etheridge Knight, whom he described as an important Afro-American poet, too little known by poetry audiences, who was then currently, serving a prison sentence somewhere in the mid-west. I cannot now recall whether Kinnell also recited Etheridge's poems from memory, as he had his own, or simply read them aloud, but I do remember being powerfully moved by the language and imagery of "He Sees Through Stone" and "The Idea of Ancestry." Those two poems, even more than Kennell's own, struck a deep chord in me.

People and events that year conspired to change the course of my life from a future of doing basic physics research under Defense Department sponsorship to a very different one of teaching young people and writing poetry. The Vietnam War and anti-war protests, the debate that raged on campus about the ethics of weapons research at MIT, the intoxicating late 1960s counterculture that permeated the air I breathed whenever I ventured outside the Institute's walls, and, not the least, Denise Levertov herself, poet and political activist, all played a role in my decision to abandon physics. The next few years, while I struggled to make my way in the world as a fledgling teacher and poet, Etheridge Knights' first slender volume, *Poems from Prison,* published by Broadside Press, was an essential text for me. It was one of the two or three books that always had a place in my backpack.

For most of the next decade I taught sciences, mathematics, and creative writing at The Group School in Cambridge, an alternative high school I had a hand in starting, which served teenagers from poor and working-class families exclusively. There I used *Poems from Prison* as one of my primary texts, along with the anthology of prison writing Etheridge had edited; later, when it was published, I added *Belly Songs* to the reading list. My students were public school dropouts, who for the most part lived in the city's housing projects. Many of them had police records. Some were on probation; others had done time, or were on release from juvenile prison for crimes ranging from breaking and entering to car theft to assault. Most of them read little, seldom if ever poems. But when they heard Etheridge Knight's poems read, they responded enthusiastically. He spoke about things they knew in a voice they recognized as "of the street."

The eldest of my first Group School students were only four or five years my junior. I looked on them as younger brothers and sisters, because their lives held many parallels with my own; but there were significant differences between us too. The projects they lived in were more run down than the one I grew up in, and life offered them less promise of escape from the condition of enduring poverty. As their teacher, I introduced them to some of the essential skills I acquired in college. I showed them how to express themselves clearly, how to quantify things and how to observes the world around them, formulate and test hypothesis, and draw conclusions. They reciprocated by sharing their lives with me; in doing so they helped me to remember, re-experience and to analyze in a new light my own childhood and adolescence. My Group School students were my inspiration to write the poems that became *The Buffalo Sequence,* my first poetry collection (Copper Canyon Press, 1977), composed during lunch hours at a coffee shop around the corner.

Rereading Etheridge's poems with these students gave me new insights into his work. They understood as perfectly obvious the metaphor that had wide currency at the time, put forward by the Black Panthers, among others. It described Amerika (spelled with a "k" taken from Klu Klux Klan) as a police state/prison in which blacks, specifically, and poor people generally, were incarcerated. This metaphor was elaborated to include then President Richard Nixon and FBI Director J. Edgar Hoover as the prison wardens, and local and state police forces, and the National Guard in the role of prison guards. With but a short leap of the imagination, the descriptions of prison life in Etheridge Knights' poems, served my students as chronicles of their lives, too. They recognized in the "old black one / who sits under prison skies ..." ("He Sees Through Stone") the long-time housing-project residents wise with years, who sat in their courtyards closed in by towering brick walls, the perimeters patrolled nightly by police cruisers. They too had their "Doer[s] of things [they] dreamed of doing, but could not bring [themselves] to do. ... Young men they had raised to the stature of neighborhood heroes, who as they stood helplessly by, were brought low by authority of the night stick, hand cuffs, service revolver ... and judges' gavel. They knew many Flukums, who "couldn't stand the strain ... / wanted inner and outer order, so / ... joined the army where U.S. Manuals made / everything plain— even how to button his shirt / and how to kill the yellow men." And they had watched their own or their friends' sisters "disappear in the dark streets / to whistle and to smile at the johns." When I read Etheridge's poems aloud they would nod their heads approvingly, as if to say "Right on! Tell it like it is."

It wasn't until 1976 that I first had the opportunity to hear Etheridge recite his poems and to meet him in person. This was at Clark University, in Worcester, Massachusetts, the city where I was doing poetry-in-the-schools, while on sabbatical from The Group School.

Hearing Etheridge *say* his poems aloud was a revelation; until that evening I didn't fully appreciate the extent to which he fashioned them primarily to be spoken. It made me realize that the poem on the printed page was a transcription of an oral entity he had composed in his head to be spoken and heard, and only secondarily to be written down, read. All poetry originates in the urgent need to speak and communicate, but that evening I understood what I had only partially intuited from his poems on the page, that, for Etheridge, the impetus to make poems was an urgent need he had to communicate via the *spoken* word. And this realization left me to marvel more than ever at how effectively his fashioned speech worked on the printed page, too. In the years following that first reading, I had the good fortune to hear Etheridge say his poems aloud many times in both public and private settings; each occasion was a moving, memorable one.

I use the term "poetry reading" guardedly when talking about Etheridge's performances. The image of him standing before a lectern, reading aloud from typescript or an open book is incongruous; and to describe what he did as recitation from memory has connotations a shade too literary. He preferred to describe his unique manner of intoning poems as "saying" poems. "Now I'm going to say a poem ..." was typically how he would begin; and to hear Etheridge "say" his poems was to experience a kind of performance art rooted in the oral folk tradition of African Americans.

Etheridge would use the available table or lectern as a place to rest his books and manuscripts; then, as he began to say the poem, he would step away from it toward the open stage, where he had free range to move and an unobstructed view of the audience and they of him. Etheridge used his body as an expressive instrument, illustrating his poems with movement and gesture in a natural, improvisational manner. There was nothing self-consciously theatrical about his stage presence; he didn't 'act' the poem out, nor did he intone it in such a way as to add emphasis solely for dramatic effect. Once into it, Etheridge would be in constant motion, pacing as he declaimed, pounding out with his footfalls the measure of his speech. One memorable evening I heard him recite "Ilu The Talking Drum" to such accompaniment: his feet stomping out the rhythms on the floorboards: "kadoom, kadoom doom, kadoom doom doom...."

Etheridge had many occasions to say his poems on college campuses, in public libraries, at academic conferences. They were paying gigs after all, sometimes paying very well, and he always needed money; but his natural preference went a different way. He was more at home saying his poems to an audience gathered in a neighborhood community center situated in the heart of an urban ghetto, or on a street corner among a group of idle men trading "toasts," or holding forth in the back corner of a crowded barroom—such as at Circe's Bar in Worcester, where for a time in the late 1970s, he presided over the Worcester Free People's Workshop.

His conception of poetry was as a form of individual expression among "free" people. He subscribed to the "What's alive is poetry, the rest is literature" school of poetics. To make poems designed for scholarly exegesis and classroom discussion was never his intention. He believed in a democratically pluralistic poetry in opposition to elitist aestheticism. On his forays into the academic world, he frequently performed the role of a subversive, one with a populist political vision. His very presence, saying his poems, served to bring the life of the street outside into the classroom or lecture hall. He knew this and took pleasure in the role. He liked to stir things up and provoke argument, which he often did with the mischievous glee of an adolescent cut-up, masterfully undermining the teacher's authority.

Etheridge spiced his reading programs with jokes and anecdotes, meant to evoke wry smiles and laughter, with folk parables and spontaneous commentary. He teased and chided audiences to respond. He had an Orwellian ear for the abuses of language, especially by politicians, and liked to share the latest examples that had caught his attention on TV news or in the newspaper, offering audiences his impromptu personal analysis of government deception and political cynicism. As Etheridge was fond of saying, he was born with a "finely tuned bullshit detector."

The point of his jokes and parables, as frequently the point in his poems, was to present race as the central issue of life in America. Ironically, the occasions he was afforded to do this mostly took place before white audiences on college campuses. With remarkable generosity of spirit, but not without a hint of irony, Etheridge shared with listeners his vision of America as seen through the eyes of a black man who grew up poor, had served time in prison; whose survival depended upon his wits and goodwill toward others.

An Etheridge Knight poetry reading was a mix of performance art, entertainment, and instruction. In this regard, he was a precursor of popular rap groups such as Run DMC, who describe their Hip-Hop genre as "edutainment." (Rap, Etheridge liked to point, out draws upon the same tradition of African American street poetry as his own poems: shine, playing "the dozens," toasts …) For college audiences brought up on textbook examples of poetry, Etheridge's work on the page, but especially heard spoken aloud, was a lesson in the narrowness of culturally determined academic definitions. Etheridge expanded the boundaries and enriched the possibilities of what is considered poetry by bridging the oral and written traditions. He served as a forceful reminder that poetry had its origins in the art of the spoken word.

2.

I got to know Etheridge Knight as friend by virtue of the fact we were both present on the Worcester poetry scene at the same time. Soon after his Clark reading, Etheridge took up with Charlene Amorelli, a Worcester native, and settled there for several years. They eventually got married and had a son, Zak. For my part, after my two-year residency ended, I returned to The Group School, but stayed in close contact with the friends I'd made in Worcester, all of them poets: Mary Bonina, Mary Fell, Chris Gilbert, and Fran Quinn … even though I lived an hour drive away in Cambridge.

The poetry community there, driven by the dynamo of the Worcester County Poetry Association, was remarkably active for a city its size. It was also very intimate, everyone knew everyone else; each local poet had the opportunity to meet each new visiting poet who passed through town; and almost all took part, at one time or another, in the Free People's Poetry Workshop, which Etheridge had established and led while he lived there. Sharing the same small circle of friends, Etheridge and I soon became friends also; and that friendship grew stronger toward the end of his Worcester tenure when I started dating Mary Bonina and visited the city on a more frequent basis. Mary, a poet and community activist, was a friend of Charlene's and prominent in the Free People's Workshop; in fact, when Etheridge and Charlene ultimately left Worcester for Memphis, it was Mary along with Chris Gilbert who assumed leadership of the ongoing workshop. (Chris later won the 1983 Academy of American Poets' Walt Whitman Award for his first book *Across The Mutual Landscape;* he died at 58 in 2007.)

3.

> I been confused, fucked up, scared, phony
> And jive
> To a whole lot of people …
> Haven't you?
>
> In one way or another?
>
> —"Cop-out Session"

Honesty and sometimes brutal frankness were traits Etheridge had in abundant supply; these he applied unsparingly to himself as to others. That he had many faults, he freely admitted, and he didn't shy from cataloging them, privately to friends, publicly in poems such as "Cop-Out Session" and the sarcastic "Welcome Back, Mr. Knight: Love of My Life." After his release from the penitentiary, Etheridge remained a prisoner of his addictions, against which he struggled desperately. When they got the better of him, when he bottomed out, he often hurt friends and loved ones, those he cared most dearly about. But it is a testament to his character that later, after he had recovered, he was able to make it up to them. His sincerity, winning personality and generosity of spirit would shine through once again and gain him forgiveness.

It was a mark of his unguarded vulnerability that Etheridge invited others to criticize his behavior and attitudes whenever they found fault. This characteristic, combined with his frequent public self-admonishments gave the impression that he hid nothing of himself from public view, that the private and public Etheridge Knight, the man, and the persona were one and the same.

It is only now, after his death that I've come to question this perception of him and to wonder how well I really knew the private man. Now, when I think back on all the occasions when I spent time with him, I realize that we were rarely alone but almost always in the company of friends and fellow poets. Etheridge liked to surround himself with people, and we were attracted to him as moths to the source of brightest illumination. I was invariably left with the feeling on each of these occasions that I had just had a private audience with Etheridge, despite the presence of others; and I now suspect that every person who spent time in his company was left with much the same feeling.

I can remember only one time when I glimpsed another, more private side of Etheridge. The occasion was a picnic one sunny summer day. Etheridge, Charlene, Karl, her son from a previous marriage, and their infant son Zak in one car; Mary (we were still dating then, not yet living together, our marriage several years off), my son Andrai, then four years old, and myself in another car, all drove to Bolton Dam State Park south of Worcester. For once, Etheridge wasn't at the center of a crowd of poets proclaiming, extemporizing; instead, he was a doting father and husband, relaxed, enjoying the company of his family and friends.

There was nothing particularly memorable about our conversations that day. We did the ordinary things people who are picnicking do. We threw Frisbees and played softball with the two older boys. We grilled hot dogs and hamburgers, ate potato salad, munched on chips and drank beer. We stretched out on the sand. The sun beamed down on us. We drank more beer and rapped about this and that while keeping watch over on Andrai and Karl, wading in the pond, and on baby Zak seated at the water's edge, patting the waves that lapped at his feet. Etheridge seemed a happy man that day; the demons that haunted him kept at bay.

I didn't see Etheridge for the next several years, having moved back to Cambridge with Mary. Mutual friends among the Worcester poets, kept us informed about Etheridge's whereabouts and doings. We learned that in the interim, he and Charlene had moved to Memphis, where their marriage foundered. She returned to Worcester. Based on reports we heard, Etheridge kept on the move, never settling in one place for very long. Etheridge became obsessed about access to his son

Zak after the breakup. He wanted to maintain a relationship with him, to visit him whenever he was giving a reading in the area, but Charlene resisted, and the more she did so, the stronger his obsession became.

We would get unexpected phone calls from Etheridge during this time, at all hours of the night. They were characterized by a moment of silence on the other end of the line until Etheridge ascertained he had dialed the right number, gotten the right person; then his unmistakable voice would boom out the receiver, "Hey, brother Mark!" or "Hey, Mary Bo-ni-na!" He'd be calling from Memphis, Indianapolis, and Philadelphia ... wherever he might be and be thinking about Charlene and Zak. He'd be holed up in a room somewhere, alone, drunk or high, hungry for talk and for news of friends; above all hoping for a fresh scrap of information about Charlene and Zak. It was Mary he would want to talk with more than me, their friendship-predated mine, ran deeper; and after all, Mary had been Charlene's friend. Etheridge would invariably turn the conversation to the subject of Zak. Did Mary think there was a prospect that Charlene would relent and allowing him to visit his son, he'd ask? I didn't seem to matter to Etheridge that Mary was no longer living in Worcester, hadn't spoken to Charlene in several years and that anything she did know about her, or her intentions regarding him, was secondhand knowledge.

Sometime in the mid-1980s Etheridge turned up unexpectedly in Roxbury, where he informed us—another phone call in the night—he was living in a halfway house. Boston was close enough to Worcester without being too close. He told us he was intent on rehabilitating himself, kicking his drug and alcohol habits and winning back Charlene's favor so that she might allow him to visit Zak whenever he wished. We saw Etheridge no more than a half-a-dozen times while he was living in Roxbury, then he dropped from sight. again

The next time Etheridge resurfaced in Boston, was in the company of my old friend, poet Elizabeth McKim. Mary and I saw a lot of the two of them during the late 1980s; although, again, rarely in what one could call intimate settings, just the four of us. Typically, the occasion was a gathering of mutual friends, a poetry reading, or a benefit for a political cause. It was a period of relative stability and happiness for Etheridge. He and Elizabeth were a good match, their relationship appeared to be a mutually nurturing one, they seemed happy.

Etheridge nevertheless continued to move about frequently during this time. He always had to struggle to make a living as a poet and he often depended on the generosity and advocacy of well-placed friends.

His job opportunities in Boston were severely limited, when he got a poetry gig in another city, off he went. Sometimes, when down on his luck, he'd go off to Yaddo for an extended stay. Then, when he returned to town, there would be a gathering of friends and poets orchestrated by Elizabeth.

There was a predictable pattern to these get-togethers. First there would be a lengthy period of convivial mingling, eating, and drinking, as guests arrived, got introduced or reacquainted. At some point, everyone would gather in the living room and get comfortable. The sofa and all available chairs would be occupied, people would be seated on the floor, others standing ... then, an impromptu Free People's Poetry Workshop would commence, with Etheridge at the center of things.

One never attended these affairs without bringing along a poem to recite, a song to sing, an instrument to play, a joke, parable, or anecdote to tell. It didn't matter whether you composed it or brought a passage written by someone else to read. The tone of these gatherings, set by Etheridge himself, was always one of inclusiveness; and they weren't restricted to only artists. The expectation was simply that you'd bring something you felt was an expression of yourself to share. Everyone was expected to participate in whatever way she or he felt comfortable; and usually most everyone present did get into it.

Etheridge held court at these events, in part by force of personality, in part because seeing him was the occasion for getting together. He would talk about his recent travels, tell anecdotes about poets he'd encountered, and share news and gossip of friends he'd seen. He'd expound on the significance of some detail in the news that had captured his attention; he'd talk politics, pick apart a recent odious instance of government doublespeak; but the focus of the evening would always turn to personal expression. Etheridge would begin; he'd recite a new poem he'd composed, and then would prod others to do their thing. As each took his/her turn, it was left for Etheridge to pass judgment. Following the saying of a poem, the singing of a song, the performance of a piece of music or a dance, he'd nod his approval; say, "Uh huh, uh huh;" or utter, "I hear you." His remarks, it was understood, were meant was not a commentary on the craft or aesthetics but on the accuracy of the perceptions, the forthrightness and sincerity of what had been shared. A good time was always had on these occasions, but something more, too: one was left with a feeling of communion, a sense that, through Etheridge's agency, your circle of like-thinking friends had just been enlarged, the bonds strengthened.

4. Last Visit

Like most other summonses from Etheridge, the last came with no forewarning: one late Thursday afternoon in mid-December (1990) I got a phone call from Elizabeth. The two of them were in town for several days, she informed me; having a few friends over that evening to her Brookline apartment. Was there any chance Mary and I might drop by too, she asked? "Etheridge very much wants to see you."

The summer before, Fran Quinn had delivered the news that Etheridge had been diagnosed with lung cancer and that doctors had given him no more than a year to live. After learning that, I'd harbored the fear that I would never see Eth alive again, as he was no longer living in Boston, hadn't been for more than a year, but was back among his family in Indianapolis (where Elizabeth had gone, too, after she learned of the diagnosis, to be with him, to help nurse him). Fran had called to invite us to Worcester, where Etheridge had surfaced to visit his son Zak. But we couldn't make it there on short notice; that's when Fran deliver the bad news. Because of Etheridge's cancer diagnosis, Charlene, had relented, allowing visits Zak, now twelve years old.

This time, November, when Elizabeth called, I was determined not to miss what might very likely be my last opportunity to see Etheridge. "We'll have to come by late," I told Elizabeth. "Mary won't be home from work before 9:30 PM." "No, that won't work out," she responded. "Etheridge will be too tired by then; he doesn't have much stamina." Then, Etheridge got on the phone. He suggested that we drive up to Peabody on the weekend, as he would be there all of Saturday and most of Sunday, alone in a hotel room, while Elizabeth was busy leading a poetry workshop for North Shore teachers (the reason for the trip East). Left unspoken, but nevertheless perfectly clear in talking to him, was that Etheridge wanted to see us one last time to say "goodbye" in person. And, as if further incentive might be needed, he added that Chris Gilbert was planning to drive up on Sunday. We could visit then, he said, and see Chris, too.

Little of Etheridge's characteristic vitality came across over the telephone. His voice sounded weak, his words slurred. I'd never had any difficulty understanding his southern drawl in face-to-face conversation, but occasionally, over the telephone, if his speech was slurred from drinking, I did have to ask Etheridge to repeat things and then I needed to listen closely.

403

Driving north to Peabody late Sunday morning, Mary and I shared our apprehensions. We feared the frail ghost of Etheridge's former self would greet us. We didn't look forward to finding this old friend, who'd always been such a vital, stimulating presence in our lives, sapped of strength, his body ravaged by cancer.

Our destination was a Marriott Hotel on the edge of the sprawling Liberty Tree Mall in Peabody, just off route 128, "America's Technology Highway." To get to it from the exit, we had the cross the mall parking lot, a vast expanse of asphalt, eerily vacant that Sunday morning during the Christmas shopping season.

Etheridge greeted us at the door of his third-floor room, a smoldering cigarette in hand. He was alone. Elizabeth had already gone off to her gig. It was a small rectangular box of a room, fitted with two twin beds, a bureau, night tables, desk and chair, and an armchair. Magazines, newspapers, a shirt, among other things were strewn about on the bed nearest the door, as was Etheridge's cloth book bag, with papers spilling from it, and a hardbound copy of *Bloods,* the recently published collection of oral histories by black Vietnam vets. On the bureau stood a bottle of red wine, three quarters empty, a glass tumbler that showed signs of use, and an assortment of pills in vials. The room's one window, set in the far wall opposite the door, offered a view of the mall and parking lots. Etheridge sat down in the armchair to the right of it, beside the far bed. He faced the large color television, mounted on the wall in the corner of the room to the other side of the window. Mary took the one other chair, and I made myself comfortable on the edge of the bed nearest the door.

The TV was on when we entered the room, volume up loud, tuned to *Face the Nation.* Etheridge fumbled with the remote, muttering about the "politicians telling lies," as he tried to turn it down. It took him three tries before he finally succeeded. He didn't turn the TV off but kept it playing quietly in the background throughout our entire visit, leaving it on even when we went downstairs for an hour to the dining room for some lunch.

Right off, Mary asked Etheridge how he was doing. "I'm in pain all the time," was his answer. "I have to take morphine and several other painkillers. It's ironic," he said. "The doctors now give me prescriptions for the same drugs I used to steal." He admitted that he continued to drink—anything, he said, to dull the pain. He told us, Saturday had been a bad day; he was left alone in the room for most it, and he'd drunk too much. Etheridge said, "I get scared, you know?" His eyes had that glazed, inward-turned look I've come to associate with people suffering acute, chronic pain.

On the drive up from Cambridge, I'd been haunted by the memory Ron Schreiber's lover John MacDonald, slowly dying of AIDS in their apartment around the corner from ours; the many months he lay in bed unable to move, his flesh gradually withering away until he was skeletal. But although Etheridge appeared to have lost weight, he looked better than I had anticipated. It showed in his face, neck, and legs: thin but not gaunt, in contrast to his barrel chest and slightly swollen belly.

Etheridge gave us a chronology of his illness: He'd had a case of the flu, which lasted throughout the previous spring. He'd begun to think he might once again have pneumonia. This prompted him to get a chest x-ray done, which revealed the cancer lodged in both his lungs. It had since metastasized in his liver, accounting for the abdominal swelling. "I'd quit smoking and drinking if I wasn't so weak," he said apologetically. "But to do that now, I'd need to go into a detox center." He had, indeed, pressed his doctor to admit him to a detox program, he told us, so that under supervision he might quit his bad habits and perhaps prolong his life, but the doctor had refused him, saying, "What would be the point, now!"

Etheridge always spoke disdainfully of the medical profession— "jive-assed doctors," he called them. He'd spent a lot of time over the years seeking their attention in VA hospitals and clinics, and he felt he'd suffered many abuses at their hands. (Elizabeth would remark months later after his death, sifting through her file of letters from Etheridge, that she was surprised to find so many had been addressed to her from detox centers or half-way houses.) And now Etheridge was dependent once again on the profession for his treatment and medications; but he told us with a gleam in his eyes, he was hedging his bets by also using "alternative" approaches to combat his cancer. And he spoke glowingly about the herbal infusion he was presently taking.

Ever the storyteller, Etheridge relished the fact that this remedy had a tale that went with it: A chemist had slipped and fallen while mountain climbing. Saved miraculously from certain death by an outcropping of rocks, the man vowed he would, for the remainder of his life, devote his talents to benefit humankind. The herbal concoction, with the consistency of molasses that Etheridge was now imbibing, was a result of the chemist's research. It increases oxygenation of the blood, Eth told us, and gave him strength—the only thing that did. But, he complained, his supply was presently used up, which accounted, he said, for the weakened state we found him in.

This was the first occasion Mary and I had had to see Etheridge in about a year and a half. After a period of what had appeared to us to be stability, living in Brookline with Elizabeth, Etheridge began to abuse drugs again and bottomed out. This led to their break-up, with Etheridge leaving town. Until the call from Fran Quinn the past summer, our knowledge of Etheridge's doings had come through Elizabeth, who, despite her anger and hurt, had continued to monitor his whereabouts via mutual friends and acquaintances. She would call us from time to time with reports: He was living in Philadelphia; then in New York City; then back in Philly, where he was hit by a car and hospitalized for months; ultimately, he got himself transferred to a VA hospital in Indianapolis, where his mother and sister lived.

Visits with Etheridge always included listening to him tell "war stories," of which he had an ample supply. This visit was no exception. He proceeded to relate the gory details of his accident: He was crossing a street in Philly when a car, driven by a teenager, turned the corner and barreled down on him at high speed. "For once, I wasn't drunk or high," he professed. "The kid looked at me; I looked back at him…. We both knew he was going to hit me. You know how they say your whole life passes before you in those situations. Well," Etheridge went on, "that wasn't the case with me. I was PISSED! I looked that kid dead in the eye. I only wished I had a gun at that moment. I was so-o-o-o mad." The car knocked him down, he told us, and dragged him some distance. As a result, his left leg was badly mangled below the knee, with much of the skin scraped off, the flesh torn.

The horrors of his tale continued throughout the four months of his hospitalization, under VA "care." He was given one skin graft that didn't take because an infection set in, an infection, which lasted for months, resistant to antibiotic treatment. In the end it was the physical therapist, who administered his daily whirlpool baths at the Indianapolis VA hospital, who cured him.

Etheridge delighted in this irony. A lowly female technician, using what in his eyes amounted to a folk remedy, cured the infection that had defeated every effort of the scientifically-trained, "jive-ass," male doctors. Etheridge was eventually given a second skin graft, which took this time. "It looks pretty mean," he said, and proceeded without a moment's hesitation to show us, drawing up his pant leg, pulling down his sock, and rolling up his thermal legging. (He wore thermal underwear in that hot stuffy hotel room!) Always one to provoke a reaction in his audience, Etheridge looked us each in the eye. He seemed to take morbid pleasure in our revulsion. His leg was a grisly looking mass of scar tissue. I quickly looked away.

Etheridge went on to tell us he was presently putting his affairs in order. He described the unpleasant task of making up a will. This he was able to accomplish, he said, only with badgering and encouragement from Elizabeth, and with the aid of a lawyer. Fran Quinn would be his literary executor. "Fran likes to do that kind of thing," he said. Then he talked at length about his children.

Squaring accounts with all the people whose love and friendship had given special meaning to his life was, Etheridge indicated, his chief concern right then; and his own children topped the list. He reported with obvious satisfaction that things had gone well between him and Zak the past summer; and he was pleased that now his 20-year-old son, Bambata, and 22-year- old daughter, Tandi, the offspring of his marriage to Mary McAnally, had both come to Indianapolis to be near him. Etheridge told us with pride that he had been instrumental in getting Bambata, a midshipman in the Navy, reassigned from the Persian Gulf to a National Guard base in Indianapolis, using his terminal illness as the pretext. By Etheridge's account, his son was very grateful to the "old man" for extricating him from "Operation Desert Shield" and the then imminent war in that far corner of the world.

Company and conversation seemed to revive Etheridge's spirits. His sense of irony grew sharper, the familiar mischievous sparkle returned to his eyes; although, from time to time, a wave of pain or fatigue would wash over him and the glint would momentarily fade.

Etheridge suggested we go downstairs to the dining room for a bite to eat; he was hungry. Once seated there, his foremost concern, after glancing at the cafe menu which listed finger foods, soups, and wine, was whether he could order hard liquor. He had a hankering for a glass of vodka and orange juice. "I'm a vodka drinker," he informed us, "I drink wine if I have to, but it gives me a sour stomach." (I'd noticed a half-empty pint bottle of Smirnoff's upstairs in his hotel bathroom. This surprised me, as I remembered him always with a beer can in his hand.)

Etheridge was anxious that the front desk knows our whereabouts in the event Chris Gilbert should call or arrive while we were out of the room. Armed with assurances they would be on the lookout for Chris, and with a plate of food and a drink on the table before him, Etheridge settled into relaxed conversation again. But, when Chris hadn't shown up after about an hour, he again showed concern. He wondered out loud whether Elizabeth had given the wrong highway exit and Chris was now lost. Just then Chris stepped into the hotel lobby, visible from where we sat. "Chris!" Etheridge shouted excitedly, "We just conjured you up!"

Chris joined us in the dining room, where we remained to eat and talk for a while longer. It had been about two years since either Mary, or I had seen him. He had since moved to Providence; we had a lot to catch each other up on, news and gossip to share. When Etheridge grew weary of sitting in the lounge, we all returned upstairs to his room, where we talked languorously through the rest of the afternoon, touching on many topics.

Etheridge took up the subject of people who had been especially important to him as mentors, colleagues, friends: Dudley Randall, of Broadside Press, his first publisher, whom he had recently visited; Gwendolyn Brooks, who encouraged him to write in prison, and his former wife Sonia Sanchez, of whom he said, "We stay in touch" … and he mentioned running into Audre Lorde at a poetry conference recently.

Next, Etheridge expounded on Robert Bly and the men's consciousness movement, a familiar topic of conversation between Mary and him, as they had both attended several of Bly's Great Mother conferences back in the 1970s. Chris then offered his observations of the Great Father conference he had recently attended in Minnesota. Etheridge chimed in that he sometimes worried about his old friend Robert's absorption with the cause of men's liberation. "I warned him not to get on a mission," Etheridge said. "It's not good for a poet; it narrows your vision." For emphasis, Etheridge pressed the flattened palms of his hands to either side of his face, suggesting blinders, and added: "You lose perspective."

Something on the television, still audible above our lively banter, sparked Etheridge to talk about the earthquake prediction for the Midwest an astrologer had made not long ago. He was relieved this prognostication hadn't come to pass, but said he felt sorry for the people he knew who had picked up and left Indianapolis for fear of it. He and Elizabeth had given serious thought to fleeing themselves, he admitted. Living on the 23rd floor of a high-rise housing project had made them both uneasy. A structure built specifically to house poor people, he chuckled wryly, didn't inspire much confidence in its soundness.

Insecurities about the firmament, superstitions, mythology ... one topic led to another. We soon found ourselves talking about the persisting popular belief in UFOs. Etheridge remarked: "It's *all* folklore, you know. It's a living thing—the legends, the stories that people say. All those academic folklorists I met in Pennsylvania, they just think folklore happened in the past—what people thought, talked about, made stories about fifty years ago. They don't see it still happening all around them today."

Chris, drawing on his training as a psychologist, interrupted Etheridge at one point to praise his slow, thoughtful manner of speaking. "Thinking out loud" was how he described it. Etheridge savored each word, Chris said, choosing with precision the apt phrase to characterize a situation. And Chris gave as example the expression "sidled away," which Etheridge had just used in an anecdote about a slimy local politician trying to extricate himself from a potentially embarrassing situation.

Etheridge deflected Chris' praise with a laugh, noting that some people find his southern drawl hard to understand. Northerners, he said, were always impatient with the slow, deliberate manner in way he formulated his thoughts. "They're always trying to finish my sentence for me," he said. "Even Elizabeth gets impatient with what I'm getting to saying; but" he chuckled, "I just tell her she's got to wait."

At various times throughout the afternoon, Etheridge mentioned recent honors, which had been bestowed on him and tributes paid him by his fellow poets. Among these he ranked high the reading he'd had the privilege to deliver at the Library of Congress. Now, he spoke of another, which had taken place in Indianapolis only months ago and had special meaning for him: Etheridge had received his bachelor of arts degree from Martin Center College, and in the same ceremony was named the college's first poet laureate.

Over a period of years, with frequent interruptions, Etheridge had taken classes at the small liberal arts college situated in his mother's Eastside Indianapolis neighborhood, at the same time as he was leading a poetry workshop there—one of his legendary Free Peoples' Workshops. To have at last earned a college degree, to have had his mother and sister in the audience when it was bestowed on him, and to be named poet laureate by the people of his own community were, to hear him tell about it, of greater personal significance than the many other awards and honors he'd gotten over the years. Etheridge pressed into each of our hands a photocopy of the Indianapolis *Star* news report of the event. These he took from a book bag, stuffed with them. Titled, "Master of words is now man of letters," the article featured a large photograph of Etheridge dressed in cap and gown, Elizabeth standing at his side. It showed him holding his eyeglasses in one hand, his face all scrunched up in a vain attempt to suppress tears, daubing his eyes with the handkerchief he held in his other hand.

In Etheridge's company, the hours had speeded by. The sun outside the window was now low in the winter sky. Much as we wanted to put off the weighty finality of saying goodbye to Etheridge, that time had arrived. Chris offered to stay a while longer, so there was no worry of leaving Etheridge alone; and, anyway, Elizabeth was expected shortly. Mary and I, each in turn, exchanged last words and bear hugs with Etheridge; then lingered in the doorway talking with Chris. Etheridge meanwhile sauntered over to the TV and turned up the volume again. I thought this strange at the time; especially since Chris was staying on to keep him company. Afterwards, I wondered whether Etheridge hadn't done this as an unconscious defense against loneliness, the images on the screen, the voices, offering the illusion they were actual people present in the room, filling the spaces we had left vacant.

Outside, Elizabeth pulled into the lot just as we were about to drive off. We exchanged greetings but talked only briefly. She was tired after a full day's work, and anxious to see how Etheridge was faring. For our part. we were eager to head home and be alone with our thoughts. We all knew *we three* would be seeing one another again.

Heading home, we had to cross the mall parking lot, a disorienting experience following our visit. The frenzied atmosphere of Christmas shopping season enveloped us as we drove into a virtual sea of cars, parked and parking; the hundreds upon hundreds of spaces, all empty when we had arrived were now occupied or being contested. We inched our way in traffic toward the mall exit, thinking how ironic this was after the long afternoon we spent with our dying friend, whose life represented the antithesis of consumerism. Etheridge, to use his own words, "traveled light:" He'd been poor his entire life; he lived frugally, dressed simply, owned little more than his books and his personal papers. He had a hearty appetite to be sure, not for microwave ovens or VCRs, but instead for such essential pleasures as good food and drink, the company of friends, good conversation. And, we realized, as we merge with the highway traffic streaming south, that our memories of this afternoon spent in Etheridge's company, the quality conversation we would always cherish … were his parting gifts to us.

Postscript: March 11, 1991

Chris Gilbert phoned this afternoon; my son Andrai took the call and gave me the message he'd left to call him back. I waited until Mary was home from work and we'd eaten dinner before dialing the number. In the meantime, I tried to think what he might want: maybe he was planning a visit to Boston and wanted to arrange to see us; maybe it was to discuss the changes I'd suggested to one of his poems he'd submitted to *Hanging Loose;* maybe it was to discuss the upcoming reading at the Boston Public Library he and Mary were scheduled to give next month ... every reason surfaced but one. I kept putting out of my mind the thought he might be calling with bad news about Etheridge, which turned out to be the case: Etheridge was dead. Chris learned from Fran Quinn that he had died a few days ago in Indianapolis.

Post-Postscript: November 1991

A phone call from Elizabeth: She wanted assured me that, although Etheridge may be physically gone from her life (our lives), he has nevertheless been letting her know, in no uncertain terms, that his spirit is still around; doing so in ways that bear his unmistakable signature as poet and trickster.

She told me he had visited her in Denver recently in the guise of a brown moth (symbol of the soul of the dead). This occurred in a season when one doesn't expect to find moths about, in a crowded restaurant where she was seated alone at a table. It(he) singled her out from among all the people to circle round and round, then settled on the tabletop across from her.

Other evidence Elizabeth gave had to do with a potted plant they'd kept on the landing in her Brookline apartment to greet visitors. She told me Etheridge had found it as a bare stalk in a Roxbury rubbish heap sometime during his last year. He had retrieved it, she told me, brought it home, repotted it, watered it regularly, and restored it to life, putting out healthy new shoots and leaves. Now, suddenly, it had mysteriously vanished.

The last instance had to do with fried chicken, a favorite food of Etheridge's. At the recent memorial for him, held at Roxbury Community College, where Etheridge had taught a poetry workshop, the plate of fried chicken set out on a table at the back of the room vanished, again mysteriously, while the testimonials were being given:

411

a sure sign, Elizabeth felt, that Etheridge was still around and up to his old tricks.

I thought to myself: "Eth left us his poems; he deserves the fried chicken!"

At The Information Desk

Barbara B. Lewis

By her desk I stand, waiting on line to ask which plays this branch library has on its shelves by Ed Bullins.

"His last name—is it spelled with an *E?*" she asks.

"No," I answer. "With an *I.*"

Her question has surprised me. It is even a bit alarming.

If the head librarian in a major Boston branch has no idea how to spell the last name of an important contemporary playwright, a seminal writer who came of age with the Black Arts Movement, rising to national and international status as minister of Culture for the Black Panther Party, a frequently produced playwright on the East and West Coasts. His work was produced all over the country, in California, uptown in Harlem in New York, midtown at Lincoln Center, and downtown at Astor Place on the East Side, and at New Federal Theatre, on the Lower East Side, where Woodie King, coming out of Detroit, was the impresario. With all those credits and more behind him, still Ed Bullins had a hard time maintaining his popularity into the 21st century.

After the time spent on the west coast where he earned his academic credentials in theatre, completing a masters in playwriting at San Francisco State and working closely with the Black Panther Party before moving to New York, establishing himself uptown in Harlem and also in the downtown theater, working closely with Joseph Papp, the Shakespearean and avant-garde impresario, and with Woodie King downtown at New Federal Theatre. In the 1990s, Bullins was named Distinguished Writer in Residence at Boston's Northeastern University. He was there during the years that August Wilson was affiliated with the Huntington. Both playwrights hailed from Pennsylvania, Bullins from the streets of Philly, and Wilson from the hills of industrial Pittsburgh, two very different but storied, pivotal nodes in America's Black Diaspora continuum. Both writers appreciated and valued the work of the other but they may have been pitted, one against the other, in a kind of battle royal, a competition popular in and surviving from slavery days. Its agenda has always been one-upsmanship, with the prize of bragging rights going to the onlookers, but none of the participants winning anything.

In *Invisible Man,* Ellison includes a short story in which blacks are made to fight and hurt each other in a battle royal scenario, a holdover

413

from slavery, with the goal being that of pleasuring the owning class with the satisfaction of seeing blacks diminish and hurt each other as they vie and compete for a nonexistent prize. Early in the novel, blacks are made to fight for bragging rights in a contest that neither can win, with the goal of their fight being to provide the onlookers with the joy of black pain and diminishment their fight pleasuring white onlookers eager for the reward of black pain.

Once again, African Americans, of any and all ages, younger and older, male and female, in severely subordinated status, are made to occupy the bottom of the collective barrel, often finding themselves in the punitive grip of a vengeful Karen or at the dead end of a gun in the hand of a rabid neighbor, whose great great uncle may delighted in the pleasure of a down-home lynching party when bored and needed some revving up on a Saturday night. Bullins, who, on occasion, might be loud and raucous in his denouncements, knew and wrote about encounters on the edge. In his mind's eye, he saw those faces, heard those voices as he journeyed home, after dark. He commiserated with the collective pain, as he too was more and more overlooked, pushed into the no longer at the forefront, no longeEver since curious explorers from across the seas planted their roots deep in a stolen Eden, the labor and muscle, the creativity of national growth and expansion has been largely black and other. Labor under the lash and heel, subordinated muscle, subordinated creativity, subordinated song have been the engine and creative wherewithal positioning America to reach new economic, political, and cultural heights, era after era. In practically every area of endeavor, in sports, business, music, fashion, science, and the media, etc. the voice and resolve of the other is the creative basis spurring on growth.

In the last century and in the new one recently born, the writing is clear on the wall. People once enslaved in this country and not yet fully free of that ormer status—Blacks or African Americans, whatever the preferred term, are still being relegated to the lower if not bottom rung of notice, of life, pushed aside, overlooked, forgotten, quickly dismissed. Bullins suffered that. It pained him, and he fought back as hard as he could. He upped his decibel level, made some pugilistic moves to counter the pain of neglect and disregard. Two years ago, he left this dimension. What Ed Bullins gave, the trajectory he followed, his disappointment, how he fought with grit, his heart pushing through pain, aspiring, to tell the truth as he witnessed it inside blocks still bloody, from the butchering of dreams, bodies and hopes decimated on urban streets east and west, north and south in the African Diaspora.

Let me end with the first time I met Ed Bullins. It was at St. Marks in the Bowery, Tenth Street and Second Avenue, New York. Lower East Side. Upstairs in the old Dutch Church. There was a little theater. His play wasn't being performed. I forget whose was. But there he was. He asked me some questions. He wanted to know my history. I told him. My mother taught school and my father worked in the post office, the big one on 34th Street and Eighth Avenue. The one with writing all around the frieze indicating the promises and pledges it upholds as its creed re delivery and public promise. "You are classic," Ed said. No one had ever told me that before, and I was taken aback. Two good jobs. That was solid middle class, back in the day. Ed had seen the black community, studied it from inside out, first in Philadelphia, where he was born in the thirties, during the Depression. The post office was what guys he grew up with aspired to. He wanted something different, something more, and he achieved that. He wrote new possibilities for his time. He understood cities and what they bred, what they could give rise to, what they could change and expand in the make-up of a people at a given time of crush. From Philly, he went to San Francisco, where he pushed open and wide some new doors by writing other realities, by celebrating alternative options, by extolling a culture arriving at new places in city spaces. First Los Angeles, where he went back to school, began writing and getting published. Then he moved to San Francisco where he continued his education, started writing for the theater, and became friendly with the founders of the Black Panther Party, becoming their Minister of Culture. After San Francisco, he flew back east, devoting more time to the theater, starting uptown in Harlem. With Robert Macbeth, he worked at the New Lafayette Theater on Seventh Avenue in Harlem, then he ventured downtown to Astor Place, where Joseph Papp had established a major theatrical venue, only blocks away from where the country's first black theatre opened in the 1820s, coincident with the time when blacks were recognized as free, no longer legally enslaved in the state. For them, being able to tell the stories they wanted to share, stories in which they had dignity and status were the stories that mattered, and they chose to take on the stories of Shakespeare, which were widely known and credited with dignity were the tales and sagas they chose to enact. But rather than let them do so, the audiences in New York stormed the theater, trashing it, and fighting with the performers, which ended with the actors being carted off to jail, and the theater destroyed. Allowing blacks status in the theater was not an end devoutly to be wished. On the contrary, they were to be kept firmly in subservient circumstances.

Ed Bullins rallied against that on east and west coasts, and he wrote with dignity and love about men and women fighting against the diminished circumstances in which they were cast. Ed was drawn to the light. He craved knowledge and understanding. And he wanted to share. His work, his words, his insight is brightest in the light of the true and enduring fight for better. Shortly after I came to Boston, back in 2004, I went to South Bay to do some shopping. Ed came into the Stop-N-Shop there. No one noticed him. No one came up to talk with him or shake his hand. No one thanked him for all the work he had done, all the careers he launched. He was just entering the store, and I thought: There are giants in our midst, walking the same paths we are. Maybe Ed knew before he passed how important it was for him to come and walk among us for a time and let us know some of what went into spelling his name, creating his legacy. And maybe, just maybe, a few writers and theater folk in the next and subsequent generations will keep his work and name alive. And, hope against hope, maybe a future librarian or two will no longer puzzle their brains over how to spell the name of this playwright and author but will know its exact spelling—and might even be a fan.

John Mulrooney, *Spooky Action,* Dos Madres Press (2003), 107 pages

Mairéad Byrne

In terms of using language to build relationship between the known and unknown, Aristotle championed the ability to make metaphors above all else. Keats, in his concept of Negative Capability, perhaps influenced by studies in electrical science at the time, valorized the capacity to be a receptor, to operate "in uncertainties, mysteries, doubts, without any irritable reaching after fact and reason." With the term Objective Correlative, T.S. Eliot proposed the clustering of objects or external events as transmitters of otherwise inchoate emotion. Actually, Aristotle, Keats, and Eliot surfaced rather than expounded on the terms of metaphor, Negative Capability, and Objective Correlative. But the terms, and the values of the concepts they represented, were taken up by poets and scholars.

Einstein's *"spukhafte Fernwirkung"* or "spooky action at a distance" also surfaced somewhat casually, in a letter to Max Born in 1947. Unlike the positive exemplarity of metaphor, Negative Capability and Objective Correlative, "spooky action at a distance" was a repudiation. Author, teacher, steel guitarist, and film producer John Mulrooney doesn't explain his choice of title for his first full-length book of poetry. Patrick Pritchett, in his blurb on the back cover of the book, provides that service: "Einstein spoke dismissively of 'spooky action at [a] distance,' the idea that separate objects could somehow share a simultaneous condition across space and time, or what is sometimes referred to as quantum entanglement."

Einstein's repudiation of entanglement implied a repudiation of quantum mechanics at the time, entanglement being a defining feature. Since Einstein, however, quantum entanglement has been detected in ever larger objects, nearly or barely visible to the naked eye; and the 2022 Nobel Prize in Physics was awarded to Alain Aspect, John Clauser, and Anton Zeilinger for their work on quantum entanglement. John Mulrooney's *Spooky Action* has the feel of a poetry developed over a long time. His adoption of the example of entanglement, and conversion of Einstein's term to a positive, signals his poetics of connectedness, systematicity, influence, and relationship. Now that we have the term, we can see that we need it, for this book and for contemporary poetry and experience.

At odds somewhat with the book title, poem titles in this book are generally very explicit, if a little stand-offish in relation to the poem. They seem more interested in themselves. Six announce themselves as poems: "Poem for Joe Ceravolo and the Bee Gees," "Poem Over Plough and Stars," "Poem Next to Summer," "Poem After Solstice," "Poem on Madonna's Birthday," and "Poem on the Epiphany." There are six cantatas: "Cantata for Mitrovica Stars," "Cantata of Pareidolia," "Cantata Under Parker's Statue," "Cantata After Bunting," "Cantata With Flight," and "Cantata in which you can have a 2 KB representation of a 2 TB database and you can use that image to get real results—the memory works that way."

There are additional forms: "Meditation on the Real," "A Short Mute History of Locusts and Cicadas," "A True Account of the Ghost of John Kenneth Galbraith" (which title honors both Galbraith and Frank O'Hara/Kenneth Koch). And other direct tributes to people, "After Ange Mlinko," "Autumn Walk After Jodorowsky," "On Amtrak, After Hearing Gerrit Is Gone"; and especially places "New Year's Eve, Gloucester Harbor," "Rustcraft Road Revisited," "Zero Lines at the Böll Cottage," "Oedipus Rex at Sheepshead Bay," "Dawn, Lower County Road," and "Heard at Oakes Cove." Boston, Cambridge and Massachusetts saturate the work but also Brooklyn, New York, Shanghai, Senegal, Kosovo, and Ireland.

The material identity of a thing and its connection to another thing are in constant tension. The texture of the poetry can be so material: the place names, people, signs, streets, businesses, grit of the city. But then there is the phantom too, what was or will be there. And the tension between these forces. How one thing is like another thing, even when it is not. How things or words that most resemble each other may be false or a play, like "Sakyamuni & Vanzetti" or "Sacco & Vairocana" ("Cantata Under Parker's Statue"). How one thing resembles no other thing as much as it resembles itself. And even then there are differences:

a day in which the shape
of another day fits
perfectly like a you-sized
disguise of you
          your own face
covered by this face
a like any other you know
but haven't seen

like the faces in the hedgerows
you can no longer discern
a blank like any other
like the day
we went to that store
in the thawing snow
but that store was closed
the shafts of sunlight
finding their way beneath
the bridge the highway
that spanned the river
astonished the roofs and gutters
the whole day was
revealed as the day that
other days had only
been the placeholder for
so that even when we
went back out into the light
and the familiar territory
it was new—a familiarity
that had not happened
before.

("Cantata of Pareidolia")

In this poetry, similes are more dynamic than commonly allowed. For a start, the simile is unexpected, even unlikely, e.g., "a sound like lost luggage" on the very first page of the book ("New Year's Eve, Gloucester Harbor"). Without simile, i.e., relationship/connection, no matter how elusive, the poem can't move forward. For example, "Apparent Wind" opens with a statement, "I am in a boat and the boat / I am in—," but there the poem halts until propelled forward by simile: "the boat is headed / up a wave like someone or / something going up a hill—Sisyphus or Jack and Jill, / penitents on the Camino / de Santiago." The poem stalls again. Another simile is drafted in: "The boat I am in / climbs a clean sheet of water / like a salamander scurrying up / a clean sheet on a clothesline / in a backyard a long time ago." And then there is a woman, "despondent about / some trouble the salamander / knows nothing of," and the poem is underway for almost five pages, spooling out of itself.

Similes are used like roundabouts to wheel the poem off in possible directions, sometimes returning it to base (which is never a base). In

"Meditation on the Real," dreams offer a brief shore leave or reprieve from the real while other thoughts vanish

> like a child pickpocket
> in a crowd on the Staten
> Island Ferry who ran off
> with your wallet—
> your money, your credit
> and identity and
> your picture of
> you in front of
> the pictures of
> the yellow harbor
> and the temple garden—
> the gentle constructions
> the mind makes and
> offices eventually accept.

The child pickpocket runs off with the poem too, its short lines offering no resistance, the very weak first words facilitating invasion. The line starts in the middle in a sense, and sometimes ends there too, cushioned on both sides by vulnerable articles, prepositions and conjunctions in a rejection of the conventional bulwarks of strong first and last word. The poem becomes Borgesian, charging itself with each image and each image within each image.

The terrific poem "Wallahi le Zein," dedicated to Filip Marinovich, points in its title to Mississippi Record's release of Matthew Lavoie's collection and compilation of Wezin, Jakwar, and Guitar Boogie from the Islamic Republic of Mauritania, *Wallahi le Zein* (2010/2021): "an immersive entry into this music: gnarled and virtuosic electric guitars weave hypnotically throughout melismatic sung poetry and exclamations, pulsing hand drums, party chatter, buzzing rigged desert sound systems, and all manner of the ambient sounds of Nouakchott wedded to oversaturated cassette in all its swirling, breathing, psychedelic glory" (https://www.mississippirecords.net/). This shorter poem, written in lower-case tercets, with long lines (mostly sparked on the most peripheral of words, e.g., "and," "but," "how," "of," "that," "at," "the"), has intense visual as well as sonic energy. Lines such as "at the edge of Boston wailing for our demon lovers / or waiting for Corita's tank to screech across the sky / or sorrowful fumbling with our trembling actor hands" remind me of Hart Crane, both *White Buildings*

(”Legend”) and The Bridge, "Down Wall, from girder into street noon leaks, / A rip-tooth of the sky's acetylene; / All afternoon the cloud-flown derricks turn …" ("Proem: To Brooklyn Bridge"). Whatever about Coleridge.

One of the takeaways for me from this book is that it's still possible to live a rich life and to leave a rich legacy of influence. A rich life is not to say an easy life, "when you build a road you know / there will be fighting—when you build a wall you had best / already made your wreathes—the republic of thought knows // the face of children crack and leak the refugees / of the next war" ("Wallahi le Zein"). Many rich lives are invoked and the book, of 34 poems, has 12 poems with dedications to poets and musicians, including two to John Wieners and one, "Cantata for Mitrovica Stars," to international peacemaker Padraig O'Malley, the subject of the documentary film John Mulrooney co-produced, *The Peacemaker* (2016). The book as a whole is dedicated to the poet's wife, Rachel.

This is poetry for an age of desolation. You know there is a love song underneath. That is the landscape but not the argument. There is no thesis, antithesis, synthesis. Only one poem, "Entanglement at Solstice," connects directly to the book's title. I'd like to quote from it but the shortest quotation I can manage is 61 lines. In any case, even when it is spelled out, to say that the poetry in this book demonstrates entanglement or spooky action at a distance is a step too far. John Mulrooney doesn't demonstrate; he places where it is possible to find. You have to look. Even the cover of the book is self-effacing. At first, second, or third glance you might see an unremarkable blue/indigo cover with some patterns. But it's a celestial map. It's great to see this book on SPD's Bestsellers list. I hope there will be a second printing soon.

Notes on the Boston occult school: Sex, Magick, and the Art of the Poem in the work of Gerrit Lansing, Stephen Jonas, and John Wieners

Peter Valente

Reading the work of Gerrit Lansing, Stephen Jonas, and John Wieners reminds me that the ghosts are real, the game is dangerous, they're out tonight, the secret workers, and they're queer; and there is a spirit world operating in the urban landscape, songs are heard in the streets of the city, in dark corners where love burns; there is a light in these poems, also transformations, the visceral effect of vision, latent desire aroused. David Grundy writes, in "Queer Shoulders at the Wheel" that "Wieners, Jonas, Marshall, Spicer, Joe Dunn, and Robin Blaser formed what their latter-day comrade Gerrit Lansing would dub 'the School of Boston ... an occult school, unknown.' With the exception of Dunn, all were openly gay, and their preferred haunt was Beacon Hill, a historically bohemian district now heavily gentrified but then still clinging to the red-light grittiness that in the nineteenth century had earned it the moniker Mount Whoredom...."

The poems show us such a devotion, a votive, (gnosis), the poets seeking the gold in the mud, like modern day alchemists. These poems also strike a balance between intellect and emotion. The games of youth are risky, the risk each poem must be, so respect the order of the gods and goddesses, desire, seduction, genital illumination; also, magick, through which one discovers the secret formulas for transformation. Finally, there is the music of the poems, the play of syllables in the mind.

Sex, magick and secrecy had a long history in the Western religious imagination. From the early Gnostics to the Knights Templar to the Cathars of medieval Europe, esoteric orders often been accused of using sexual rituals as part of their hermetic magical arts. Aleister Crowley, in *The Law is for All,* writes: "The sexual act is a sacrament of Will. To profane it is the great offense. All true expression of it is lawful; all suppression or distortion of it is contrary to the Law of liberty." These Boston poets were interested in the unknown, magick, even what is "criminal" (in esoteric terms this is the meaning of the sign of the Beast) in the eyes of society ("happy criminals in love, united in a rhythm simple as a poem").[1] Furthermore, in his *Confessions,* Crowley wrote: "[T]he detestable mysteries of sex were transformed into joy and beauty." This is the essence of the XIth degree of the O.T.O which dealt with homosexual magical practices. Lansing, in "Conventicle" writes, "A god is of the nature of the slime" that will appear suddenly as "Water Lily and the Child." From the slime emerges a delicate and beautiful image, that suggests youth and elegance. In "Festive Song (The New Year)," Lansing writes about the lovers that they "make sharp love and live in shocks of light." They seek out the sacred places, where magick can happen, in the night transformed into the bright light of illumination, where men encounter men,

> each eager for the other's pleasure,
> faster and faster,
> mouth to body fastened,
> enjoyment like forever and then at the same time time shot off
> > into eternity's gullet.

For Lansing, "sex is rhymed angelic motion." The men during sex are no longer men but gods, their ejaculation is likened to "time" shooting off into the throat of "eternity." It is a striking image. The poem also highlights the relationship of man, who is bound by time, to an experience of eternal arousal. Man can transcend his material limitations through tantric sex practices and experience a sense of this eternal. In "In the Light of the Tinctures" Lansing writes:

> (How mysterious!   What I just wrote as if it were future
> > Seems to be what has happened already
> and I realize that time
> > (I had said it before but forgotten)
> is not where we really are.

As a result of these magickal practices, the link with the material world and time is broken and the eternal is experienced. One goes beyond the self, the ego. Furthermore, Lansing speaks of his "pain and out of body bliss" and calls on the "Great Woman" [perhaps, the Whore of Babylon or the Earth Mother] to give him courage. This suggests the Shamanic idea of bilocation, where the soul leaves the body and enters the spirit world where it gains supernatural wisdom. It also suggests astral travel. The Orphic is suggested: "Once gone down the hell hole /

---

1. Lansing, from "A Simple Fire of Wood"

there is no turning back." Lansing also speaks of the "golden reversion." Poets in the gnostic tradition, like Jonas and Lansing, are "thrown back upon an earlier revelation" that is "better / suited to its times than this inchoate present."[2] In "Advertisements of the Tribes" Jonas speaks of a prehistoric time when man known as a "Hunter / drew bison on the cave walls // altamira / buttocks as fine as any Ruben."

For Lansing, the act of writing is entwined around sex and magick: "Mournful angels spire down his black syntax / to health. Mad and warm as children, they splash / And couple in the joyous summer sea." To perceive all things as different from each other, as well as the same, is what certain spiritual teachers maintain is a fundamental truth, although one difficult to fully understand, despite its apparent simplicity. Holy men are thought to have bright and glistening auras. But members of certain occult traditions set out to absorb all experiences, which they regard as equal, and this produces an interesting metaphysical reaction: their auras appear *black,* less "pure," which is desirable in certain occult orders [thanks to the late Richard Gernon, a member of the O.T.O, for this description of the aura]. Therefore, health emerges as a result of using the "*black* [my emphasis] syntax."

For Jonas, knowledge is derived from "an audacious willingness to experience."[3] He writes, addressing the reader in an intimate, conversational manner, "consider w/me for a moment the phenomenon of / the burning bush." For Jonas, the burning bush is "all consuming but is not / itself consumed." Herein is "the Divine Seed / manifested to the beholders." This is not the gross material fire but the spiritual flame. Jonas continues, "we (momentarily) approached / The Palace of the King, / after the descent from the Mount of Vision;" Man has arrived at this point of revelation. The "Divine Seed," is the flame that consumes itself but is not itself consumed, that gives birth to and illuminates the poem, but only for a moment. Lansing writes in "To the Boy Charioteer," "Emerging into sunlight / I dance with capability; my feeling is a waterfall / that spends without exhaustion of the snow." For both Lansing and Jonas this expenditure without loss is a result of working the body energy divine, accessing the solar energy that resides in the heart. For Jonas, to "make the poem" is to look "into the heart of light," the light of knowledge, the mystic rose blooming in the heart of man as he approaches the "The Palace of the King" or goes to meet

2. All quotes by Jonas are from poem LXVI from an untitled series unless otherwise noted.
3. From "Three Dance Moods for Ear"

that "queen with the gone stick," his angel, his demon brother. He urges the reader to be "discreet / (upon the street)" but "in the pad ... / let the bedsprings creake. / Marvel. Question.," add petals to the rose of self-knowledge through magick and exploration of the tantric mysteries. Finally, when asked, "did you *make* him / YET?" the poet replies, "Hell noe / besides, he's straight." With success comes failure. For Jonas, "the search for truth can mislead us thru many corridors / of false leads" because "The Divine is beyond our eager notions." Lansing writes in "The Gold in the Mud," that "our knowledge exceeds our having minds" but this is not "madness but logic of the rites of whatever seasons come to be." In this respect Magick is akin to the logic of dreams. For Crowley, the point of magickal ritual is that through repeating various movements and gestures according to the logic of the ritual, one could enter an alternate space, and achieve an ecstatic union with God.

In *The Journal of John Wieners is to be called 707 Scott Street,* Wieners writes that he was reading the *Book of the Law* by Aleister Crowley and studying Arabic poetry and mysticism; he was also drawing cards from the Tarot as a guide to his life: "I pick one every day and it is the day. Sets the tone. Unleashes a chain of events that I love on, off. Capricorn. The land and the sea. The narcotic and the natural." He quotes Jung: *magic is the science of the jungle.* For Wieners the darkness, that is a prelude to light, is a source of fear from which he eventually emerges, scarred but with the poem. Wieners writes in "The Acts of Youth," "And with great fear I inhabit the middle of the night / What wrecks of the mind await me, what drugs / to dull the senses, what little I have left, / what more can be taken away?" His life and the poem merged. After much pain and humiliation, Wieners emerges from the darkness, with a vision of "Infinite particles of the divine sun." And the poem is done. Lansing writes: "It is night and the poem is ready to end and reform into dawn."[4]

For Wieners, love is idealized as in a poem like "Chinoiserie," filled with a sense of glamour and fantasy:

> Boats are propelled by poles of bamboo
> Held in the hands of dreamers, the holds
> > are heavy
> With fruit and dates; and they paddle
> > through clouds
>
> > of azure drifting in canals of heaven.

---

4. Lansing, from "In the Light of the Tinctures"

And in "Feminine Soliloquy," Wieners writes of "A Venice where floods of onanism took hold. / This self indulgence has not left me. / Normal relations seem mild." For Wieners, Venice is a world of fantasy and decadence. Arthur Symons wrote about Venice: "A realist, in Venice, would become a romantic by mere faithfulness to what he saw before him." Wieners is a lyrical poet and his search for love often leads to tragedy and pain since he experiences the clash between the ideal and the real. But from suffering the poem is born. Wieners writes of this necessary suffering as part of the initiation of the poet in *The Journal of John Wieners is to be called 707 Scott Street:*

> The magic forest is always full of adventures. No one can enter it without losing his way. But the chosen one, the elect, who survives its deadly perils, is reborn and leaves it a changed man. The forest has always been a place of initiation; for there the demonic presences, the ancestral spirits, and the forces of nature reveal themselves. There man meets his greater self, his totem animal. And thither the medicine man conducts the youths of the tribe in order that they may be born again through gruesome initiation rites, as warriors and men.... It holds the dark forbidden things— secrets, terrors, which threaten the protected life of the ordered world of common day.

In a poem written on the Winter Solstice, 1964, entitled "Steve Magellanstraits" [the reference is to Stephen Jonas) Wieners implores the "Black magician of the night" to "dive into the secrets of the sea" to retrieve a "golden fish" "so that we may know/ the currents of the inky storm / to come." In Buddhism, the golden fishes symbolize happiness, conjugal unity and fidelity; it also refers to the auspiciousness of all living beings in a state of fearlessness, without the danger of drowning in the ocean of sufferings and being able to freely and spontaneously migrate from place to place. Ultimately, for these poets, the *"making"* of the poem is concerned with the possibility of consummation; their subject is always desire.

Wieners concludes "A Poem for Vipers" in this way, writing about the Law of the poem for which the poet is bound:

> We lie under
> its law, alive in the glamour of this hour
> able to enter into the sacred places
> of his dark people, who carry secrets
> glassed in their eyes and hide words
> under the coats of their tongue.

426

There is the oath of secrecy that initiates (poets) must swear to keep when they join an occult order (their vocation as poets). The secret is in the "eyes" and words are hidden under the tongue. In Wieners' poem, the secret is contained in the visual; presumably the eyes are glassy because of the influence of drugs or tears. In the latter case, the source of the pain is kept a secret, hidden from the light. But "sacred places" imply the secret world where the initiates go to consummate their acts of love.

Jonas echoes the idea of secrecy when he writes, "the Secretum Artis / remains w/God & unpublished." The Poem (as opposed, in Jonas's formula, to the poem), the divine logos, remains "unpublished." The poet "makes the poem." In other words, receives it by dictation and never through intention. It is not predetermined and where it goes "is anybody's guess ... venus, mars, the kitchen sink, south station."[5] In his final work, "Orgasms / Dominations" Jonas would answer the question "how do you write a poem" with "you don't it comes to you" and furthermore "It is not enough today / to say / 'write.'" This word can only, like the rational mind, approximate what occurs, which is, in a sense, not enough. Furthermore, he writes: "concerning the Lower to the Higher [as above so below] have I come to speak / of a grace above all // normal grace / recognized in the heart." Here one can use the image of the rosy cross of the Rosicrucians to reflect on the nature of this grace. Each petal of the rose upon the cross signifies the acquisition of inner knowledge and as the rose continues to bloom there is a fuller realization of the Great Work,[6] resulting in a state of grace not normally recognized, because of an order that cannot be reducible to terms outside its own.

Gerrit Lansing refers, in "The Compost," to "the Men of the Secret, / Who care for the compost in winter, / Waiting to ready the fields," where offerings are made, where "work" is "undertaken without prospect of gain." "Beyond grace" Jonas writes, "I transgress not. / "make poetry" is my aim. // goldmaking / I leave to the cracks." The poem is never in the service of the "goldmakers," the false alchemists who claim to transform lead into gold and thus claim knowledge of the Divine agency. For them the secret of money is that it's shit and it's as if they "were / to defecate" and then from this expect to achieve

---

5. From "Orgasms / Dominations" part 1
6. In a June letter from 1962 Jonas writes to Gerrit Lansing that, "the whole picture of the Great Work is clear." In 1967 Jones, during the writing of Orgasms, Jonas writes to Lansing, "I allow the, what I term "poetic judgment," [to] take precedent over my formal judgment."

"salvation." Furthermore, in "Conventicle," Lansing writes "The people of the Phoenix do not say "the Phoenix" / and we do not name the Mystery that weaves a parsley garland // for the temples of the lusters." Jorge Luis Borges writes in "The Cult of the Phoenix," that this secret group were alternately known as "the People of the Practice" or the "People of the Secret," and they can be "traced back no farther than to Hrabanus Maurus," the 9th century Frankish Benedictine monk, poet and theologian. Borges notes that "The name by which the world knows them is not the name that they themselves pronounce" and that their rituals are secret.

In "The Music Master (*after a Mozart divertimento*) Jonas writes, "Use / the music of / the streets." He says, "you must / hear yr language spoken." These poets of the Boston Occult School were concerned with the language of the poem and its relation to music; the ability of music to suggest an alternate space outside of language. Jonas concludes the poem: "In short, the music / is more explicit than the lyrics." The reason for this is that music can signal that which is beyond words, using the medium of language. The music transcends the limits of meaning. And thus more "explicitly" states what cannot be otherwise said. Where the words are fragments of an original unity, the music alludes to the unbroken state of origin. It represents desire.

In "Poem for Painters" Wieners' language is not stationary but fluid. In the following lines, Wieners' description of the rising sun over the rooftops and his emotional state occurs in terms of color:

> The sun also
> > rises on the rooftops, beginning
> > w/ violet. I begin in blue
> > knowing we are cool.

Bill Berkson, quoting Gertrude Stein, writes, "A writer should write with his eyes." The description of the sun begins with violet and furthermore, Wieners writes, "I begin in blue / knowing why we are cool." "Blue" suggests a state of despair but to "begin in blue" also suggests Wieners is using language as a painter would; he is speaking about the tone of the poem as expressing an emotional state. Here "knowing" is also related to the color "blue," and this is not intellectual knowledge but self-knowledge, gnosis. The following is the block of prose-like poetry, from "A Poem for Painters," that signals a change in scale from what came before, and this introduces a different kind of music. The block of poetry is like a freeze-frame, a way of grounding the poem, that changes the rhythm, and slows down the tempo of the poem:

> South of Mission, Seattle,
> over the Sierra Mountains,
> the Middle West and Michigan,
> moving east again, easy
> coming into Chicago and
> the cattle country, calling
> to each other over canyons,
> careful not to be caught
> at night, they are still out,
> the destroyers, and down
> into the South, familiar land,
> lush places, blue mountains
> of Carolina, into Black Mountain
> and you can sleep out, or
> straight across into States

Wieners, in this excerpt draws a kind of map of his travels across the U.S. Charles Olson famously wrote, "I take SPACE to be the central fact to man born in America."[7] Speaking of "sleeping out" and being "careful not to get caught" suggests Jonas' "audacious willingness to experience."[8] In "A Poem for Vipers" Wieners wrote "The poem / does not lie to us." Furthermore, he writes: "Let us stay with what we know." The above passage is literally and figuratively, a real travelogue in scale. In his imagination, Wieners moves from the enclosed space of the Hotel Wentley poems to the wide-open fields of America; it is a trajectory from the local to the universal; from the microcosm to the cosmic. The scale of the poem grew larger to encompass a wider field of emotional experience. The poem is governed by the breath not the meter and through varying the music. The placement of the words on the page also suggests the extension of the line in a painterly manner:

> At last the game is over
> and the line lengthens.

The unexpected extension of the second line to the right of the page is not merely an affect; it shows, in a subtle visual way, that the line has changed, moved, the scale of the poem has shifted. These

---

7. Both Wieners and Lansing were friends of Charles Olson (Wieners was his student at Black Mountain College) and in their own ways, follow Olson's dictum, "the poem itself must, at all, be a high energy-construct and, at all points, an energy-discharge."
8. From "Three Dance Moods for Ear"

visual effects in the poem have their analogue in painting. Wieners opened the space of the poem. In language Wieners is able to suggest a visual space. In this respect, like Jonas, he can signal that which is beyond words.

In "Stanzas of Hyparxis,"[9] Lansing writes "Something is hidden. There are no other words.... But the solar heart defines the blood / How far out you go / it is within." For Jonas "the quest begins & ends w/in." All other attempts "to prod / further would be to multiply the deeply wooded." Gerrit Lansing also writes of the difference between rational and spiritual constructions, language and what cannot be said in words; in "For An Unlikely Love," he writes, "I praise the canyons no bridge spans / but eagles fly across." Here, the bridge suggests a rational structure, but the eagle suggests spiritual navigation. In this, Lansing as well, posits something that is "unlikely" but not impossible, that which is beyond speech or language, "the golden sunlight of the midsummer mystery."

Reading these Boston poets, I am reminded of Jung's *Mysterium Coniunctionis*: the game of Carl Gustav Jung that naming is gaming; Rimbaud's vowels, "Being Beauteous"; also, Kenneth Anger's Magic Lantern Cycle or Initiation into the Mysteries. For these poets, there is an order behind reason, a field of interlocking words in the invisible made manifest in the poem. The magickal world is a field of correspondences with which we interact, are part of. These are the poets as priests, who seek out the "sacred" places to perform their "priestly" acts. They are poets who are not afraid to enter the darkness, where the gold of experience is found. They are adept at this alchemy. Grundy writes, that this Boston "Occult School" turned "conditions of marginality and enforced secrecy into tools of power. This is not necessarily the queer poetry we've been taught to expect: pre-AIDS, pre-Stonewall, yet not in the least way closeted; experimental yet anti-elitist; coterie but defiantly lower class." Finally, reading the work of these poets remined me that every man and woman is a star must follow his/her orbit. AUMGN.[10]

---

9. Hyparxis means subsistence, existence. The 7th Oracle of Zoroaster is "Containing all things in the one summit of his own Hyparxis, He Himself subsists wholly beyond."
10. AUGMN was a secret word formulated by Aleister Crowley in *Magick in Theory and Practice,* and "uttered by the Master Therion himself as a means of declaring his own personal work as the Beast, the Logos of the Aeon.... The cardinal revelation of the Great Aeon of Horus is that this formula AUM does not represent the facts of nature." This recalls the XIth degree of homosexual magick.

"the great and wonderful high blank of no purpose": On *All This Thinking: The Correspondence of Bernadette Mayer and Clark Coolidge*

Peter Valente

While reading *All This Thinking: The Correspondence of Bernadette Mayer and Clark Coolidge,* I thought about the time when I decided to pursue the life of a poet, right out of college, after I graduated in 1992 with a degree in Electrical Engineering from Stevens Institute of Technology. I first published poems in those xeroxed, hand-stapled mags that were still coming out of San Francisco in the 90s such as Lyric& (ed. Steve Carll), *Angle* (ed. Brian Lucas), *ÄnTənym* (ed. Avery E.D. Burns) and Kevin Killian and Dodie Bellamy's *Mirage* #4 [Periodical]; later, I published some work in softbound magazines like Lee Chapman's *First Intensity,* Burt Kimmelman's *Poetry New York,* and Ed Foster's *Talisman: A Journal of Contemporary Poetry and Poetics.* I attended many readings at the Poetry Project, and elsewhere in NYC, while commuting from Jersey.

I read everything I could get my hands on and encountered many of the books from publishers such as Rosemarie and Keith Waldrop's Burning Deck, Lyn Hejinian's Tuumba Press, Steve Clay's Granary Books, Annabel Lee's Vehicle Editions, Geoff Young's The Figures, and many others, including Angel Hair, who originally published John Wieners' *Asylum Poems.* During this time, I sent some of the collages that I was doing to John M. Bennett, publisher of the mag *Lost & Found Times,* who wrote on them, and sent me photocopies to give out for free. In the late 1990s, with a couple of friends, I published a zine of poetry are artwork; the poems were Xeroxed, and the pages were stapled together; we published friends as well as some better-known poets; we only published four issues. We basically Xeroxed a few and gave them out to friends; a few went to the Poetry Project in NYC. As a young poet I was told I should start a zine because it was a way to get in touch with other poets. These early experiences in publishing my own work and the work of others taught me about community; this was important for a young poet (I was 23 years old at the time), living in New Jersey and working in a bookstore. I learned that there were poetry scenes and a sense of community throughout the United

States and in Europe: this led to my correspondence with Kevin Killian, Gustaf Sobin, William Bronk, Gerrit Lansing, and others.

I had published poems in Peter O'Leary's *LVNG*, a magazine he gave out for free. This led to some correspondence with him in the early 2000s. He was living in Chicago at the time, and I was in Jersey. Two years ago, I emailed him asking for PDFs of my letters because I wanted to see what I had written (during several moves, my copies of the letters were unfortunately lost). In our letters we spoke of the poetry scene, readings we attended, the nature of poetry and the poet's role in the world; we talked about books we were reading, music we were listening to; I remember the excitement of receiving a letter in the mail and sitting down to read it, and the energy that consumed me when I wanted to get it all down in my response, everything I wanted to say. But is that possible? Can you say everything you're thinking and feeling? Email has completely erased that thrill of correspondence, or perhaps it's better to say that it has morphed into something different.

Here I think it would be useful to speak of some of Mayer's and Coolidge's early works to create a context for their concerns with language and the nature of poetry in these letters. Mayer had explored ideas about language and image in her book *Memory*, republished by siglio press in 2020. It contains around 1,100 photographs along with 31 poetic journal entries; each day for the month of July, 1971, Mayer would take photographs, using up a roll of film; she wrote in her journal: "take pictures for a week, say, then put them away don't even show them around for a year & see what you remember & a week's diary too." I remember imagining each line (or groups of sentences) as images being spliced onto the page, the page itself as if containing a sequence of frames in a film: Mayer is "writing writing pictures of." The "cuts" in the text are quick and often discontinuous, concerned more with recording "states of consciousness" than with a linear narrative. Bernadette and her friends are seen performing various tasks, or alone reading, or in a car, etc. and these images are hinted at in the text, as though they were brief and discrete moments in the continuous flow of consciousness. The relation of the photographs to the text is asymmetrical and dynamic. The space between the text and the images is where thought occurs; it is associative, rather than logical, and leads to alternative readings. As a reader we are asked to interpret multiple realities that occur simultaneously and to see, or rather, feel, resonances, in the spaces between the image and the text (sound). Light, time, language, memory: these are the central concerns in the book. Mayer often speaks of light, until it acquires a kind of eternal quality: "the light in the white room looks like itself, all the lights ... between black & white is blue, all is light." *Memory* was originally published in 1975 by North Atlantic Books.

About an early book *Polaroid* (1975) Coolidge wrote, "I picked a set of words—prepositions, connectives of various kinds, which's and that's and conjunctions—and thought I would limit myself to those," but eventually nouns and adjectives started to appear and determine the course of this work; the longer lines start about midway through the book. This gives *Polaroid* an "outer dimension," which gets it away from "language as language." *Quartz Hearts* (1978) was a longer "prosoid" work. Coolidge, writing about *Quartz Hearts,* says, "It is in very sense a hinge work, reflecting a fresh interest in sentence as axial structure, the final movement of *Polaroid* had pushed me toward, the prosoid's lengths would explore in full." (In the course of the letters, Coolidge would speak of a "longwork," which was eventually published in 2112 by Fence books as *A Book Beginning What and Ending Away*) Furthermore, *Quartz Hearts* constitutes a "meditation on the state(s) of things, in other words words." There is also a list of the books and music that were used in the making of the poem; these included Gertrude Stein's Stanzas in *Meditation,* Gerry Mulligan's earliest quartets from the early '50s, Kerouac's *Desolation Angels,* Beckett's *The Unnamable, Texts for Nothing,* and *Watt,* Thelonious Monk's "I should care" (his solo on Columbia), and Beethoven's late quartets. In *Quartz Hearts,* Coolidge writes, "I don't sense I state." The poem is not pre-determined, or based on a sensual apprehension of reality, but as if "received" from outside; the poet is the medium for the message (In the letters, Mayer and Coolidge speak about this idea of a "dictated" poetry) *Own Face* was published in 1978 by United Artists (it would later be republished by Sun&Moon in 2000). This book was concerned with real-life events, with friends, and with observations of the past. The abstract quality of the early works gives rise here to meditations on the self and memory.

What is seen in these early works, and the ideas they would develop in the letters, is what distinguishes Coolidge and Mayer from so many other poets of their generation: their poetry, especially the longer works, have the intensity of personal expression as well as intellectual force; they are concerned with both the nature of words as language as well as the self and memory. In the letters Mayer and Coolidge write about the details of everyday life (Mayer is pregnant with Max, her third child during the early part of their correspondence and in a later letter Susan and Clark's daughter Celia has her first period) and they also speculate about the nature of poetry, the function of the poet in relation to the world, solitude versus community.

All This Thinking: The Correspondence of Bernadette Mayer and Clark Coolidge contains the letters from September 1979 to October 1982. They show the strength of Mayer and Coolidge's unique relationship in the poetry world. As the correspondence begins in '79, Mayer is 34 years old, and Coolidge is 40. For both Mayer and Coolidge, the poem is a kind of high-energy beast. Many of the letters are about the momentum of writing, and how to retain that energy over the long haul of the poem; how to say EVERYTHING in the poem; how to get the poem up off the ground into the atmosphere. But this requires a concern for limits as well as freedom in language; Coolidge writes about "the big thing that can never be closed, we can enjoy fiddling with closing all the near and thus smaller things." As if the sum of all we think and feel can only be approached but never fully realized in the poem. But for Mayer it is also important to remind herself of "where I am and what I am." She continues, in the letter of March 25, 1980: "to write about one's self is one way to find something you can tell the truth about…." You "have to let language take over" despite the "lapses" of memory. In the letter of November 19, 1979, Mayer speaks of the "'unending feeling' of Kerouac's prose, writing past any ending, continuing to write, keeping up the momentum until you can't any longer." Mayer is concerned with memory, how that plays out in a work. Both she and Clark, as well many other poets of their generation, were influenced by Kerouac's language in *On the Road,* that sense in his prose, of a mounting energy and rhythm. It would lead them to explore the possibilities of the longer prose work, Mayer with *The Hunger Journals,* and Coolidge with *A Book Beginning What and Ending Away.*

Coolidge responds, in the letter of December 6, 1979, to Mayer's thoughts on memory and the writing process; he says that maybe when you come to the end of a work, "your mind is already 'to one side' enough, or full of what comes next enough, that you're in the wrong position to see what stands back there (?)" Here, I'm thinking of a jazz solo; the shapes and arcs, the various ways the sound can alter or bend; how a certain turn in the soundscape can lead you to a completely new dimension. You have to keep going and never look back. And the point is to keep moving through the poem, not to get stuck. Coolidge writes "I agree with Kerouac that lots of Shakespeare's best stuff seems written in an inspired rush, almost unblotted (as he says), like many of the Sonnets how the first two (or sometimes four) lines look like out-of-the-blue shots that he later fills in and develops, rounds off to (amazing actually) wholes." It's the thought that keeps you moving, the changes in thought, or the extensions: "Duncan is always talking about 'the tone-leading of vowels' but what about the thought-leading of words/sentences." Sound as Thought. Mayer elaborates on Coolidge's ideas about the momentum of the poem: "... that writing (poetry) is always having to be that process of not knowing what you think, what you're going to say, and of finding out as you go along, something I just can't teach my students ... which is why the mind must be empty, gertude-stein-wise."

And for Mayer, this involves a central distinction between her and Coolidge's work and those of the Language poets; in Mayer's letter of "May 23 OR SO," 1980, she writes:

> So I figure you can denude the language of sense and grammar too, the one thing you
>
> have to leave is the language's own impulse (as you say) like the muscular impulses of a human to speak, & the power of the impulse to write, its lushness if you will, I mean the language's, & that is where, I think, they [Language Poets] get confused about emotional matters.

For Coolidge, the problem is seeing language as a kind of blueprint to be tampered with but getting "close enough to the language to allow it its power"; "you can't maintain a distance from the language, for this passion—both—ways to be operating. It's a victim/victor sort of thing, so hard to talk about. But we've both felt the grip of the beast, and also the willfulness of our own grip to extend and possess." For Mayer and Coolidge, the Language poets get caught up in the trap of language games, and they forget the almost ecstatic pleasure that comes with the impulse to write, the obsessive desire to get it ALL done on the page.

But life can intrude on the poet's solitude and interrupt all that thinking about poetry. Mayer was director of the Poetry Project from 1980 to 1984. Living in New York during this time she becomes aware, as she writes in her letter of December 13, 1980, of "American culture, in the sense of the disparity between rich, poor, etc." The frenetic pace of living in the city has its effect on her. She had formerly lived with her husband at the time, Lewis Warsh, in relatively rural Lenox Massachusetts before moving to New York because of work. Her frustration comes out in the letter of September 2, 1980: "However my thought is these imponderable messes are what we are all in one way or the other, whether life is peaceful (as I hoped it could be, yet I went ahead and succumbed to what Alice [Notley] calls 'whynotness' & had 3 children) or whether it is not peaceful yet apparently peaceful and still not peaceful."

Her demands at the Poetry Project overwhelm her at times; her having to constantly write letters, trying to get grants, dealing with the "politics" of the poetry scene at that time; and then there is the problem of choosing readers to read at the Project. How to determine whose work is good or bad, or who is worthy of reading at the Project, and should it be a solo reading or with others. Coolidge tries to help in the letter of September 8, 1980: "As we've discussed before it becomes harder to read other (especially younger, living, etc.) poets anyway, in fact the poetry scene seems in such a knotted mess right now I can't deal with it except as a Mess.... Fairness is the first wall you run into." But it is the relationship with her children "that is so radically sane and permits me to see clearly what is my work, self, life etc. and what is something else, extraneous, or overblown." But all these responsibilities nevertheless impinge on her freedom to write: "I'm often expected to attend 3 or 4 readings a week and I say no I've gotta do my work, so the sum of what I'm saying is that a whole lotta people seem to have lost their perspective about why (or what) are we writers." Finally for Mayer the problem with New York,

> is that I don't want to feel overwhelmed or frenetic about every thing & person, I want to have time to think about it for myself and though I'm learning to do a lot of things I don't know how to do, and then I get to see especially psychological messes I would never otherwise know about, still I want to be alone, to be waiting to see what happens without that...

And Coolidge is no fan of New York city in the late '70s, early '80s; in the letter of August 4, 1981, he writes: "Also I realized very clearly lately just how much I hate New York City. It seems the end of things. Especially the Lower East Side, about the most depressing place I know." During this time Coolidge was living in Hancock, Massachusetts, far removed for the poetry scene in New York. Both Mayer and Coolidge are like poet-monks; they essentially prefer the solitude to write and think. This reminds me of the reason why some poets prefer to live in a rural setting rather than a big city. I moved to North Carolina almost ten years ago, to a rural environment, after years of living in Jersey and going to New York. Away from the frenetic pace of the city,

I could finally hear myself think; here was finally the quiet space where I could think and write. But that desire for a certain energy in the big city never leaves you, and so I often travel to New York to see friends.

On July 26, 1981, Mayer wrote Coolidge a letter asking him if he would read with John Cage at the Poetry Project on October 7th at 8pm. He doesn't respond. Mayer writes more letters to him, growing increasingly worried about his silence: "Only thing is I feel so close to you that it's hard for me to write write sensibly & to try on a small page to respect your silence when I just want to hit you! I want to jolt you out of your thoughts!... And I can say that I know about your writing & and all about it and everything ... Please I hope you feel better, I often think it would be wonderful to have someone to talk about what I think about writing at this moment, I don't." On August 4, 1981, Coolidge finally responds: "I know I'm fighting a big depression ever since we got back from Peru, something I'll have to fight through somehow. I especially don't want any choices at the moment, they drive me to immobile distraction.... Anyway, thanks for asking me to read, but I just can't. The main reason is I have nothing I want to read." I think it's safe to say that most, if not all poets have, at one at point in their writing life, felt the same way, as they thought about their work, and about the life they chose to lead as writers. Such a kind of existential crisis is part the writing life. In one of the last letters included in this book, May 8, 1982, Coolidge writes:

> And what is the importance of what we're doing? I keep getting the strong but indefinite feeling that its beyond what we say about what we do. Certainly not publishing, careers, desires for fame or the right response. Not even glory ... Authorship seems a very odd title for such a doer.

Eventually their correspondence resumes and Coolidge gives a solo reading at the Poetry Project. They continue writing to each other until the letters begin to trail off in 1987 and finally end in 1995.

All This Thinking: The Correspondence of Bernadette Mayer and Clark Coolidge is an important book as it shows the relationship between two of our most important and influential poets at important periods in their lives. They talk about issues that are continually relevant to contemporary poets: what is the role of a poet in her/his community; what is the relationship between language and the self; what are the issues surrounding publishing one's work; what are the challenges between life's responsibilities and the solitude required to write. During the time covered in the letters, Mayer published *Midwinter Day* and *The Desires of Mothers to Please Other in Letters;* Coolidge published *Own Face,* a book that marked a turning point in his work, and *Mine: the one that enters the stories.* Mayer also talks about writing a book called *Utopia* (eventually published by United Artists in 1984), a book that the jaded New York poets attacked as irrelevant.

Mayer, in the letter of February 6, 1982, speaks about how she conceives of utopia in terms of language:

> Surely writing could conceivably never stop, I would hope so, I would hope it could be so—to be such a lunatic would be sublime, thus the silence we speak about. Someday someday has to do that work of never stopping, of going as fast as it can be gone to the point, dare I say it, of eliminating existence at all so that, and that would be an interesting moment, which gets gotten to sometimes in poems, or in Proust, you've finally gotten to the end of reminiscence and all experience and certainly all knowledge (if you have it)—well actually poems do this all the time I guess, like Rimbaud—and get left with the great and wonderful high blank of no purpose at last but a mind wherein you can know exactly (ha!) how you and everyone else too exists in the world at this time (not times but breathing). Oh I am being pretentious, I hope not, because I do mean it.

It's a wonderful passage in which she speaks of that ecstatic feeling of being totally possessed by the language, until the ego is blurred, and a new world is visible on the horizon; it is a way of conceiving of a utopia as involving a selfless regard for others. There is so much to explore and think about when reading the correspondence of two of our most influential and important poets. And for this reason, I am glad *All This Thinking: The Correspondence of Bernadette Mayer and Clark Coolidge* is in the world.

Lund, Elizabeth (2023) *Un-Silenced*, Červená Barva Press

bg thurston

Many in the poetry community recognize Elizabeth Lund for her perceptive interviews and stellar reviews of poetry books. Elizabeth is also a remarkable poet, as is evident in her recently released full-length collection, *Un-Silenced,* published by Červená Barva Press.

The poems in *Un-Silenced* portray a family tragedy. They comprise a story difficult to tell but ultimately one that must be told. This book is broadly based upon the murder of the author's aunt by her uncle. As the book unfolds, other people and situations involving domestic abuse are revealed. Because of its private nature, this all-to-common, yet silent trauma is usually confined within a family, remaining secret not only from society but also kept from the victim's friends and relatives.

The book is organized into three sections. The first, titled "The Secrets She Kept," contains poems that deal with Elaine's death and the shock her family experiences in their attempt to understand how it could have happened. The past and present collide within poems that portray the swirling emotions of hope, fear, despair, and finally the fateful boiling over of rage. The push/pull of personalities and the intimate power struggle that leads to her murder brings the realization that Elaine could neither escape nor survive her marriage. One of the most haunting poems in this section is "Refrain": *the family removed all his guns / thought they'd removed all his guns ... all but one / the newspaper said / all but // one.*

The second section, "A Chorus Rising," delves into other women the author has known whose lives have been impacted by violence. Personal instances of abuse are voiced by women who have ended up in prison as well as experiences drawn from the poet's life. In the first poem, a barred owl appears and questions *who comes for you?* Several of these poems portray the actions and thoughts of abusive perpetrators. The motivations that cause this behavior are rendered in disquietingly beautiful lines such as these two stanzas taken from "Skins:" *He begins at the top / guiding the knife / till an unblemished / body appears in his hand. // Fruit by fruit, a new Eden / emerges. He is God / and flawless Adam.*

In the third section, titled "The Niece Finds Her Voice," the niece grapples with the emotions of loss and comes to the resolution to give Elaine her voice and an identity as more than a victim. There are questions that deal with the speaker's unease and the disquieting vulnerability that grief bestows upon daily life. Images of circles appear in many of these poems, echoing the frustration that comes from the inescapable sense of mortality and the inability to alter outcomes that seem inevitable. Yet the speaker survives her losses and rebuilds her sense of place in the world. In the poem, "Revisiting Lowell Street," she hears the admonition: *Don't let fear become your shadow. / Anger buries you alive.* A command is revealed in the final lines of this poem: *Owl slowly circles above, watching / You—keep writing her story.*

The poet deftly weaves symbols throughout these poems. Mysterious owls appear and reappear—often as soothsayers and harbingers of danger, offering messages of advice or protection. Apples become the subject of several poems, bringing with them their laden history of Eden and temptation. The penultimate poem, "Your eyes will be opened …," is a marvelous sestina that demonstrates how this form can capture obsession and shapeshift it within its repetitions of six perfectly chosen words.

These finely wrought poems will leave their haunting impression upon the reader. One of the poems that I have found myself reading countless times is: "In the dream he's a blacksmith."

In the dream he's a blacksmith

and she is a child, cradling
an old horseshoe no one will miss.

A small black pony stamps his feet.
Smoke sways on the ceiling.

Come closer, he says.
See the girl in the fire?

The pony snickers S-O-S.
Shall I put you in the fire, too?

He swings her onto his table,
beats the red glow thinner.

Every thief must be tamed or broken.
Two cold nails in her hand.

440

In the end, it is Elaine's husband who becomes the consummate thief, robbing his family of their beloved mother and aunt, after he selfishly stole her dreams, self-worth, and ultimately her life.

Having worked with victims of domestic violence, I can attest that this issue continues to be a perverse societal trauma lurking within too many relationships. A victim's mental and physical wellbeing withers from the shame and steady erosion of their confidence. If they are fortunate, they manage to find a way to escape their situation. If they are not, the consequences can be deadly.

Elizabeth Lund has written a beautifully defiant book that honors her aunt. *Un-Silenced* is a memorable collection of powerful poems you will never forget. These poems offer strength and courage to those who need it.

Tony Trigilio (2023), *Craft: A Memoir,* Marsh Hawk Press

Marc Meierkort

Pay attention. Look. Listen. Words and ideas and images float through the ether wanting to be claimed, or re-claimed, by a consciousness intent on creating beauty and meaning in an otherwise strange and contradictory landscape we call reality. It's in this landscape, a landscape that "can't be contained by the limited logic of everyday language," where poet Tony Trigilio finds his voice, his center for being, his raison d'être, where language becomes his "ticket into community."

In his new book, *Craft: A Memoir,* part of Marsh Hawk Press' Chapter One Series, Trigilio composes a unique look at the avenues of influence upon which a poet walks, highlighting the intersection of life and art, where writing becomes a function of seeing and listening, as fundamental to a daily human existence as breathing. For Trigilio, a daily writing practice born out of the rhythms of everyday life becomes a playground where he can erase any distinctions between writing and living, where poetry can encompass the autobiographical, and the autobiographical can be addressed poetically.

This is not your typical book on craft. Yes, there is discussion of typical writing concepts like narrative, voice, persona, and character, but Trigilio's approach to these topics is on the more esoteric side. His perspective is one not often found in a book on craft, as his interests lean toward "blogging, psychic channeling, documentary writing, arcana, and meditation" as areas of poetic inspiration.

All areas of Trigilio's life are fair game for generating poetry. Whether playing music, meditating, teaching his college courses, or balancing work responsibilities and personal relationships, Trigilio has created for himself a rhythm to living where ideas for writing can come from anywhere. What enables Trigilio to access and harness the language required for poetry is his commitment to a daily writing practice, a discipline which he learned from watching his college roommate, Mitch Evich (to whom the book is dedicated). It's in the sustained, intentional dedication to writing every day where Trigilio can be "attentive to the needs of the artistic imagination," which allows for "individual pieces of writing [to] grow into manuscripts through regular sessions of writing and revising."

Two of Trigilio's poetry collections, *Historic Diary* (BlazeVOX, 2010) and *Proof Something Happened* (Marsh Hawk, 2020), are excellent examples of documentary poetics, the materials of which "tend to be the overlooked details of everyday lived experience." The focus of *Historic Diary* is a journal Lee Harvey Oswald kept while living in the Soviet Union, and *Proof Something Happened* dives deep into the story of Betty and Barney Hill, whose alleged 1961 abduction by aliens in the White Mountains of New Hampshire is arguably the most famous and compelling of alien abduction stories. Establishing a daily journaling practice opens up new possibilities for Trigilio's poetry, allowing the familiar ("the overlooked details of everyday lived experience") to blend with the arcane (conspiracy theory and alien abduction), permitting him the freedom to weave "personal experience, informed by the historical record ... to create a realistic emotional landscape" for the work as a whole.

I found Trigilio's advice for creating this "realistic emotional landscape" to be the most valuable in the book. When I'm making poems, I'm constantly worrying about the language more than the emotion, producing work that can feel stilted and off-putting. But Trigilio's comments about vulnerability struck a nerve with me. While discussing his approach to a particular poem, Trigilio talks about accessing Oswald's emotional state regarding his father by reflecting on his own relationship with his father: "I had made myself vulnerable enough—as a psychic medium might—for both Oswald's and my own identities to be superimposed on one another in a poem." He goes even further in talking about vulnerability: "I need to be unguarded enough to allow myself to be taken over (almost) by the persona at the core of the poem.... If I make myself too vulnerable while channeling the voices of other, I risk disappearing."

For me, expressing emotions can be daunting and downright scary. But if I want poems that are emotionally truthful, then I need to push myself out over the cliff a little bit. I need to not just allow, but harness, an awareness of my own vulnerability so I can write the kind of poems I want to write. Trigilio's willingness to show his own vulnerability in explaining how he utilizes it to enhance his own writing struck at the heart of my own writing journey. That you can assume a persona while also being personal and emotionally present in a poem is a wildly appealing idea.

I've read this book three times now, each time in one sitting. At 108 pages, it's a literary snack, but an energizing, thought-provoking, and comforting snack. It makes me want to write. It makes me want to commit to a daily journaling practice (which I have finally done). It makes me want to stop, sit quietly, and open my eyes, ears, and mind to the world around me. I've loved Tony Trigilio's poetry for years now, and this book offers valuable insights into his writing process and how he seamlessly incorporates it into his daily life. This is a book on poetic craft unlike any other, written with generosity and kindness, with authenticity and compassion. Like any great teacher, Trigilio helps you discover your best writing self. Sharing personal experiences that have fed and sustained his writing, he hopes that you too will find a path to the center of your own artistic imagination.

Pay attention. Look. Listen. Read this book. Then read it again.

WHO IS WHO

Indran Amirthanayagam is a poet, editor, publisher, translator, and youtube host. As a U.S. diplomat he has worked in Africa, Asia, Europe, and North and South America, and received several Superior Honor and Meritorious Honor awards for his work. The author of 23 books of poetry, Amirthanayagam writes in English, Spanish, French, Portuguese, and Haitian Creole. He has received fellowships from the Foundation for the Contemporary Arts, the New York Foundation for the Arts, the US/Mexico Fund for Culture, and MacDowell. He publishes poetry books at Beltway Editions and edits *Beltway Poetry Quarterly*. A new bilingual collection of his creole poems, *Powèt Nan Pò A* (Poet of the Port) will be published by MadHat Press in 2023.

Sharon Amuguni is a writer and artist whose practice includes poetry, papier-mâché, and paper arts. Her work was featured in Mass Poetry's Raining Poetry project, with an excerpt of her poem "Ghost" stenciled outside of the Jamaica Plain Branch of the Boston Public Library. She is currently a MASS MoCA Assets for Artists Worcester 2023 Cohort grantee.

Cassandra Atherton is a widely anthologised Australian prose poet and an award-winning interviewer. She has published 30 critical and creative books and has interviewed public intellectuals including Noam Chomsky, Camille Paglia and Harold Bloom. Cassandra is the successful recipient of many national and international grants and is currently working on a book of prose poetry on the atomic bomb with funding from the Australia Council. She is a commissioning editor for Westerly magazine and associate editor at MadHat Press (USA). Cassandra co-authored *Prose Poetry: An Introduction* (Princeton University Press, 2020) and co-edited the *Anthology of Australian Prose Poetry* (Melbourne University Press, 2020) with Paul Hetherington. She is a Professor of Writing and Literature in Melbourne, Australia.

Jennifer Barber's most recent collection is *The Sliding Boat Our Bodies Made* (The Word Works, 2022). Her previous books are *Works on Paper, Given Away*, and *Rigging the Wind*. She is a co-editor, with Fred Marchant and Jessica Greenbaum, of the anthology *Tree Lines: 21st Century American Poems* (Grayson Books, 2022). In 1992 she founded the literary journal *Salamander* and served as its editor through 2018. She is the current poet laureate of Brookline.

Daniel Bouchard's most recent poetry book is *Spider Drop* (Subpress). He works in publishing.

Mairéad Byrne is the author of six poetry collections, nine chapbooks, two plays, four collaborative books with visual artists, and a lot of journalism. A native of Dublin, she is a professor of poetry and poetics at Rhode Island School of Design in Providence.

Linda Carney-Goodrich is writer and teacher whose work has appeared in *Nixes Mate Review, Anti-Heroin Chic, Muddy River Poetry Review, Literary Mama, WordGathering, Gyroscope, City of Notions: An Anthology of Contemporary Boston Poems,* and is forthcoming in *The MacGuffin* and *Soul-Lit.* Her poems have been displayed at Boston City Hall through the Boston Mayor's Poetry Program. She is the Poetry Coordinator for the Menino Arts Center and proprietor of Home Scholars of Boston. Her first collection of poetry is forthcoming in 2024 from Nixes Mate Books.

Chen Chen's second book, *Your Emergency Contact Has Experienced an Emergency,* has been named a 2023 Notable Book by the American Library Association. His debut, *When I Grow Up I Want to Be a List of Further Possibilities,* was long-listed for the National Book Award and won the Thom Gunn Award. His work appears in many publications, including three editions of *The Best American Poetry.* He has received two Pushcart Prizes and fellowships from the National Endowment for the Arts and United States Artists. He teaches for the low-residency MFA programs at New England College and Stonecoast.

Alfred Corn published a translation of Rainer Maria Rilke's *Duino Elegies* in 2021. His latest book, *The Returns: Collected Poems,* premiered on April 7th, 2011, at Pentameters Theatre, London, UK, in a production directed by Daniel Rickman.

Maxine Chernoff is the author of nineteen books of poetry and six books of prose. Her newest book is *Light and Clay: Selected and New Poems* (MadHat Press, 2023). She is the winner of an NEA Poetry Fellowship, a PEN Translation Award, CLMP Editors' Award, a PEN Fiction Award, five Illinois Arts Council Fellowships, and many other prizes. Chernoff has served as faculty in the Creative Writing Program at San Francisco State University since 1994.

Cheryl Clark Vermeulen is poet, editor, translator, and educator. She is the author of the poetry book *They Can Take It Out* (The Word Works, 2022) and chapbooks *This Paper Lantern* (Dancing Girl Press)and *Dead Eye Spring* (Cy Gist Press). Her poems and translations appear in journals *The Mantis, Gigantic Sequins, Bombay Gin, American Poetry Journal, Heavy Feather Review, Drunken Boat, Caketrain, Jubilat, Sixth Finch, Third Coast,* among others, and the anthology *Connecting Lines: New Poetry from Mexico.* She received an MFA from the Iowa Writers' Workshop. She is Poetry Editor for *Pangyrus* literary magazine and Visiting Associate Professor in Liberal Arts at Massachusetts College of Art and Design. Originally from Illinois, she has lived in Boston, MA, since 1998, now with her husband, twin boys, and pets.

Amanda Cook continues to be changing in a changing world. She has traded sourdough starter for sour beers, back-up singing for ukele online, and social events for succulents. Her house is messy but her company is good. Her book *Ironstone Whirlygig* was published by Bootstrap Press in 2018.

Susan Donnelly's newest poetry collection is *The Maureen Papers and Other Poems*. Its title poem sequence was the 2019 co-winner of the Samuel Washington Allen Award from the New England Poetry Club. The author of *Capture the Flag, Transit, Eve Names the Animals,* and six chapbooks, she has published in *The New Yorker, Poetry, Agni, Poetry Ireland Review,* and in many other journals, anthologies, textbooks, and online. Susan offers poetry classes and individual consultations from her home in Arlington, Massachusetts.

Wendy Drexler is a recipient of a 2022 artist fellowship from the Massachusetts Cultural Council. Her fourth collection, *Notes from the Column of Memory,* was published in September 2022 by Terrapin Books. Her poems have appeared in *Barrow Street, J Journal, Nimrod, Pangyrus, Prairie Schooner,* and *The Threepenny Review,* among others. She's been the poet in residence at New Mission High School in Hyde Park, MA, since 2018, and is a member of the board of the New England Poetry Club.

Magdalena Gómez, Poet Laureate of Springfield, MA (2019–2022) and Academy of American Poets Laureate Fellow (2021–2022) received the Latinas 50 Plus Literature Award at Fordham University in 2019, and the Latinx Excellence on the Hill Award from the Black and Latino Legislative Caucus of MA at the State House. Her memoir, *Mi'ja,* was published by Heliotrope Books in May 2022. She is a 2023 recipient of a National Association of Latino Arts and Cultures, NFA award. Gómez was the first poet commissioned by the Springfield Symphony Orchestra, MA. latinapoet.com, mijamemoir.com.

Lea Graham is a writer and translator who lives in Hyde Park, NY. She is the author of two poetry collections, *From the Hotel Vernon* (Salmon Press, 2019) and *Hough & Helix & Where & Here & You, You, You* (No Tell Books, 2011), an edited collection *From the Word to the Place: Essays on the Work of Michael Anania* (MadHat, 2022) and three chapbooks, *Spell to Spell* (above/ground Press, 2018), *This End of the World: Notes to Robert Kroetsch* (Apt. 9 Press, 2016) and *Calendar Girls* (above/ground Press, 2006). She is an associate professor of English at Marist College.

Holly Guran, author of *Twilight Chorus* (Main Street Rag), *River of Bones* (Iris Press) and two chapbooks, received a Massachusetts Cultural Council award and coordinates a popular Boston reading series. *Now Before and Ever* (Kelsay Books) will be published early in 2024. Her work has appeared in journals including *Poet Lore, Santa Fe Literary Review,* and *Salamander.* Selections from her narrative poems, based on a 19th-century correspondence between a mill girl and the editor she married, have been performed in Boston and at the Lowell National Historic Park.

Tiffany Higgins is a writer, translator, and Fulbright scholar whose research and writing focuses on traditional peoples in the Brazilian Amazon, especially as concerns their river-forest homes. The Pulitzer Rainforest Journalism Fund and the Banff Centre for the Arts have supported her work. She was the 2020 Annie Clark Tanner Fellow in Environmental Humanities at the University of Utah. Her narrative journalism and poetry appear in *Granta, Guernica, Poetry,* and elsewhere, and she is the author of two collections of poems. She is finishing a manuscript of translations of the poetry of Márcia Wayna Kambeba of the Indigenous Kambeba people of Brazil.

Sabine Huynh is a French poet, novelist, essayist and literary translator born in 1972 in Saigon, Vietnam. She grew up in France and has lived in England, the United States, Canada and Israel. She has published a dozen books, including the poetry collection *Kvar lo* (Éditions Æncrages & Co, 2016), which won France's 2017 CoPo Poetry Prize, and the novel *Elvis à la radio* (Éditions Maurice Nadeau, 2022), which won the 2023 Jean-Jacques Rousseau Prize for Autobiography. She holds a PhD in Linguistics from the Hebrew University of Jerusalem. She has published more than twenty translations, including major works by Anne Sexton, Gwendolyn Brooks, Uri Orlev, and Ilya Kaminsky. She won the 2022 Alain Bosquet Poetry Prize for her translation of Kaminsky's *Deaf Republic.* Some of her work has been translated into English by Amy Hollowell, including *Dans le tournant/Into the Turning* (Éditions Christophe Chomant, 2019), and her new poetry collection, due out in May 2024 (with Éditions Bruno Doucey). She is currently translating poetry collections by Diane Seuss, Alice Oswald and Diane di Prima, among others, for French and Belgian publishers. The poems in this issue were translated from *Parler peau,* published by Æncrages & Co in 2019 along with paintings by Philippe Agostini. Her website is sabinehuynh.com

A.M. Juster is the poetry editor for *Plough.* His poems and translations have appeared in *Poetry, The Hudson Review,* and *The Paris Review.* His most recent book is *Wonder and Wrath* (Paul Dry Books 2020) and W.W. Norton will publish his translation of Petrarch's *Canzoniere* next year.

Robert Kelly is the author of many books, mostly of poetry, but also fiction, drama and essays. After the five-volume Island Cycle (various publishers), the most recent works are the long narrative poem *The Cup* and the *Collected Short Stories* (both from McPherson & Co,), and the most recent collection of poems, *Linden Word* (Black Square Press). He lives in the Hudson Valley with his wife, the distinguished French translator Charlotte Mandell.

John Kinsella lives on stolen/unceded Ballardong Noongar boodja/country at 'Jam Tree Gully' in the Western Australian 'wheatbelt'. He has lived in UK, USA, Ireland and Germany, and taught at Cambridge University (where he remains a Fellow of Churchill College), Kenyon College, Tübingen University, the University of Western Australia, and Curtin University. He has published dozens of books of poetry, including *Peripheral Light: Selected Poems*, *Divine Comedy: Journeys Through a Regional Geography*, *Jam Tree Gully*, *Firebreaks*, *Insomnia*, and *Metaphysics*. His *Collected Poems* in three volumes is in the process of being published in Australia. He has also published a number of books of criticism and poetics, including *Activist Poetics: Anarchy in the Avon Valley*, *Polysituatedness*, *Beyond Ambiguity*, and *Legibility: an anti-fascist poetics*. Over the decades Kinsella has also edited and often introduced many anthologies of poetry, as well as single-author collections. These include *The Penguin Anthology of Australian Poetry*, *The Land's Meaning: Selected Poems of Randolph Stow*, and *Dislocations: The Selected Innovative Poetry of Paul Muldoon*. He is at present compiling an anthology of poems in support of animal rights. He is strongly influenced by visual arts and music. A frequent collaborator with other poets, artists, musicians, writers and activists, he has worked with Kwame Dawes, Charmaine Papertalk-Green, Drew Milne, Forrest Gander, Thurston Moore and others. Kinsella and Kwame Dawes recently published their fifth book together, *UnHistory*. Also a writer of short fiction, experimental novels, cross-genre works and plays, he has a particular interest in 'verse theatre', and has written and had performed/broadcast a number of such works. He has frequently written for the Marlowe Society in Cambridge, UK. John Kinsella identifies as a vegan anarchist pacifist of almost four decades, and is a committed environmental activist. He works towards a poetics of decolonisation, human rights, identity rights, and animal rights.

Natasha Labaze enjoys writing poetry and teaching. Her poems have appeared in the online literary magazine *Tanbou*. "Love Letter to Haiti" was featured in the *Bronx Biannual*, Issue 2. Natasha loves performance poetry. Her poem "I Iunger," about the 2010 earthquake in Haiti, was published online by the Women Writers of Haitian Descent. She also performed "Hunger" for an arts fair and a fundraiser for Haiti. In 2015, she performed her poem "A Moment of Silence" for a local poetry and art exhibit, *Lines Connecting Lines*.

Danielle Legros Georges is a creative and critical writer, and literary translator who works in the fields of contemporary U.S. poetry, African-American and African-diasporic poetry and literature, Caribbean/Latin American and Haitian studies. She is the author of several books of poetry including *Maroon* (2001), *The Dear Remote Nearness of You* (2016), and *Island Heart* (2021), translations of the poems of 20th-century Haitian-French poet Ida Faubert. The former Poet Laureate of Boston, her work has been supported by fellowships and grants from institutions including The American

Antiquarian Society, the PEN/Heim Translation Fund, the Boston Foundation, and the Black Metropolis Research Consortium.

Barbara B. Lewis, PhD, directed the William Monroe Trotter Institute for the Study of African Diaspora History and Culture, UMass Boston, 2004 to 2019. Now retired, she is pursuing her interests in playwriting, poetry, and fiction. Before coming to UMass Boston, she chaired the theatre department at the University of Kentucky, Lexington, taught at New York University and also at Lehman College. Born in the North, she grew up between New York, South Carolina, and Canada. Drawn to other languages, she has traveled in Europe, South and Central America, West Africa, Asia, the Middle East, and the Caribbean. Her doctorate is in theater history and literature. She also earned a masters in creative writing and translation, focused on French. In 2019, she was accepted into the Play Lab program at Company One, led by Kirsten Greenidge. In 2020, she participated in a Company One acting workshop. In 2021 and 2022, she joined a summer playwriting program with the Kennedy Center. Also in 2022, she enrolled in a poetry program at MASS MOCA and participated in a Renaissance Writers Workshop on Martha's Vineyard. Recently, she learned that her paternal great-great grandfather, Jeremiah Bradley, enlisted in Company B of the 54th Massachusetts, memorialized in sculpture across from the Massachusetts State House, Boston Common, Beacon Street.

Charlotte Mandell has translated half a hundred books, including works by Mathias Énard, Jonathan Littell, Jean-Luc Nancy, Maurice Blanchot, André Breton and Philippe Soupault, and, most recently, Marcel Proust. She is currently translating *Guerre*, a newly discovered manuscript by Céline, and *Déserter*, the new novel by Mathias Énard. *Speaking Skin* is forthcoming from Black Square Press. See more at charlottemandell.com

Lívia Maria Natália de Souza Santos, or Lívia Natália as she is known, has a doctorate in Theories and Criticism of Literature and Culture from the Universidade Federal da Bahia, and is a professor in the Literary Theory department at the Universidade Federal da Bahia. She is the author of many poetry collections, including *Água Negra* (2011), *Correntezas e Outros Estudos Marinhos* (2015), *Água Negra e Outras Águas* (2016), *Sobejos Do Mar* (2017), *Dia Bonito pra Chover* (2017), *Em face dos últimos acontecimentos* (2022), and *Sobejos do Mar* (2023). Her poetry has been widely anthologized.

Ellen McGrath Smith teaches at the University of Pittsburgh and in the Carlow University Madwomen in the Attic program. Her poetry has appeared in *The Georgia Review, The New York Times, The American Poetry Review, Talking Writing, Los Angeles Review,* and other journals and anthologies. Books include *Scatter, Feed* (Seven Kitchens 2014) and *Nobody's Jackknife* (West End Press

2015). Her chapbook *Lie Low, Goaded Lamb* was published in January 2023 by Seven Kitchens Press as part of its Keystone Series.

Marc Meierkort is an Adjunct Professor at Columbia College Chicago, as well as Managing Editor for the poetry magazine *Court Green*. He earned an MFA in Poetry from Columbia in 2022, where he was the inaugural Efroymson Editorial Assistant for *Allium, A Journal of Poetry and Prose*. A Pushcart Prize nominee, recent poems have appeared in *Allium, New Note Poetry,* and *Red Ogre Review,* among others.

Gavin Moses is from Pennsylvania. His poems have appeared in *Appalachian Heritage, A Gathering of the Tribes, Wick, The World, Long Shot, Icarus, Quatro, In the Tradition* (Harlem River Press), *Aloud: Voices from the Nuyorican Poets Café* (Henry Holt), and *Changer L'Amerique* (Le Temps Des CeRises/Maison de la Poesie). He has degrees from N.Y.U., Columbia University Graduate School of Journalism, and Harvard Divinity School. Gavin was on New York City's first actual National Poetry Slam Team (1991), is founding member of both New York's Poets 4 and Boston's Langston's Legacy poetry collectives. He was nominated for the Pushcart Poetry Prize.

Mark Pawlak is the author of nine poetry collections and the editor of six anthologies, most recently *Reconnaissance: New and Selected Poems* and *Poetic Journal* (Hanging Loose, 2016) and *Natural Histories* (Červená Barva, 2015). Pawlak's work has been translated into German, Japanese, Polish, and Spanish, and has been performed at Teatr Polski in Warsaw. In English, his poems and prose have appeared widely in anthologies such as *The Best American Poetry, Blood to Remember: American Poets on the Holocaust, For the Time Being: The Bootstrap Anthology of Poetic Journals* and in the literary magazines *New American Writing, Mother Jones, Poetry South, The Saint Ann's Review,* and *The World,* among many others. His essays and memoirs have appeared in such journals as *Arrowsmith, Jacket,* and *spoKe*. His latest publication is the book-length memoir *My Deniversity: Knowing Denise Levertov* (MadHat Press, 2021). Pawlak supports his poetry habit by teaching mathematics at the University of Massachusetts–Boston and lives in Cambridge, Massachusetts.

Melissa Peters' poems have appeared in literary and art journals including *DoubleTake, Denver Quarterly, Spoon River Poetry Review, Poetry Northwest,* and *Northwest Review*. She received an MFA from New York University and works in New York City. She is currently completing a manuscript entitled *All Cities are Fragile.*

Anne Riesenberg is a writer, photographer and Five-Element acupuncturist living in Newcastle, Maine. Winner of *Blue Mesa Review*'s Nonfiction and *Storm Cellar*'s Force Majeure contests, a Pushcart and Best of the Net nominee, her work can be found in *Pleiades, Rogue Agent, Posit, Heavy Feather Review, What Rough Beast,* and elsewhere. *The Palace of Unbearable Feeling,* her chapbook of visual poems, was recently published by Lily Poetry Press.

Guy Rotella is Professor of English emeritus at Northeastern University, where, for twenty-six years, he edited the Morse Poetry Prize. His books include *Castings,* on monuments and monumentality in postmodern poets.

Alex Simões is a poet and performer. His books include *minha terra tem ladeiras* (Caramurê, 2022), *assim na terra como no selfie* (Paralelo 13s, 2021), *trans formas são* (Organismo, 2018) and *Contrassonetos* (Mondrongo, 2015). In addition to participating in poetry gatherings, literary festivals, and multilingual events both in Bahia and beyond since the 1990s, Alex has been conducting performances, including "você tem seda?" and "a cappella de Waly," blurring the boundaries between art and life, between poetry and other languages, in what he calls poeformances. His blog is toobitornottoobit. blogspot.com

H. Preston Soss abandoned his law practice in 2016 to write full-time. He has won *Writer's Digest* poetry prize awards in 2015, 2017, 2018, and in 2019 a First Prize in Poetry, with three 2022 WD Honorable Mentions and two poems of his chosen as Finalists for the Montreal International Poetry Prize in 2022. In 2017 he founded, and has since curated, the Artful Dodgers Poetry Series at the historic Montauk Club, established in 1891 in Park Slope, Brooklyn, New York, still boasting many of its original Victorian design elements, to provide a platform for artists to be heard. Twitter: @poetsoss

bg Thurston lives on a sheep farm in rural Massachusetts. She has taught writing courses at Lasell University/Village and online for Vermont College. Her third book of poetry, about the history of her 1770's farmhouse, is titled: *The Many Lives of Cathouse Farm/Tales of a Rural Brothel* and is forthcoming in 2024 from Červená Barva Press.

Joseph Torra is a novelist, poet, memoirist, and editor. His novels include *My Ground Trilogy: (Gas Station, Tony Luongo, My Ground), They Say, The Bystander's Scrapbook, What It Takes, What's So Funny.* Poetry books include *Keep Watching the Sky, After the Chinese* and *Time Being.* Memoirs: *Call Me Waiter* and *Who Do You Think You Are? Reflections of a Writers Life….* He edited the journals *lift magazine, Let the Bucket Down, a Magazine of Boston Area Writing,* and the poetry of Stephen Jonas.

Márcia Wayna Kambeba, of the Indigenous Kambeba people of Brazil, is a poet, photographer, singer, and educator. She was the first Indigenous Ombudsman of Belém do Pará in the Amazon, and, with a master's degree in

Geography, is currently a doctoral student in Linguistics. Her books include *Ay kakyri Tama (Eu moro na cidade), O lugar do saber, Saberes da Floresta, Kumiça Jenó: Narrativas Poéticas dos Seres da Floresta,* and *De almas e águas kunhãs.*

Peter Valente is a writer, translator, and filmmaker. He is the author of eleven books and the translator of Gérard de Nerval's *The Illuminated* (Wakefield Press, 2022) and Antonin Artaud's *The True Story of Jesus-Christ: Three Notebooks from Ivry* (Infinity Land, 2023).

www.ingramcontent.com/pod-product-compliance
Lightning Source LLC
Chambersburg PA
CBHW020147090426
42734CB00008B/719